DOMESDAY
A Search for the
Roots of England

DOMESDAY
A Search for the Roots of England

MICHAEL WOOD

BBC BOOKS

Published in Great Britain by BBC Worldwide Ltd,
Woodlands, 80 Wood Lane, London W12 0TT

First Published 1986
BBC Classics edition first published 1990
This edition copyright © Michael Wood 1999
The moral right of the author has been asserted

ISBN 0 563 55127 5

Commissioning editor: Sheila Ableman
Project editor: Katy Lord
Designer: Linda Blakemore
Picture researcher: Sarah Matthews
Cover design: Senate

Set in Bembo by Pheonix Photosetting, Chatham
Printed and bound in Great Britain by Butler and Tanner Ltd, Frome and London
Plate section printed by Lawrence Allen Ltd, Weston-super-Mare
Cover printed by Belmont Press, Northampton

CONTENTS

What task could be more agreeable than to tell of the benefits conferred on us by our ancestors, so that you may get to know the achievements of those from whom you have received both the basis of your beliefs, and the inspiration to conduct your life properly?

William of Malmesbury, c. AD 1125.
(William's father was Norman, his mother Anglo-Saxon.)

PREFACE

Where does England come from? How did it come about, this intricate association of rights, obligations and allegiances which we call the nation? Of all the historical documents which survive from the English past, Domesday Book conceals most mysteries and holds most answers. The product of William the Conqueror's survey of England in the dark days of 1086, Domesday Book is the nearest thing to a photograph of the ordinary people of this country we could hope for from so long ago; it is, as it were, the 'family album' of the English people. It is an administrative document – and who was not switched off history at school by that prospect? – but it does what chronicles, biographies and literature cannot do: it represents us with a pattern of living social relations in terms of land and labour for an entire population. And indeed, from Domesday Book onwards, England has the most detailed and complete record of the lives of the mass of the people of any nation. At first sight such material may seem forbidding and off-putting when compared with the wonderfully vivid and accessible poetic and historical literature created in early England. Much of Anglo-Saxon literature, for example, with its riddles, its speculations on fate, its juxtaposition of the heroic with the transient in life, manages to convey to us across the thousand years something of the character of people: ruminative, pragmatic, individualist, aware of the insecurities of life, people who do not set too much store by material things. But Domesday Book enables us to balance that picture by giving an insight into the roots of that society, its social classes, land ownership, money and power, economy, agriculture, yields and rents; the material forces which still influence people's lives today.

Much of the argument in this book is based on the work of professional scholars in the field, and I hope my bibliography makes clear my main debts to them; the translations are mine unless otherwise stated. I have thought it helpful to include a glossary of difficult terms which crop up frequently. I should also add that all references to English counties are to the pre-1974 boundaries: in this book Rutland and Huntingdonshire still exist! Likewise I should point out to those born after about 1970 that the money system in use for the previous 1300 years was 12 pennies to the shilling and 20 shillings, or 240 pence, to the pound (£.s.d.): there is no point in giving modern equivalents, but in the tenth century you could buy a good cow for 20d; average annual income for a smallholder was 6s at the time of Domesday, going up to 11s in rich south-western shires like Wiltshire, and down to 3s per annum in Yorkshire and the north – times don't change! So a wealthy aristocrat's estates might yield several hundred pounds a year – the equivalent in purchasing power in 1999 of, say, £2 or £3 million per annum.

This book was originally written for the 900th anniversary of William the Conqueror's Domesday survey which was celebrated in 1986. Anniversaries of course are often thought-provoking affairs, even at the level of birthdays, let alone novocentenaries. They make us, individually or collectively, look afresh at our changing relation to our past. The Domesday anniversary certainly did that, from national events down to the activities of the smallest local schools, groups and societies. But, as always, it is less easy to sense the drift of history when one is right in the middle of it. Now that fifteen years have passed and we stand at the beginning of a new millennium, it is plain that England and Great Britain have gone through more dramatic and far-reaching changes than could ever have been foreseen in the mid eighties. Now, with the growing success of nationalist parties in Wales and Scotland, the breakup of the union of 1707 is being widely canvassed; new questions are being asked about English identity, which has become the object of much soul searching among historians, journalists and writers.

Of special interest here is the question of the origins of the English state. In this book these origins are shown to be a creation of the Anglo-Saxon kings of the ninth and tenth centuries, thus firmly rooted before the Norman conquest. Allegiance to this state, the growth of a group feeling acknowledging English law under an English king, was achieved early on. A shared idea of English identity stemmed from the growth of this feeling. National identity in history also comes about through a sense of a shared past; despite the cataclysm of the Norman conquest and the death or removal of almost the entire English ruling class, this sense perpetuated itself strongly in the common culture of the people. Strongly enough for 'Englishness' to re-emerge in the later Middle Ages. So, the Anglo-Saxons and their Norman successors made England, and gave it workable institutions which proved extremely durable and long-lasting. Shaped by its history and culture, the national identity never depended on race as such, but rather on a common sense of custom and language, which in an open society can be wide and inclusive, as we have seen in our own time with the influx of large numbers of immigrants from the Commonwealth. An identity always in the making, but never made. This book describes the beginnings of that making.

INTRODUCTION

The most extraordinary historical record in the world can be seen today in the Public Record Office in Chancery Lane, London. Look at any page and you will not take long to fall under its spell. It is an account of England drawn up 900 years ago in 1086, and written up in the next twelve months; 888 leaves crammed with column after column of facts about eleventh–century England and its people. Some people called it 'The Great Survey', 'The Inquisition', 'The Book of Winchester', 'The Great Description of England', but there is one name which has stuck since the twelfth century – Domesday Book. 'Doomsday is what the man in the street calls it in the English language,' said a Norman writer of that time; 'that is, to us, "The Book of the Day of Judgement", for its verdicts are just as unanswerable.'

Astonishingly, the whole thing was transcribed and written up by one man. But though the book was prepared for a foreign overlord, the Norman William the Conqueror, the work was done by a native Englishman – or at least by someone who had lived in England long enough to be familiar with the native forms of English place names. The parchment (sheepskin) pages are still supple and creamy yellow, easy to turn, pleasing to use; the writing is astonishingly clear – an almost cursive Latin hand-writing, stylish, with even a touch of flamboyance in the long descenders, especially the '7'-shaped Anglo-Saxon shorthand for 'and'. The book is easy to use, too, as the eyes get used to the abbreviations, with the red ink markings for each individual heading, and the red line through most of the 13,400 place names to guide the eye to them.

The book acquired the power of a talisman as soon as it was made. By the thirteenth century an illustrated version had been produced in the manner of the illustrated Gospel books of the time: fitting for what was, after all, a kind of secular sacred book. Originally held in the King's Treasury at Winchester, Domesday Book was later moved to Westminster where it was kept under lock and three keys in a great old chest, which still survives. Up to the third quarter of the eighteenth century it was little used by scholars; indeed, to consult it the student had to pay a fee of 6s 8d, and 4d extra for every line copied. Not surprisingly, little progress was made in understanding this extraordinary record until 1783, when Abraham Farley published his famous edition of the Latin text after forty years of 'almost daily' work on the book. It would be too expensive a task to undertake today, but fortunately his transcription was so painstaking and accurate that making a new one would be superfluous, and

Farley's version of the text is still in use. His text is reproduced, for example, in the new Phillimore editions of Domesday, shire by shire, which has at last made the book available to everyone at a modest cost – an undertaking of which Farley, if not William the Conqueror, would have heartily approved. Domesday was moved to the Public Record Office in the nineteenth century, and has since been the subject of numerous studies by modern scholars who have shaped our present ideas about late Saxon and Norman England: Round, Maitland, Seebohm, Vinogradoff, Stenton, Douglas and many others. It was rebound in 1954, and again in 1986, when – a pity perhaps – 'Great Domesday' was divided into two parts; but though no longer physically one, it will remain forever Domesday Book.

No other country in the world possesses such a detailed single record from so far back in time. Here, in utterly hypnotic detail, is a cross-section of English society twenty-seven generations ago. With the text of Domesday in one's hand, it is possible to go back to the local courts in that terrible year of 1086, with its torrential rain, cold, famine, ruined wheat and fruit crops, 'dreadful thunder and lightning', and be there as King William's commissioners asked their questions and drew up their picture of the people they had conquered. Here are the hill farmers of Devon, the open-field ploughmen of Berkshire, the wealthy Fen farmers by the Wash, the itinerant shepherds of Wharfedale. Here are the herring fishermen of Yarmouth, the eel netters of Ely and Wisbech, the lead miners of the Derbyshire Peak, the iron smelters of Corby, the salt boilers of Droitwich and Nantwich; the burgesses of Norwich, Chester and 110 other towns; the freemen in East Anglia and slaves in the West Country; with all the various classes of society in between – sokemen, villeins, bordars, cottars and the rest – the elaborate gradations of Old English society faithfully reproduced by the Norman surveyors. Here are forests, woods, meadows, pastures, open fields at Garsington in Oxfordshire, a garden (overgrown) at Langport in Somerset, a vineyard at Lacock in Wiltshire, a fruit orchard at Church Knowle in Dorset; here are churches, mills, hawks' eyries, and even (at Wilcot in Wiltshire) 'an excellent house with good vines'; here are rents paid in fish, eels, 'blooms of iron', horses, falcons, wheat and barley, 32 hogs of bacon, 16 sesters of honey, 480 hens, 1600 eggs, 100 cheeses, 240 fleeces and even 'a pair of white gloves'.

At first sight dry as dust, the pages of Domesday Book teem with life. They tell us about the real people who lived in England 900 years ago: the woman Leofgyth at Knook in Wiltshire, 'who made and still makes gold embroideries for the king and queen'; 'miserable' Aelfric of Marsh Gibbon in Buckinghamshire, a free landowner in 1066 who held his land for a rent in 1086 'with a heavy heart'; his near neighbour Aelfgyth 'the girl', who held a few acres off Godric the sheriff at Oakley, on condition that 'she taught his daughter how to embroider'; Maccus, a smallholder of Viking descent at Cockerington, near Louth in Lincolnshire, who shared 80 acres or so with an English farmer called Eadric; the woman Asa from Scoreby in the Derwent valley east of York, who 'held her land separately and free from the domination and control of her

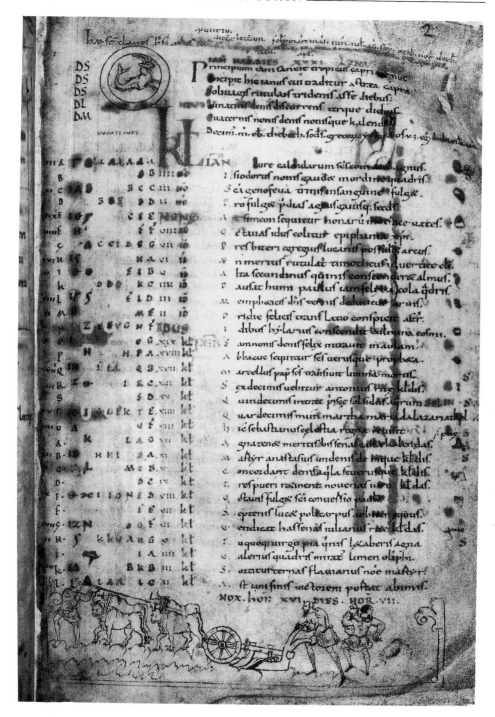

The Domesday workforce: a drawing of rural labourers on an eleventh-century
Anglo-Saxon calendar.

husband Beornwulf, even when they were together, so that he could neither give, nor sell, nor forfeit it; but after their separation she withdrew all her land, and possessed it as its lady' (scandalous to the Norman commissioners); the Norman doctor Nigel at Bartestree in Herefordshire; Hugh 'the interpreter' at Bathampton in Somerset; Toki, the dispossessed Danish freeholder of Rolleston in Leicestershire; the female slaves at Leominster; and the 127 semi-free small-holders at West Ham, the depressed real-life East Enders of 1086.

Behind such astonishing and remorseless detail, it is not hard to imagine a gallery of characters to set beside Chaucer's Canterbury Tales. Instinctively we feel that this is the recognisable ancestor of modern England. The population may only have been two million in 1086, as against fifty million now; the mass of the people – 90 per cent of them – may have worked the land compared with only 1 per cent or so now; the biggest city then may only have held 25,000 people, where today's London alone has three times the population of the whole of Domesday England: but it feels like the same country. This, we sense, is the authentic village England of the wholemeal bread television adverts and the intercity rail posters: the 'real' England which waits just beyond the high-rise blocks and the commuter jams at rush hour. We imagine it as 'traditional' England: unchanging, timeless, rooted in ideas of community, co-operation, closeness to the land, extended families full of neighbourly care and local loyalties.

Timeless, unchanging rural England: a photograph from the early twentieth century.
In fact the rural story from before Domesday up to the present has been one of mobility, destruction and change.

But did such an England ever exist? Nine hundred years on from the compilation of the Domesday survey, what is the connection between its world and our own? And where did the world of Domesday come from? What are the roots of the society and the social order portrayed in the Conqueror's survey? The argument of this book is that some of the fundamental traits in English culture – for instance, marriage, property and inheritance customs, and what has been termed 'English individualism' – are rooted earlier than Domesday in a time when an idea of 'Englishness' and a sense of the unity of English culture was already established. But it is only because of the existence of Domesday itself that it is possible for us, nine centuries on, to delve deeply into English social history far beyond 1086. That search is the theme of this book, which does not attempt to summarise what Domesday contains. Instead it presents a view, inevitably selective, of the thousand-year-period from the late Roman world in Britain – when the roots of the manorial system in Domesday can be discerned – to the fourteenth century, when that system began to break up. It presents a series of close-ups of certain landscapes, certain places and certain characteristic medieval societies as they existed before and after Domesday. Later developments, from the Tudor period to the present day, are alluded to by way of a conclusion, for the historical processes which shaped Domesday England are still working themselves out, and at the same time the English people are now experiencing changes as complex and far-reaching as any in earlier periods. What the 1000th anniversary of Domesday will hold is still too early to say.

PART ONE

BEYOND DOMESDAY: THE SAXON AND CELTIC PAST

Above The 'Great Domesday' (open), along with the 'Little Domesday' which covers East Anglia.
Previous page The funeral of Edward the Confessor, 6 January 1066: the end of Anglo-Saxon England.

1

'THE GREAT SURVEY' OF 1086

Domesday Book was written in 1086, twenty years after the defeat of the Anglo-Saxon army under King Harold at Hastings. The Norman invasion of England had been led by Duke William, later 'the Conqueror', leader of a former Scandinavian-speaking province of France. The Normans were relative newcomers to the European scene, descendants from pagan Viking adventurers who had settled in the Seine valley in 911. The Anglo-Saxons on the other hand had created one of the great civilisations in the Dark Age 'barbarian' West. King Edward the Confessor, whose childless death in January 1066 precipitated the Norman attack, had the oldest pedigree in Europe. Like his great predecessors, Alfred, Athelstan and Edgar, he was a member of a dynasty which claimed to be (and perhaps was) descended from a warrior called Cerdic who was thought to have led a band of Anglo-Saxon raiders into Southampton Water soon after AD 500. In the succeeding five centuries the Anglo-Saxons, though a racial minority compared with the native Celtic-speaking Britons, created a unified culture in low-land Britain which they called England ('Angle-land') with sophisticated forms of taxation, coinage and chancery, a remarkable vernacular literature, and a standardised language, the ancestor of today's English, the most widespread tongue now in use throughout the world. It is therefore not surprising that the Anglo-Norman historian Ordericus Vitalis, born in 1075, remarking on the arrogance of the Norman rulers of his day, said that 'they had forgotten that the country they had conquered was far older and richer in its achievements than their own'.

England in the eleventh century was not only old but also wealthy. 'Many times richer than Normandy in wealth and in military strength,' wrote William's biographer William of Poitiers. One of the chief sources of this wealth was wool, which England may have exported to Europe. Though Duke William had a claim to the English throne through his aunt, the Norman mother of Edward the Confessor, and proclaimed himself Edward's chosen heir, nevertheless it was the richness of the country which was the great attraction to the Normans in an era of opportunist expansion which took their militarist aristocracy as far as Sicily and Antioch. The takeover of 1066, as Ordericus put it, was 'not by hereditary right but in desperate battle with much spilling of people's blood'. The background to our story, then, is this violent conquest of an older culture, rich in achievement but past its most creative period, by a young, brutal and warlike state on the verge of momentous growth. This is the context of the extraordinary events surrounding Domesday Book.

King William I spent Christmas 1085 at Gloucester, one of the old residences of the Anglo-Saxon kings. He held court for five days and then spent another three days on church business. At this point – round about New Year's Day 1086 – the *Anglo-Saxon Chronicle* continues the story:

After this, the king had much thought and very deep discussion with his council about this country – how it was settled, and with what kind of people. Then he sent his men over all England, into every shire, and had them find out how many hundred hides there were in the shire, or what land or cattle the king himself had in the country, or what dues he ought to have each year from the shire. Also he had a record made of how much land his archbishops had, and his bishops, abbots and earls – and though I relate it at too great length – what or how much everybody had who was occupying land in England, in land or livestock, and how much money it was worth. So very strictly did he have it investigated that there was no single hide nor a yard of land, nor indeed (shame it is to relate but it seemed no shame to him to do) one ox nor one cow nor one pig was left out, and not put down in his record: and afterwards all these writings were brought to him.
Translated G. N. Garmonsway.

These were desperate times. The twenty years since the Battle of Hastings had seen war, hunger and pestilence. The country had been criss-crossed by armed forces plundering and devastating wherever they went. In some areas – Yorkshire, the Welsh borders, the West Midlands – the population would be marked for generations by fire and sword. Recurring attacks of plague and cattle murrain were compounded by bad weather and crop failure. Famine was always around the corner: in 1082 the *Anglo-Saxon Chronicle* singled out a particularly bad one as 'The Great Famine'. Amidst all this the hard-headed King William saw his own practical needs as paramount: to maintain his armies with supplies, and to pay them; and to raise even larger forces to fight his French and Breton enemies, to subdue the Welsh and the Scots, to keep the conquered English in subjection and to counter the continuing threat from Denmark. He would milk the English dry if he could. Soon after Christmas 1083, for instance, he had imposed 'a great and heavy tax' over all England at a rate of *6s* on each hide of land: a geld which would have brought him in about 21,000 lb of silver – the size of the huge Danegelds or army taxes raised under those other foreign occupiers, Canute and Harthacnut, earlier in the century. In the winter of 1085 William had raised the biggest forces yet, so that, as the *Anglo-Saxon Chronicle* put it, 'people wondered how this country could maintain that army'. William's solution to this problem was to disperse the army over the country and billet it on his vassals, so that each had to provision a set number of troops according to how much land they held. 'Certainly in his

Right The *Anglo-Saxon Chronicle*'s account of William's 'deep discussion' (line 15: '*deope spaece*') in Gloucester, 1085, from the Laud manuscript of *c.* 1122, now in the Bodleian Library, Oxford.

þis land mihte eall þone here afedan. Ac se cyng let to scyfton þo
ne here geond eall þis land to his mannon. ⁊ hi feddon þone
here ælc be his land efne. ⁊ men heafdon mycel ge swinc
þæs geares. ⁊ se cyng let awestan þ land abutan þa sæ. þet
gif his feond comen upp. þ hi næfdon na on hwam hi fen
gon swa rædlice. Ac se cyng ge axode to soðan þ his feond
ge lætte wæron. ⁊ ne mihten na ge forðian heora fare. þa
let he sum þone here faren to heora agene lande. ⁊ sum
he heold on þis lande ofer winter. Ða to þam midewintre
wæs se cyng on gleaweceastre mid his witan. ⁊ heold þær his
hired. v. dagas. ⁊ syððan þe arceb ⁊ ge hadode men hæfden
sinoð þreo dagas. Ðær wæs mauricius ge coren to b on lun
dene. ⁊ willm to norðfolce. ⁊ rodbeard to ceaster scire. hi
wæron ealle þæs cynges cleriecas. Æfter þisu hæfde se cyng
mycel ge þeaht. ⁊ swiðe deope spæce wið his witan ymbe þis
land hu hit wære ge sett. oððe mid hwylcon mannon. Sen
de þa ofer eall engla land into ælcere scire his men. ⁊ let
agan ut hu fela hundred hyda wæron innon þære scire.
oððe hwet se cyng him sylf hæfde landes. ⁊ orfes innan þā
lande. oððe hwilce ge rihtæ he ahte to habbanne to. xii. mon
þum of þære scire. Eac he let ge writan hu mycel landes
his arceb'. hæfdon. ⁊ his leod b'. ⁊ his abb'. ⁊ his eorlas. ⁊
þeah ic hit lengre telle. hwæt oððe hu mycel ælc mann hæf
de þe land sittende wæs innan engla lande. on lande. oððe
on orfe. ⁊ hu mycel feos hit wære wurð. Swa swiðe nearwe
lice he hit let ut aspyrian. þ næs an ælpig hide. ne an
sulung landes. ne furðon hit is sceame to tellanne. ac hit
ne þuhte hi nan sceame to donne. an oxe. ne an cu. ne an
swin. næs belyfon. þ næs ge sett on his ge write. ⁊ ealle þa
ge writa wæron ge broht to him syððan.

time,' says the *Chronicle*, 'people had much oppression and very many injuries.'

So Domesday Book was born not out of a dispassionate enquiry into the land of England, but out of military necessity. The king's greed was proverbial: he 'oppressed the poor'; he was 'so very stark and deprived his subjects of many a mark of gold and more hundreds of pounds of silver, that he took with great injustice . . . for greediness he loved above all'. So it was, according to this contemporary, that 'he ruled over England, and by his cunning it was so examined that there was not one hide in England that he did not know who owned it, and what it was worth, and then set it down in his record' (*Anglo-Saxon Chronicle*). Domesday Book is that record. 'Great Domesday', the final version, is the abbreviated account of most of the kingdom; 'Little Domesday' (in fact physically hardly smaller) comprises the more detailed returns for East Anglia which were never incorporated into the final volume, presumably because the writing up of the survey was left uncompleted at William's death in September 1087. What 'writings' William was shown before he left England for the last time late in 1086 is debatable – perhaps an edited version of the returns, like the 'Little Domesday'. 'Great Domesday' itself must have taken about a year to write, and can hardly have been begun before autumn 1086.

Above William the Conqueror, a detail from the Bayeux Tapestry: 'too relentless to care though the world might hate him.'
Right A page from the Exon Domesday, the more detailed account of the returns from the south-western shires. It is still kept at Exeter Cathedral, where it was annotated by the scribe of the 'Great Domesday'.

Until 1907 the *Anglo-Saxon Chronicle* was the single reliable literary account of the great survey. Then a text was discovered in a Bodleian Library manuscript which had been written in the very year of the survey. Its author, Robert Losinga, Bishop of Hereford, must have been present at the 'deep discussion' in Gloucester after Christmas 1085:

In this, the twentieth year of his reign, by order of William king of the English, there was made a survey [*descriptio*] of the whole of England, that is to say of the lands of the several provinces of England, and of the possessions of each and all of the magnates. This was done in respect of ploughland and habitations, and of men both bond and free, both those who were cottagers and those who had houses and a share of the arable land; and [it was done] in respect of ploughs and horses and other livestock; and in respect of the services and payments due from all men in the whole land. Other investigators followed the first; and men were sent into provinces they did not know, and where they were themselves unknown, so they might be able to check the first survey and if necessary denounce its authors as guilty to the king. And the land was vexed with many calamities arising from the collection of the royal money.

This remarkable discovery precisely confirmed the *Anglo-Saxon Chronicle*. It also added two new pieces of information: first, that two successive circuits were made by the commissioners to check on possible fraud; second, that the survey coincided with a tax levy. This last point seems to be alluded to by the *Chronicle*, for the 1086 entry says that before the king crossed from England to Normandy he 'levied very heavy taxes on his subjects – upon any pretext, whether justly or unjustly'. So both sources insist that the last year and a half of the Conqueror's reign was marked by extortionate taxation, which seems to have been tied in with the making of the Domesday survey. Indeed, from their combined testimony it must be assumed that the actual inquiry coincided with the levying of a new geld like that of 1084. This may well be confirmed by the presence of tax rolls bound up in the set of south-western returns known as the Exon Domesday, still preserved in Exeter Cathedral today, for these are almost certainly tax returns for the south-western shires from 1086. Unique as Domesday was, it was compiled as another massive piece of financial extortion was taking place.

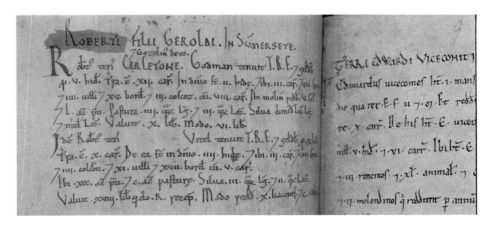

The Domesday survey describes the whole of England south of the Tees and the Westmorland fells – the limits of practical rule achieved by the Anglo-Saxon kings of the tenth century. It is likely that there were seven 'panels' for seven circuits – Kent and the south-east (I), the south-western shires (II), the East Midlands (III), the central Midlands (IV), the West Midlands (V), the North Midlands, Yorkshire and Lincolnshire (VI), and East Anglia (VII). By a fantastic chance, the questions which were asked of each hundred court have survived in a related text known as the Ely Inquiry, which is now preserved in a late twelfth-century version in the British Library.

Here follows the inquiry into the land made by the king's barons, on oath of the sheriff of the shire and of all the barons and their Frenchmen, and of the whole hundred, the priest, the reeve, and six villeins of each village; in order [they asked] the name of the estate; who held it in the time of King Edward; who holds it now; how many hides; how many ploughs on the demesne [the lord's land]; how many among the men; how many villeins; how many cottars; how many slaves; how many free men; how many sokemen; how much wood; how much meadow; how much pasture; how many mills; how many fishponds; how much has been added or taken away; how much, taken altogether, it used to be worth and how much now; how much each freeman or sokeman had or has. All this [to be given] three times, that is, in the time of King Edward, as it was when King William first gave the estate, and as it is now; also whether it is possible that more [revenue] could be taken from the estate than is being taken now.

There can be little doubt that this account contains the only surviving record of the official instructions given to the commissioners: these were the actual questions put to every group of jurors, who were required to swear on oath the truth of the figures. Indeed the Ely text also gives the names of the Domesday jurors for the areas it covers, for example:

In the hundred of Thriplow the following men gave sworn evidence: Ralph, the reeve of this hundred; William of Cailly; Ralph of Barrington; Theobald, the man of Hardwin; Stanhard of Hauxton; Godric of Fowlmere; Aelfric of Thriplow; Sigar the steward, and all other Frenchmen and Englishmen of the hundred.

At root, then, the inquiry was intended to be a record of estates or manors, with over twenty questions asked about each manor at three different periods. Though the inquiry followed closely the raising of another heavy tax, it was essentially unconnected with it. But at the same time Domesday was ultimately about tax in general: wherever you look in the book you find money. In each case the point of the questions was the value of the estate in terms of taxation, 'and whether more can be got from it than is being taken now'.

Scholars now think that the making of Domesday had three separate aims. One was to provide the king with an exact record of local contributions to the king's geld, Danegeld or Heregeld, the one great Anglo-Saxon tax which could be levied uniformly over the whole country. Each entry in Domesday usually begins with a statement of the estate's liability in terms of geld, an assessment given in accordance with a system used before

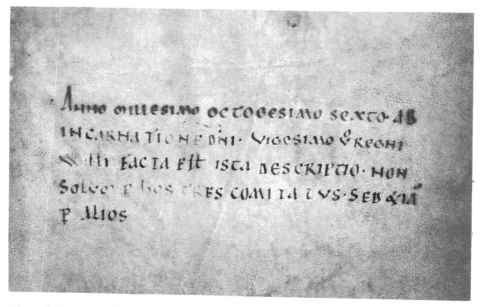

The colophon (or tailpiece) from the 'Little Domesday': 'In the year one thousand and eighty-six from our Lord's birth, and in the twentieth year of the reign of William, this survey [*descriptio*] was made, not only in these three counties [Norfolk, Suffolk and Essex] but also through others.'

1066 – in English areas based on the unit known as the hide, in Danish ones on the carucate.

But Domesday also had a more general military and fiscal purpose. The crises of the mid-1080s show that the king had every reason to obtain precise and accurate information about the exact holdings of his feudal lords – presumably the problems of billeting his army in the winter of 1085 highlighted this. So although Domesday gives little information about feudal organisation, and misses out key facts such as the amount of knight service owed by each landowner, it is different from all earlier geld inquisitions in that below shire level it is arranged according to the holdings of the military hierarchy – not by hundreds or parishes, but by tenants. The second purpose of Domesday Book was to reveal the resources of the newly established feudal order in England: the king could learn exactly what was held by his vassals, and how much revenue they had.

Thirdly, Domesday had a legal purpose. The years since the Conquest had seen the violent and unjust seizure of land on a vast scale. Surviving records of trials show that these must often have been the subject of court cases. For example at Kentford in Suffolk a trial was held in 1080 concerning the possessions of the church of Ely, which had been 'almost totally destroyed by the unjust exactions of [King William's] officials'. In many places there had been continuous litigation since the Conquest, and

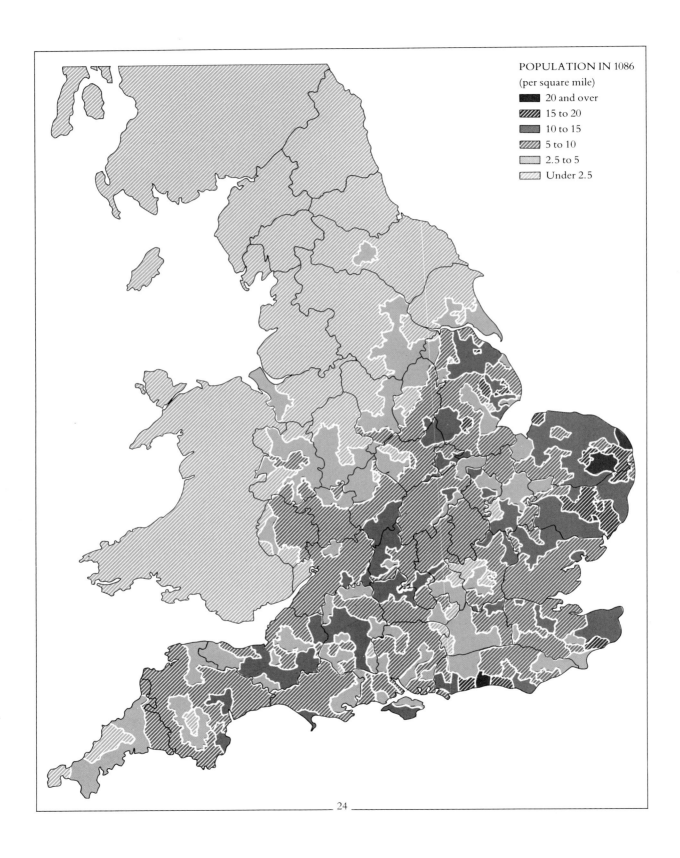

POPULATION IN 1086
(per square mile)

- 20 and over
- 15 to 20
- 10 to 15
- 5 to 10
- 2.5 to 5
- Under 2.5

ownership of many places was still in dispute. William, of course, saw himself as the legitimate successor of Edward the Confessor, and wanted Domesday to provide him with a record of England before 1066. But he was also anxious to legalise the great changes which had taken place since the Conquest. Domesday Book therefore contains constant references to the disputes which had arisen over ownership and possession, claim and counter-claim, and in the accounts of several shires, such as Yorkshire, Lincolnshire and especially Huntingdonshire, the disputes which came up for settlement before the circuits and the local juries are actually entered in the finished product.

Domesday, then, was a tax or geld inquest, a feudal record and a judicial statement. But it is more than all those things for its scope was so much wider. It was the unique product of a unique occasion, perhaps the single most dramatic event in British history – the Norman Conquest of 1066. It was the Conquest, and the chaos, violence and uncertainty which it entailed, which had given form to the king's desire to obtain the fullest possible information about the kingdom he had won. Domesday Book not only described the conquered country to a king who never learned to speak its language, but it also recorded the tremendous changes in ownership which the Conquest had brought about.

So it was that soon the book assumed a symbolic role in English history, until in the 1170s, in the 'Dialogue concerning the Exchequer' written by the treasurer Richard Fitznigel, we learn that 'This book is metaphorically called by the native English Domesday, that is, the "Day of Judgement". For just as the verdict of that strict and terrible last account cannot be evaded by any skilful subterfuge, so when this book is appealed to on those matters which it contains, its sentence cannot be quashed or set aside with impunity. That is why the book is called "The Book of Judgement" (Domesday Book), not because it contains judgements on various difficult questions, but because its decisions, like those of the Last Judgement, are unalterable'.

Though Domesday Book is far and away the greatest single source for early English social history, it still hides many mysteries. Indeed it may be that only our present age of computers will reveal some of its underlying patterns. First of all, Domesday is not in fact comprehensive. By accident or design it fails to account for many places which are known to have existed in the eleventh century; the final version excluded even some important towns, such as the biggest of them all, London, along with Winchester and Tamworth; many smaller sites were also omitted, perhaps because they did not come into the inquiry's terms of reference. But Domesday is still so far-reaching that a picture can be gathered of English society as a whole. It shows tremendous regional variation in social structure and custom, with society graded in careful legal terminology from the free to the virtual slave. Totals vary, but in terms of heads of households the Domesday population looks something like this:

109 230	villeins (bonded peasants who pay labour service to the lord but have a share of common fields)
81 849	bordars (unfree smallholders)
5 205	cottars (similar, mainly in south)
905	burs or coliberti (relics of older servile class in south)
28 235	servi (slaves, chattels of their lords; mainly in south and south-west)
13 553	freemen (liberi homines) and
23 324	sokemen (usually, but not always, paid money, but were free to buy and sell land; 80 per cent of these were in the three eastern counties of Lincolnshire, Norfolk and Suffolk)
1 100	chief tenants
6 000	sub-tenants
15 000	estimate for clergy (1027 rural priests recorded)
6 000	miscellaneous rural workers, etc.
290 000	total rural population

To these figures we must allow at least 10 per cent for omissions – Domesday was not interested in population totals themselves but in values and tenure – so we must be dealing with well over 300,000 families in the assessed areas. How can we turn that into a reasonable estimate of English population in 1086? Scholars have usually guessed at a multiplier of between four and five to account for wives and children, and medieval censuses from Lincolnshire suggest an average family size of 4.68 around 1200. In this case the rural population of Domesday England south of the Tees was probably around one and a half million, and quite possibly more. There is, however, a further element of the population to be considered. Domesday Book names 112 places to which it gives or implies urban status, often calling them *civitas* (city) or *burgus* (burh). Domesday's population figures for these places suggest a 'real' total of about 111,500, but there is reason to think the 'urban' population of eleventh-century England was much larger. To start with, London is not in Domesday. This may be partly due to the fact that 'the largest and fairest part of the city' was burned down in the late summer of 1086, while the survey was still being made. London's population in 1086 was very likely upwards of 25,000. The *Anglo-Saxon Chronicle* says that many other towns were burned down at that time, and though it mentions no others by name, this could help account for further omissions, such as Winchester, and the very imperfect description of many others. Winchester probably had 6000 or so people in 1086; it had been bigger twenty years before. York was a similar size at Domesday, and several other big towns, notably Lincoln, Norwich, Oxford and Thetford, must have had 4000 or 5000 people. About twenty towns probably had between 2000 and 4000 people, Stamford, Canterbury and Exeter among them; another twenty-five were between 500 and 2000, including Cambridge, Shaftesbury and Warwick. To these we should add

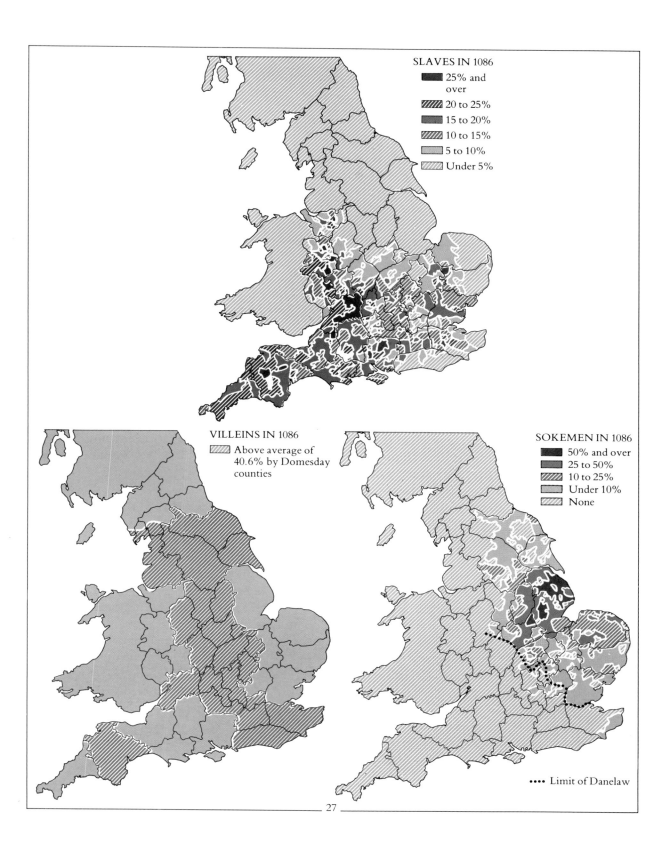

SLAVES IN 1086
- 25% and over
- 20 to 25%
- 15 to 20%
- 10 to 15%
- 5 to 10%
- Under 5%

VILLEINS IN 1086
- Above average of 40.6% by Domesday counties

SOKEMEN IN 1086
- 50% and over
- 25 to 50%
- 10 to 25%
- Under 10%
- None

•••• Limit of Danelaw

about eighty royal manors and large villages with some sort of urban nucleus and a population of less than 500. So the 'town' population of the country could have been anywhere between 120,000 and 200,000; 175,000 seems reasonable, at 10 per cent of the country, but may be on the low side.

Domesday, then, paints a picture of a sophisticated early medieval 'state' with an elaborate system of local government; a society which we now know before 1066 had the capacity and willingness for improvisation and change in its administrative ideas which is not found again until the Victorians. Some features of this state lasted a very long time – some, as we shall see, still survive – and it has yet to be precisely determined by scholars to what degree the structures of the Anglo-Saxon state influenced even the course of modern English history. It has, for example, been suggested that the resilience of the English state in the post-medieval period, and its successful avoidance of revolutionary change, owed something to the framework of government established before Domesday.

So today no one follows the nineteenth-century view which saw the Norman Conquest and Domesday as a purely new beginning, the imposition of continental sophistication on an old-fashioned, insular and under-developed backwater. Domesday may ring in the new, but its roots lie far back in time.

Until the arrival of over a million immigrants from the Commonwealth countries of Asia and the Caribbean after the Second World War, the Norman Conquest was the last – and perhaps politically the most potent – intrusion into British culture. But beyond the Normans lay Vikings, Norse and Danish, Anglo-Saxons, Romans, Celts – all of whom have left their traces on the landscape and in the historical record. This book looks at these different kinds of evidence in detail, showing how Domesday Book is a pointer towards the development of English – and British – society not only over the last 900 years, but over centuries, and even millennia, before Domesday. For example, many different social classes were revealed in Domesday, as well as marked differences between one region and another – how did this society and these differences come about? What are the origins of the social order portrayed in Domesday – the feudal manorial system? Kingship? The classes of society? Freedom? And what did freedom mean? These fascinating questions are much debated by modern historians because they are central to an understanding of the whole of British history. They also have a bearing on the problem of the origins of 'Englishness', if we can call it that: is English civilisation different from other western cultures, and if so why? When did it diverge? These are some of the riddles which lie behind the search for the roots of Domesday. In considering the idiosyncratic political growth of England in particular, English ideas about common law, property, marriage, and so on, the great Domesday historian, F.W. Maitland, wrote a century ago that it was perhaps long before the thirteenth century that 'England had taken her chosen path'. Was he right?

2
AN ANCIENT LANDSCAPE:
THE SEARCH BEGINS

A people without history is not redeemed from time, for history is a pattern of timeless moments. So, while the light fails on a winter's afternoon, in a secluded chapel History is now and England.
T. S. Eliot, Little Gidding, *1941*.

You can see Ashdown rising on the left 3 miles off as you leave Didcot on the train from London to Bristol and Wales. For the next 20 miles – almost as far as Swindon – its long green ridge runs parallel to the track, a steep 600 feet above the rich farmland through which the train speeds. When the autumn rains come you will often see Ashdown, dark and damp, shrouded

The Berkshire Ridgeway from the east, showing Uffington Camp and the White Horse.

in cloud; it is the brightest emerald green on summer evenings when deep shadows fall across the great natural hollow in the escarpment at Dragon Hill, where the famous White Horse can be glimpsed, cut into the chalk beyond the church tower of Uffington. You can reach it by exits 13 or 14 from the M4. Better still, you can walk to it, on two of the most ancient routes in Britain: on the Ridgeway from the Thames at Goring and Streatley; or on the Icknield Way from the Thames at Wallingford. On either route the walker quickly starts to see indications that this landscape has taken thousands of years to arrive at its present shape – and, of course, it is still changing: only since the war have important Iron Age field systems been ploughed away in these parts. As you walk westwards you soon begin to distinguish medieval field patterns and linchets, tumuli and ancient dykes, and the ramparts of Iron Age hillforts like Blewburton, with medieval strip fields cut into its slopes, and Segsbury with its massive ditches. You cross the relic of a more recent age of great builders, the remains of the embankments for the nineteenth-century railway line from Didcot to Newbury, which was closed in 1963 and already looks for all the world like a prehistoric boundary ditch. At East Hendred Down, where the north wind really scours up the valleys of Ashdown, you look down from the Bronze Age defence work of Grim's Ditch on to the Atomic Research Establishment at Harwell; beyond it lie the line of the Icknield Way and Brunel's track from Bristol to Paddington. It is a view once shared by Jonathan Swift and Thomas Hardy's Jude the Obscure. The landscape before you was already shaped something like this at the time of Domesday; there was probably just as much of the land under cultivation then, and not much more forest, for these parts had been cultivated since Neolithic times and cleared long before the Conqueror's day. Indeed in 1086 the villages between Harwell and Wantage were clustered more thickly than now. Other than the odd farm, little remains today of East and West Lockinge and East and West Ginge, villages created as the hunger for land developed in the tenth century, and all with sizeable populations in Domesday. The other Domesday villages are all clearly visible from the Downs: East and West Hendred (the main centre, East Hendred, an important royal estate before 1066), Ardington, and Wantage itself, centre of a hundred, and a major royal possession where King Alfred the Great was born in 849.

So from our vantage point above Harwell we can see evidence of many of the forces which have shaped the lives of the English and British peoples over nearly 10,000 years. Only scattered finds have been made from the Palaeolithic period, but the Downs have a very long and rich Mesolithic period, especially in the Kennet valley in the fourth millennium BC. By

Right By the side of the Ridgeway, there are still strip linchets – terraces made to create ploughland up the slopes of the chalk Downs; these at Bishopstone, near Uffington, are seen (above) on the ground and (below) from the air.

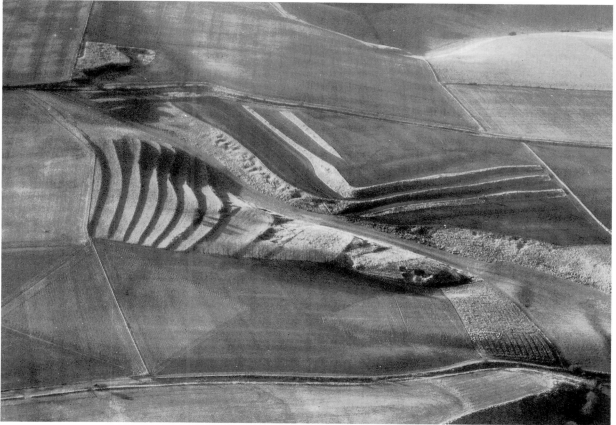

Neolithic times (the third millennium BC) the Downs were beginning to be cleared and cultivated. From then on the signs are everywhere on the ground: Bronze Age barrows and ring ditches, Iron Age forts, dykes, ways and field systems, and then the Roman, Saxon, medieval and modern overlay. Out of this intricate pattern modern field research has been able, with the aid of aerial photography, to recover evidence of farms and their enclosures which existed in the Iron Age, and sometimes fairly complete pictures of the Celtic field systems which were cultivated by the people dependent on the great hillforts on the Downs. In one case, in the fields below Segsbury hillfort, it has proved possible to reconstruct the best part of 3000 acres of the small rectangular and square Celtic fields from the first millennium BC. Indeed in some cases the prehistoric patterns can be seen to have determined the shapes and courses of later fields and ways – the present track which runs southwards to East Garston Down from Letcombe Bassett below Segsbury, for instance, is a prehistoric road.

Above Segsbury Camp on the Berkshire Ridgeway. The Iron Age field systems around it have been overlaid by medieval and later enclosures.
Left Blewburton Hill, Blewbury, Berkshire. In Domesday it was the centre of an already ancient unit of administration, which may have depended originally on the Iron Age hillfort from which Blewbury takes its name.

Air surveys and archaeology have also revealed evidence of how these lands were cultivated during the Roman period when the country houses which we call villas took over the administrative function of the Iron Age hillforts. Farms and estates had developed extensively during the later pre-historic period, and it was natural that the Roman occupiers – progressively Celticised themselves – should let the native system run in its own way. So they left the locals to till the chalk Downs, while they themselves cleared the heavier soils below the Downs for more intensive 'modern' farming methods such as the heavy, iron-tipped plough, which they introduced. Villas were built below the Downs at East Challow and Woolstone, for example, but native housing carried on right through to the end of the Roman period, with the typical pattern of villages of round huts sur-rounded by a network of small fields and pasture beyond. Further along the Downs such a site, though now destroyed, has been recorded at Maddle Farm; it extended over 75 acres and had at least one major villa-type building with tessellated pavements, subsidiary buildings and evidence of corn drying and milling. Most of the finds from the site were third- and fourth-century: whether the whole 'estate' was dependent on the presumed villa, or whether this is really a village, cannot be answered, but what was here was clearly a Celtic-Roman settlement which existed right up into the era of the English settlements, the fifth century and later, when Anglo-Saxon immigrants came to these parts from the continent.

Back at our vantage point above Harwell, the village pattern we see is predominantly the one created between the English settlements of the fifth

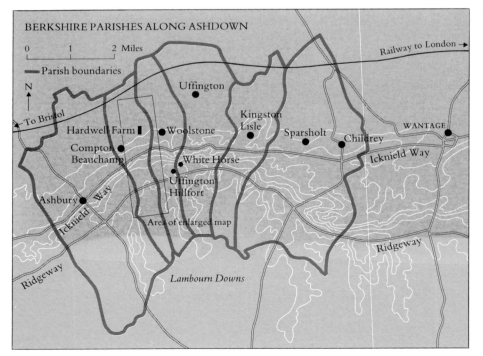

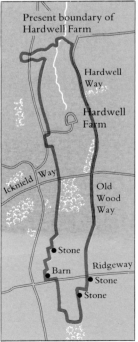

and sixth centuries, and the time of the Domesday survey. Indeed, it was probably late in this period that most of these villages we see today were created, in the tenth century as the population grew. In Domesday the villages cluster thickly along the spring-line at the foot of the Downs. It was during this period that the open-field system seems to have developed: the lands of each estate were divided into two or three great open fields which were ploughed in strips by the peasantry, a system which continued right through the Middle Ages and even into the twentieth century. The villages below us, Ardington, Charlton by Wantage, Hendred, and northwards beyond the railway Drayton and Sutton Courtenay, are of particular interest in this story. Anglo-Saxon charters – lease documents – of the tenth century from these five villages provide the first clear evidence of the classic intermixture of the common fields where, as at Ardington, 'these nine hides lie among other lands held in share; the open pasture is common, the meadow is common and the ploughland [arable] is common', and where, as at Charlton, 'the lands cannot be described on any side by clear boundary points because to right and left the acres lie in combination one with another'. The estate map of 1754 in the Berkshire Record Office shows this open-field system still in existence in Charlton. (See p. 115.)

If we walk on from East Hendred Down westwards along the Ridgeway we pass the surviving signs of these field systems in the fields of Wantage and Letcombe Bassett, below the Celtic field patterns around Segsbury hillfort. Another 5 miles or so and we come to perhaps the most extraordinary corner of this remarkable landscape. Here a great natural amphitheatre opens out with wonderful views northwards over the Vale of the White Horse. This is Uffington Down. Below is the 361-foot-long White Horse, cut out of the chalk in the Iron Age. Above is the hillfort of Uffington Castle. In the tenth century this place was known as Ashbury, and we know a lot about the character of the landscape then because of the existence of a remarkable series of Anglo-Saxon land grants whose boundary clauses describe the natural features in great detail. The charters tell us of a series of estates which follow the lines of the present parish boundaries very closely. Indeed, the great similarity between the pattern of Iron Age boundary ditches and hillforts and that of the Anglo-Saxon estates suggests some sort of continuity. Both groups exploit elongated strips of territory running off the Downs into the spring-belt below, enabling each to benefit from several different soil types. Perhaps, then, the landscape has always determined the nature of the settlements, but even the casual observer cannot help but wonder what relationship exists between these superimposed pasts – Iron Age, Roman, Saxon and modern.

The tenth-century documents for the estates around Uffington show us that, long before Domesday, the management of the countryside for agriculture was already deeply rooted. They also enable us to engage in a kind of time travel back to tenth-century Berkshire. Here, for example, are the

boundaries of Hardwell Farm – now those of the parish of Compton Beauchamp, though Hardwell Farm still exists, 500 yards west of the site of the
Roman villa at Woolstone:

First along Swinbrook, up to rush hollow, and then from the bend in rush hollow on to
Hardwell Way; along the way until it comes to Icknield Way, then from the way up on the
'old wood way' along the eastern side of Tell's Camp [an Iron Age fort in the wood, south of
the present B4507], then to a gore, and from there to a gore-shaped acre [the triangular end
of a piece of ploughland] and then along the furrow to the top of a headland, and on to a
fore-earth [headlands are where the ploughman turns his team; fore-earths are where the
headland is then ploughed at right-angles to the rest of the field] and this fore-earth sticks
into the estate; then right on to the stone on the ridgeway; then westwards to a gore, and
along the furrow to its headland, then from the down at 'ferny hill valley', to a furrow an
acre [strip?] nearer the linchet; then to the linchet, and then from the linchet at 'ferny hill
valley' to the other linchet on the south side of 'ferny hill valley'; forward then along a
furrow to a row of stones [markers] then right onto the ridgeway [again: the bounds are now
heading north]; then from there to a gore-acre; then to a headland, then to a gore-acre going
into the land [i.e. the estate], then along a furrow until it comes to a corner, and then from
there forward along a furrow until it reaches a fore-earth, and this fore-earth goes into the
land; then on to Icknield Way along the west side of Tell's Camp, then northwards over the
Icknield Way to 'Sica's spring'; then from there crossways over a furlong right on to an alder
bed at the corner of 'hedged hill brook', and along this brook until it comes to two gore-
acres, these gore-acres going into the land, then on to a fore-earth, to a headland, then right
on to 'redcliff' [riverbank] on Swinbrook, and so along the brook back to the rush hollow.
Translated from the twelfth-century copy of the bounds in the British Library.

Above Hardwell Farm, near Uffington. The stream at top left is the Swinbrook of the 903 charter, and the track running from centre top to lower right is Hardwell Way. To the left of the farm is the D-shaped moat mentioned in 1307, perhaps pre-Conquest in origin. *Above left* The Ridgeway approaching the Uffington escarpment; this route was used by travellers since prehistoric times.

The Hardwell charter takes us back to the Berkshire countryside in around AD 903, at the shoulder of the Anglo-Saxon surveyor who rode the bounds with Tata, the new owner. Nearly all the features named in this grant can still be found on the ground. The farm itself stood inside a D-shaped moat which still exists in part, though sadly the medieval longhouse 'hall' which can be seen on old photographs and maps was demolished twenty years ago: probably the site of the Saxon hall which succeeded the nearby Roman villa, though perhaps 'Hordwyll' – 'the well, or spring, of votive offerings' – had been inhabited since the Iron Age. Hardwell Way, now a deep, broad lane overgrown with trees, still leads past the farm up onto the Icknield Way, and the 'old wood way' is still there – inside a double hedge going uphill east of 'Tell's burh', the earthwork known today as Hardwell Camp. Ferny hill valley is still there, though now called Pingoose Covert, and even the alder bed at hedged hill corner leading on to Swinbrook. The numerous cultivation marks are of course gone now, but what is really remarkable about this document is that here we have all the indications of specialised agriculture, all the language of arable farming from medieval times to the present day: headlands, furrows, furlongs, gore-acres, fore-earths. With the adoption of the heavy-wheeled plough in the later Saxon period, and the growing demands of expanding population, agriculture was at an advanced stage of estate management and specialised ploughing techniques. The 903 charter shows how the layout of the estate and its exploitation were geared to the soil – a strip of land 2½ miles long and never more than 500 yards wide, running from the top of the chalk Downs to the rich soil in the vale. The estate of Hardwell Farm today has the same shape as in 903, and perhaps for over a thousand years before that. In many parts of England great changes have happened in the landscape since then. The great open fields have been enclosed, woodland and waste have been brought under cultivation, land which was ploughed for centuries has been turned into grassland for cattle rearing, and everywhere roads have cut up the ancient lie of the land. But here at Hardwell Farm a careful reading of the landscape can reveal its deep past almost as clearly as a photograph.

In 1086 the Conqueror's local surveyors, the sheriff's agents, came to Uffington to the shire hundred court at Hillslowmound – a meeting place close to Hardwell in the neighbouring parish of Compton Beauchamp. Here they heard the testimony of the local jury – six Normans and six English (perhaps they included the owner of Hardwell) – on the ownership of the manors around Uffington: the raw material of the evidence they collected would be sworn on oath by the sheriff to the regional circuit commissioners – the 'bigwigs' – at their hearing later in Wallingford.

They learned that Hardwell was held by Abingdon Abbey and that its 3 hides (here 600 acres) were lumped in with the Abbey's main holding, Uffington (in whose parish Hardwell remained up to the last century). This we learn from the *Abingdon Chronicle* as Domesday gives no separate entry

A settlement from the Roman period at Crosby Ravensworth near Shap in Westmorland. This group of stone-walled enclosures for houses, yards and corrals was probably inhabited by Celtic-speaking natives up to the fourth century. Anglian and Norwegian farmers lived nearby before Domesday.

for Hardwell. Domesday does, however, name Hardwell's tenant in 1086, a Norman called Gilbert de Colimbars. At the farm itself there was probably only a handful of peasants who did the ploughing. As late as 1307 the place is mentioned with its moat and house, courtyard and outbuildings, fishpond and dovecote, with a mere four villeins and eight cottagers. In 1086 they probably had two plough teams of eight oxen each, with perhaps one more plough for Gilbert. What happened to the Anglo-Saxon freeman who farmed Hardwell from the Abbey in 1066 we do not know. Conceivably he or his sons were now villeins in Gilbert's service, performing weekly work for him, like an English villein on one of his next neighbour William FitzAnsculf's estates, at Marsh Gibbon in Buckinghamshire, the former freeman Aelfric, now farming at a rent, 'miserably and with a heavy heart'.

Standing on Ashdown above the White Horse, then, we can take in clues about the development of the English landscape – and the life of the ordinary people – over thousands of years. History is often presented in terms of cataclysmic change: the Romans sweeping away the prehistoric past; the Anglo-Saxons driving out the Romano-British and building a new Germanic society on their ruins; the Vikings pillaging and killing the English villagers of the north and east; the Normans replacing the antiquated Old English state with the new 'modern' feudal order, doing away with old-fashioned English culture at the same time. The trouble is that history has always been viewed from the top, by the makers and doers, by the rulers and their chroniclers, by the scholars of church and state. Only in the last hundred years has the prospect emerged of reconstituting the life of the ordinary people who have lived in Britain over the thousands of years for which we have records. In a place like Ashdown the signs speak of deep continuities, and the written records and archaeology can take us back into prehistory past the homely names of Swinbrook and the alder bed at hedged hill corner. It is on this idea of continuity that this inquiry into Domesday Book is based; much of the man-made landscape described in Domesday was already very old by 1086. But, as our walk along the Downs has revealed, the documentary sources for this past – that is, inscriptions and texts, supplemented by archaeology – begin with the Romans. To them we turn first.

3
THE ROMAN PAST

How lucky you are, Britain, more blessed than any other land, endowed by nature with every benefit of soil and climate. Your winters are not too cold, your summers not too hot; your corn fields so productive, your herds innumerable, the dairy herds overflowing with milk, the sheep flocks heavy with wool. To make life all the more pleasant, your days are long and your nights short, so while to us the sun may appear to go down, in Britain it merely seems to go past!
From a panegyric to the Emperor Constantine, AD 310.

The Romans invaded lowland Britain in AD 43 and conquered it over the next few decades. As we have seen on the Berkshire Downs, the land they overran was already an old country which had been cultivated for a long time. The Romans retained the old tribal organisation of the land as the basis of their administration, founding new cities as tribal and provincial capitals, some of which are still cities today, such as Lincoln, Leicester and Winchester. Though the Iron Age hillforts were abandoned, the basic pre-Roman structure of regional and local organisation was retained, and this probably included the economic grouping of estates which had been dependent on, or contributory to, the hillforts, estates like the group around Uffington. (See pp. 32–3.)

As imperialists, the Roman governors' chief concern was to exploit the conquered land. One of their biggest sources of revenue was wool, and from the second century AD a network of villas grew up around many of the main towns as country estate centres for the handling of Britain's 'innumerable flocks' with their 'heavy fleeces', as the panegyric to Constantine puts it. The mass of the native British workforce, who spoke a Celtic language related to today's Welsh, simply worked for their new masters as 'free', tied or enslaved peasants, in the villas, farms and villages which covered southern Britain. By AD 300 the population may have reached as much as four million. In this chapter I will attempt to trace the fortunes of the Romano-British workforce through to the fall of the Roman empire in Britain early in the fifth century AD, when groups of Anglo-Saxon immigrants – who spoke the Germanic ancestor of today's English language – settled in southern and eastern Britain and imposed themselves as masters on the native population. The question we will be trying to solve is this: how much did Anglo-Saxon England – the England portrayed in Domesday Book – owe to the Roman and pre-Roman past?

Two miles east of the centre of Hitchin stands the village of Great

Wymondley. In the Domesday entries for Hertfordshire it comes first, as a royal estate: formerly gifted to the abbey of Chatteris in the Fens, it had probably been a royal possession back in the eighth century. Today, if you go past the village green and through the churchyard, you climb over a stile into an embanked and overgrown enclosure about 100 yards square; beyond it are others of a similar size, also still partly hedged and embanked. It was here over a century ago that the great scholar Frederic Seebohm came looking for continuity between Roman villa and Anglo-Saxon manor. Seebohm, attracted by chance archaeological finds in this and neighbouring parishes, had been intrigued by the remarkable regularity of the field system in the 1803 tithe map, then still in the possession of the lord of the

Above A Victorian photograph of Great Wymondley church, Hertfordshire, which has a Norman nave and chancel. There may have been continuity in the area from Roman times.
Right The 1803 tithe map of Great Wymondley, with its pattern of open-field strips overlying a more ancient rectilinear arrangement.

manor but now in Hertford Record Office. In particular he had noticed a group of fields in between the open fields and the church, fields which were used for common grazing by the villagers. One group stood out on the map and was even more conspicuous on the ground. In *The English Village Community* he wrote:

It consists now of several fields, forming a rough square, with its sides to the four points of the compass, and contains, filling in the corners of the square, about 25 Roman *iugera* – or the eighth of a *centuria* of 200 *iugera* – the extent of land often allotted to a retired veteran with a single pair of oxen. The proof that it was a Roman holding is as follows: In the corner next to the church are two square fields still distinctly surrounded by a moat, nearly parallel to which, on the east side, was found a line of black earth full of broken Roman pottery and tiles. Near the church at the south-west corner of the property, is a double tumulus which . . . may have been a terminal mound. In the extreme opposite corner of the holding was found a Roman cemetery, containing the urns, dishes, and bottles of a score or two of Roman burials. . . . Over the hedge begins the Lammas land [i.e. the common grazing]. How many other holdings were included in the Roman village we do not know, but that the village stood in the same position in relation to the open fields that it was in 1803 is obvious.

Seebohm's brilliant book fell out of favour with later generations of scholars, but now, as evidence grows for continuity, it has deservedly come back into the reckoning. Since he wrote, excavations at Great Wymondley have supported his theory. The site of a Roman villa was located in the 1930s, a mile or so north-west of the church; coins found there show that its occupants continued to use money well into the fifth century. Remarkably, Saxon pottery was also turned up on the same site. The double tumulus has not been dug; it may represent a small Norman motte inside the Roman or Iron Age bailey – there are hints of the same kind of arrangement nearby at Pirton and Bygrave. Recently, Seebohm's arguments have been taken even further with the suggestion that the whole open-field system at Great Wymondley shown in the 1803 map may preserve traces of a symmetrically laid out field grid of the late Roman period with ten *iugera* squares. Only excavation can prove this, and it is unlikely that so rigid and mathematically precise a layout would be imposed on what is assumed to be an earlier Celtic field system. We would not expect absolute regularity, but something more like the Berkshire field systems, with square or rectangular fields varying in size. Nevertheless Seebohm's point stands: do we not have here, on the ground, the remains of a Roman villa estate, perhaps with its smaller holdings for veterans, *coloni* or whatever? This was an area of high civilisation and organisation in the Roman period, and Roman coins have been found at many of the villages around Hitchin. Remarkably, at Litlington, east of Ashwell, the rectangle of the medieval manor contains in close association the medieval manor house, the Roman villa, the church and a Roman tomb adjacent to a *ustrinum* surrounded by four walls, with coin finds extending from the second to the fourth century.

The finds at Great Wymondley open up one of the most intriguing and difficult questions – perhaps the single most important question – in British history. How much of the Celtic and Roman past went into the Anglo-Saxon culture and identity? Of course the question goes beyond the survival of land organisation or administrative units such as we found at Uffington: it involves law and customs of landholding, property inheritance, marriage and so on; it touches on the question of racial identity itself. For if the roots of the manorial society portrayed in Domesday Book draw on the pre-English and even pre-Roman past, so may other crucial aspects of the English and British identity. But do they?

The Roman world is often referred to as a slave society, a term which implies that most of the actual production was done by slaves, and that most of the workforce was enslaved. This is the kind of image we are used to in Hollywood movies and TV epics. But it is a fallacy. Most production

Right Great Wymondley Priory: the late medieval barn exterior (above) and interior (below). The remains of the early thirteenth-century priory and fourteenth-century hall testify to the continuing prosperity of the area after Domesday.

in the Roman Empire – above all in agriculture, the dominant area of the economy – was achieved by peasants who were at least nominally free, even though serfdom seems to have increased during the fourth century AD, with many more people brought into different kinds of servile labour.

In the mid-third century, after a series of economic crises, the currency of the Roman Empire became worthless and the government was forced to raise most of its revenues by requisitions in kind, and to pay the army mainly in kind, with foodstuffs and supplies. Then from the 270s onwards came what the late Romans called the *renovatio*, the renewal, under the Emperor Diocletian. It was Diocletian who reorganised things into an elaborate system of taxation in kind. The first step was to hold new censuses through the Empire, in which not only was the land surveyed and assessed, but the rural population and the very farm livestock were counted.

The rules of the late Roman census varied between different areas. Censuses were carried out over a long period, and of course local customs varied: for instance where there was a poll tax, some regions exempted women, some counted them as half, and some as equal to men. But the most interesting thing from our point of view is the manner of assessing land. Obviously with such an unstable currency it was impossible to value land in straight cash terms; equally, the differences in climate, soil and productivity meant that land plots of the same size did not necessarily share the same value. So the land tax was assessed in ideal fiscal units, generally called *iuga*. In some parts of the Empire these were given in straight land measurements in a unit which we might call 'ploughlands', *iugera*: one *iugerum* was five-eighths of an acre, and 200 *iugera* (one *centuria*) was 125 acres. In sixth-century Roman lawbooks the tax assessment for 20 *iugera* of arable land (15 acres) is given as one *iuga*; but in Asia and Egypt pasture, arable land, vineyards and olive groves were rated differently, and in Syria three different qualities of arable land and two of olive groves were distinguished, rather as we grade land quality today.

The bulk of the payment of this taxation system was in kind, with an elaborate reckoning system being used to work out how much each land unit had to pay in wheat, barley, meat, wine and oil: these tax rates were published each 1 September. In the fourth century, when a sound gold currency was established, most of these payments in kind were dropped in favour of hard cash. But in the Eastern Empire as late as the early sixth century payment in kind was still levied in places to feed the troops. The payment of the tribute in cash in the Western Empire continued into the fifth century. In Britain, however, 'official' Roman rule ended after 410, and coinage ceased to be circulated after about 450. Nevertheless, as accounts of the fifth century suggest that organised civic life remained uninterrupted until the middle years, it must be assumed that the taxation system continued as a means by which local and provincial rulers could

Above Taxation in kind: Roman tenants paying up with poultry, fish and rabbits, a carving from the period of Diocletian's renewal.
Below Payment of taxes in money, from a late third-century stone carving from Italy.

sustain themselves, their élites and their armies, and that the tribute gradually came to be exacted in kind once more.

There is little hard evidence from Britain on this subject, but the general picture from many of the provinces of the Empire over the fourth and fifth centuries is clear. Complaints abound against the ruinous levels of tax – often over a quarter of the gross value of the yield was levied, on great and small alike. The result was that many people were driven out of business and much marginal land, where the rewards were poor anyway, was abandoned. In parts of Asia Minor in the fourth century 10 per cent of the land was deserted; and, astonishingly, in parts of North Africa between a third and a half of the cultivated land was deserted and no longer paying tax. This clearly would be a catastrophic state of affairs for any government, then or now, and the effects are not hard to envisage. The economy of the Roman Empire was overwhelmingly agricultural, and the great bulk of the revenues had always come from taxing land. The incomes of the rich likewise came from land, and their wealth was always invested in land. On the other hand the vast mass of the population were peasants, and the inequitable taxation system undoubtedly hit them heaviest, for they were always the ones who would be forced to sell up first. And indeed, all the evidence shows that in the late fourth and fifth centuries in many parts of the Empire the peasantry lost wealth and status. It was now difficult to rear your family; you had no chance of accumulating a few reserves; barbarian attacks – in Britain from Picts, Scots, Saxons and Angles – destroyed your crops and your stock; army units billeted on your land took more; there was the constant threat of epidemics, culminating in the terrible plague of the 540s which hit Britain hard along with the rest of the Roman world. How could a poor landholder with a few acres restock his farm and buy new tools? He could only borrow from bigger landowners around him, and if things went wrong, sell his land to his creditor and become in some way tied to a land-lord. In many parts of the Empire, therefore, an increasing number of peasant proprietors sank into the condition of being dependent farmers, tenants, as estates grew bigger and were concentrated into fewer hands. If this is what happened in Britain, too, it makes it much easier to speculate what happened to the lowland British population when the Roman government left them to their own devices and they gradually fell under the control of the Anglo-Saxon newcomers.

The history of the large estates in later Roman Britain is largely a blank. Archaeology has shown that in the third and fourth centuries villas were built in great numbers in southern Britain, especially in the wealthy sheep area of the Cotswolds where there is a villa in virtually every parish. In Somerset, around Ilchester, another sizeable group has come to light, and again around Dorchester in Dorset, where many, such as Frampton, Hinton St Mary, Tarrant Hinton and Halstock Dewlish, were richly adorned with mosaics. The great splendour of some of these country houses can be seen on the ground at Chedworth in the Cotswolds, at Fishbourne, Lullingstone, or in the British Museum where the famous mosaic from Hinton St Mary is the centrepiece of the Roman gallery. These were country manors on a grand scale. Unfortunately little has survived to give us any real idea of the extent of their estates, or how they were run; consequently all arguments about their nature have tended to work back from early records of estates covering roughly the same area in Anglo-Saxon times. It is likely that the population of Roman Britain throughout the fifth century still numbered over two million; nobody seriously supposes that anything like that figure settled in Britain during the migration period. So what happened to the mass of the workforce of Roman Britain, the dependent peasantry whose economic and social status sank during that time to the level of tied labourers?

Above right Hinton St Mary, Dorset: the famous fourth-century mosaic. This was the dining room floor of a wealthy Roman Briton's villa. The figure in the left roundel is the hero Bellerophon; that in the right one, Christ.
Right Mediterranean culture comes to Britain: mosaics of *c.* 350, depicting scenes of the Trojan War from the *Aeneid*, on the floor of a villa at Low Ham in Somerset.

The long-term effect of Roman government, then, may well have been to concentrate land in the hands of the governing aristocracy at the expense of the mass of the population at large. Concrete evidence survives which gives a clear picture of this accretion of power and land by a British landowner at this very time. It consists of a Latin life of a Roman lady from the great family of the Valerii; she became a Christian, and the Church recorded her disposal of many estates to charity. In AD 404 Melania freed 8000 slaves out of a total of 24,000 on sixty farms, villas or hamlets which she owned in the vicinity of Rome. Her other landholdings included estates elsewhere in Italy and in Sicily, Africa, Spain and Britain. She may have had well over 100,000 slaves working on her lands, maybe a quarter of a million. Unfortunately the names of her villas in Britain are not known, but her rentals show her income to have been on a scale comparable to the imperial revenues. As a comparison, the taxes of Numidia and Mauretania in North Africa in the early fifth century were 10 and 6 *centenaria* of gold respectively; the medium range of income for the senatorial aristocracy at that time – when there was still such a class in Britain too – was around 15 *centenaria* from land rents; and Melania's biographer estimates her rents to have been about that.

The structure of Melania's holdings can be imagined by reference to the Roman census records from Greece and Anatolia in the fourth and fifth centuries. These surveys show a contrast between huge senatorial estates, of which an example might be 2000 acres of arable land, 225 of vineyards and 8000 olive trees, down to scattered smaller properties: one on Thera, for example, amounted to 420 *iugera* (say 260 acres) of arable, 110 (say 70 acres) of vineyards and 580 olive trees. Whilst conditions and soil fertility varied greatly, this must be something like a middling farmer's holding in the Eastern Empire, and in this case it actually comprised three largish farms, five smaller farms and two smallholdings. On the other hand most small farms in these lists averaged about 25 acres of arable land and 5 of vineyards, with 100 olive trees. A high proportion of the smallholders were in some way obligated to bigger owners. Whilst the Western Roman Empire – and especially Britain – was very different in agrarian and social conditions from the East, in the breakdown of such minor holdings the censuses read remarkably like the documents referred to later in this book, from ninth-century France, tenth-century England, or from Domesday Book itself.

Thera: Politike farm on Paregorius' estate.
26 iugera [16 acres] of arable, 8 iugera [5 acres] of vineyards,
18 olive trees. Tenant a colonus [tied labourer] called
Theodorus, aged 30. Living with him his wife, aged 20.
Baby daughter, aged 2. One ox, 10 sheep.

The taxman would then have added something like this:

Land tax assessment for the farm, five-eighths of a iugum; poll tax rate for heads of household one and a half.

Above This mosaic from a Tunisian villa of the fourth century gives a vivid impression of the villa as a country manor house, with all its estate workers. At the top the lady of the manor receives renders of animals and produce from her tenant farmers (*coloni*).
Previous page A fresco from Pompeii gives an idea of the luxury enjoyed by Melania and the villa owners in Britain in the fourth century.

Late Roman aristocratic society continued to depend on the slave and on the semi-servile or tied peasant. As we have seen, it was not uncommon for sizeable villa estates to have had several hundred slaves or serfs. Slavery was still a big business in the later Empire, as it had been in earlier days, with the Germanic peoples providing a new source of slaves. In the East in the sixth century, Emperor Justinian's law codes indicate not the slightest change in outlook on this; similarly in the West the barbarian law codes of the seventh century – Ethelbert in Kent or Erwig in Spain – show that the system was taken over lock, stock and barrel by the newcomers. This surely included the acceptance of all the gradations of 'unfreedom' which had been devised

Conspicuous consumption: Roman grandees and their servants enjoying a country house banquet.

by later Roman society – not merely the words for slaves (*servi* being the one used in Domesday Book), but the half dozen or more terms which existed for servile peasants who were bound to a lord but not chattel slaves. Unfortunately, there is as yet no authoritative modern study on this fundamental problem of European history – that is, on how the slave-based system of the antique world gave way to the feudal world. It is agreed that slavery declined in late antiquity, though probably not very greatly. It is agreed that Domesday Book – where perhaps 10 per cent of the population may still have been *servi* – depicts the metamorphosis of the ancient system. But exactly how it happened, and to what degree the Romano-British population became the Anglo-Saxon, is still not known. Presumably the Anglo-Saxon newcomers found many estates, especially on marginal land, abandoned, or cultivated by *servi* or squatters. Some may still have been kept up by the well-to-do Romano-British owners, especially in the far west. Many others must have been cultivated even after the grand country houses of the aristocracy had been abandoned, as many were through the fifth century – doubtless absentee landlords like Melania reached a point where they lost contact with, and ceased to get revenue from, their British estates, and simply washed their hands of them. In many other cases, no doubt, Anglo-Saxon newcomers came upon semi-servile *coloni* and allowed them to continue in outlying farms as servile tenants to the larger central farm. In this way the land units farmed by the villas up to the fifth century might emerge in a slightly different form in the sixth or seventh centuries, with the Celtic population still providing labour for some Anglo-Saxon *cyning*, almost forgotten in the record, but whose continuing presence is revealed on the ground by the evidence of place names and archaeology. Two examples of such continuity can be found in the Cotswolds, and just off the Great North Road in Hertfordshire.

Right A shepherd with his sheep and goats. At least as early as the Roman period the wealth of lowland Britain depended on wool.

4
FROM ROMAN BRITAIN
TO ANGLO-SAXON ENGLAND

The parish of Withington in Gloucestershire, in the Cotswolds north of Cirencester, lies in a region covered by villa estates that were of great importance to the economy of later Roman Britain; the rich fleeces of their sheep flocks were carted to the imperial weaving mill at Winchester before being exported. Cirencester and Gloucester fell to English warbands as late as 577, but the Cotswolds north and west of Cirencester show little evidence of early Anglo-Saxon cemeteries, and it is likely that some form of

After processing in the imperial mill at Winchester, fine wool cloaks from Britain were sold in continental markets.

Romano–British rule existed there until 577, even though the cities them-selves by then were thinly populated and ruinous. Cities are expensive to maintain in any age, and by the late sixth century in western Britain local rulers may not have had the resources to maintain costly civic buildings. But the fabric of rural economy may still have survived in some form: in other areas of the Roman Empire there was a move away from the cities and into the country in the fifth century. The *Anglo-Saxon Chronicle* believed that the former Roman cities of Gloucester, Bath and Cirencester were still centres of administration when they were sacked in 577; it believed that they were governed by 'kings', and the names it gives for them (Conmail, Condidan and Farinmail) look like British – or in one case (Candidanus?) Roman – names. The attack of one group of Germanic invaders, the West Saxons, from the Thames valley into the Cotswolds in 577 did not lead to permanent colonisation. Subsequently a kingdom was established there under the overlordship of another big grouping of Anglo-Saxon settler tribes: the Mercians. The folk name of this particular kingdom, the Hwicce, is still obscure, but the name 'Cotswolds' was synonymous in the Dark Ages with the 'hill of the Hwicce', and among the 'Hwicce' names which have survived into modern times is Wychwood, the forest which separated the Saxons of the Thames valley from the Hwicce.

The Hwicce ruling family were Anglian in origin, and their armed foll-owing perhaps a mixture of Angle and Saxon. But the mass of the popu-lation of what is now Gloucestershire must have been of British origin in the seventh century, and it stands to reason that many traditions from Roman times must have carried down to the English period, especially in rural areas. With the aid of a remarkable series of Old English charters which start in the late seventh century, we can now look at what happened – bearing in mind the likelihood that whoever came to power in the Severn valley and Cotswolds in the seventh century must have inherited the social structure and sources of revenue available to the late sixth-century sub-Roman rulers who had controlled the region from the old cities. Whether this structure was based on villa estates or manors is not relevant at this stage, but it must have been there in some form. The money economy had broken down by about 450, but this offers all the more reason why local rulers should have taken pains that the 'redistributive' economy of the villa farms functioned in a way which ensured that they and their élites were sustained.

The Anglo-Saxon dynasty in the West Midlands, the Mercians, accepted Christianity in the 650s. In 679 a bishopric was established at Worcester to serve the Hwicce. Christianity had undoubtedly survived here from late Roman Britain; the great minster at Deerhurst-on-Severn overlay a late Roman building, as did the parish church of St Mary de Lode in Gloucester, which had its origins in a post-Roman timber church built into the ruins of a grand house with mosaics and wall paintings. Other churches in the Severn valley – Ozleworth, Hewelsfield and Oldbury-on-Severn – may also lie on late Roman holy sites. This makes the rapid success of the Church in the late seventh century more explicable. As elsewhere in Anglo-Saxon England and Germanic Europe, once the 'barbarian' inheritors of the Roman world had adopted Christianity they were anxious to show themselves as worthy patrons – and in return to make the most of the power offered them by the Church. They set about founding new churches or refounding old ones across their territories. To do so they had to endow the Church with land from the estates they had appropriated as conquerors of this former province of the Roman world. The Church recorded these acts in charters from the seventh century onwards, and before Domesday Book these are the most important evidence for the early history of Britain.

Around 675 Osric, king of the Hwicce, founded a monastery church dedicated to St Peter in the old Roman city of Bath. In 679 he did the same in Gloucester, endowing it with the 'tributaries of three hundreds': the later hundreds of Berkeley, Whitstone and King's Barton which St Peter's, Gloucester, held in Domesday Book. The reference to *tributarii* sounds suspiciously like a hangover from the Roman *tributum*. It is in this context that we should now look at Withington.

Between 674 and 704 the Anglo-Saxon Oshere, under-king of the Hwicce, with the consent of his overlord Ethelred of Mercia, gave 20 *cassati* (hides) of land to a noblewoman called Dunne and her daughter Bucge by the river Tilnoth – an Old English name for the Coln. The document recording this transaction, which described the land in detail, is lost; but a surviving decree of 736–7 gives the details: the minster was at a place called *Wudiadun* (Withington). Further charter evidence traces the descent of the land at Withington. By 774 the church's landholding was 21 hides; in that year Withington was granted to a holy woman called Aethelburg, descended from the royal kin of the Hwicce who by now had lost their kingly title, with reversion to the bishopric of Worcester after her death. Other documents of the tenth century show that Withington remained in the hands of the church of Worcester, as it did right up to the Domesday

survey itself, which gives a brief account of the estate: 'The same church [Worcester] holds Widindune. [There are] 30 hides there. Three of these never paid tax. In lordship are two ploughs. And 16 villeins and eight [bordars].' Twelfth-century surveys of Worcester estates enable this meagre entry to be supplemented. Withington held land in a number of places: ten hides in Cold Aston, five in Notgrove, three and a half in Dowdeswell and Pegglesworth, two in Owdeswell, three in Foxcote, one in Hilcot, one in Colesbourne, one in Upcote, one in Compton, 'and ½ hide belongs to the church'. Some of these lands can be identified in a gift to the bishop of Worcester from an abbot Headda in the 780s, and as luck would have it they are described in a detailed Anglo-Saxon land survey which goes round the boundary points of the estate, which then included the neighbouring parish of Whittington. The question now is, what was the unit of land which we have traced from the 680s to 1086? Did it have a prehistory? When did the manor of Withington originate? The question has wider relevance, of course – when did the manorial system originate, in which the whole of English society is structured in Domesday Book?

The Roman villa at Withington is about 500 yards south of the village. A mile and a half south-east of Withington villa is the large excavated villa at Chedworth; a mile north-east of Withington is the villa site near Compton Abdale; westwards at Colesbourne on the Churn there is another; north at Whittington a fourth: five villas in five adjacent parishes. All the parishes

Above Withington in 1905. The original village settlement was by the church, and the villa was 600 yards to the south.
Left The Norman doorway of Withington church; no trace of the seventh-century minster has survived above ground.

The discovery of the villa at Withington in 1811.

bear Anglo-Saxon names today, but can they really have been new creations of the seventh century? It seems extremely unlikely. In fact each of these parishes may preserve in its boundaries the outline of the Romano-British estate which preceded it. At Withington there is further evidence. Three miles north of the village is a small settlement called Whittington; though it had been severed from Withington by Domesday, it was originally part of the Old English manor of *Wudiadun*. Just over the A40 from Andoversford is a stretch of land where the remains of a small Roman town have been found. The site bears the name Wycomb, first attested in 1248 as 'Wickham'. It seems likely that this name comes from the Old English *wic*, and before it the Latin *vicus*, the smallest unit of local government in the Roman world. In other words the regional administrative centre for this group of villas was within the area of the seventh-century estate of Withington; and the twelfth-century Worcester surveys show that Withington still had a spread of outlying estates (listed separately in Domesday) including Colesbourne, Compton and Foxcote, in whose areas other Roman farms were situated. The parish of Chedworth was not part of this arrangement, and presumably controlled and cultivated the lands south of Withington to the Fosse Way. Indeed the main local administrative division here, between the hundreds of Rapsgate and Bradley, runs between Withington woods and Chedworth woods, not along the River Coln, but along the ridge which divides the two villa sites. It is not impossible that the present-day parish and hundredal division of this part of Gloucestershire goes back to Roman or pre-Roman estate boundaries.

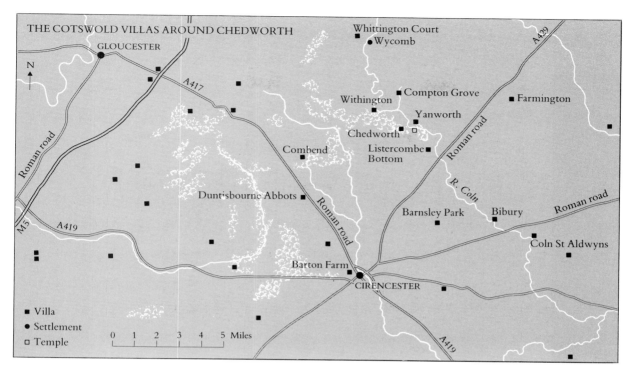

THE COTSWOLD VILLAS AROUND CHEDWORTH

N

GLOUCESTER

A417

Roman road

M5

A419

Whittington Court
Wycomb

Compton Grove
Withington
Farmington

Yanworth
Chedworth
Listercombe Bottom
Combend

Roman road

R. Coln

Duntisbourne Abbots

Barnsley Park
Bibury

Roman road

Coln St Aldwyns

Barton Farm
CIRENCESTER

A419

■ Villa
● Settlement
□ Temple

0   1   2   3   4   5 Miles

There seems no obvious reason why the area cultivated by the Roman villa at Withington should not have survived intact – as a working land unit – through the Anglo-Saxon period and later from the end of the Roman Empire. The slaves and other workers tied to the Roman estate, the British-speaking *coloni*, were still on the estate when it was taken over by a companion of an Anglo-Saxon king at some point after the fall of Cirencester in 577. Like their predecessors, the Anglo-Saxon landlords had every reason to want the old system to continue efficiently and provide them with bread, milk, meat and especially with the staple of the Cotswold economy, sheep's wool. The survival of the dependent workforce of other Roman villa estates has been postulated from the survival of groups of Welsh speakers deep inside Wessex, where, for example, one villa estate at Balchester in Hampshire had in its English boundary as late as 945 'the Welsh grazing pasture'. Further evidence of the correlation between medieval parishes and distribution of villas comes from Somerset, where the relationship of the villas at Banwell, Wrington, Butcombe and Sutton seems to be reflected in the later parishes. In some cases, such as the villa at Ditchley in Oxfordshire, a wealth of archaeological and topographical information has enabled the estate boundaries in Roman times to be plotted with accuracy against ancient woodland, boundary ditches and habitation sites; again it fits the later parish closely. It is likely that, as more Anglo-Saxon charter bounds are examined in detail, the estates they describe so minutely will be able to be pinpointed on the ground and some of their features attached to

the earlier Roman estate: for instance, a tenth-century charter from West Meon in Hampshire has a Roman villa site within its bounds, and the western edge of the Saxon estate ran along what appears to be the Roman estate boundary ditch.

When they came into Britain the Anglo-Saxons were much concerned with wealth and status. Their earliest law codes show a society with rigorous stratification and social gradations. They would not have found it difficult to fit into, and even adapt themselves to, the glaring inequalities of the Romano-British countryside with its villas, farms and *vici*. They needed to sustain their own rule; the first thing would be to take over the villas and farms and make sure that the mass of the workforce stayed enslaved or tied. How else did the Saxon word for the native inhabitants of Britain, the Welsh – *wealh* – come to mean 'slave' or 'bondman'?

The chiefdoms established in the early days of Anglo-Saxon England bore some of the marks of their continental tribal origins. But right from the start they showed themselves able to organise more than the tribe. By 600 they were already inventing traditions of rule with Roman overtones. In the seventh century, with the Latin language at their disposal, they would refer in terms recognisable to a late Roman to the elements of their complex economic structure. Large estates were evidently an important feature of that system from the outset, and became more prominent as society became more and more 'feudalised' before 1066. Only a century after the Saxons first entered the Severn valley, a petty chieftain of the Hwicce referred to the revenue of three hundreds of Gloucestershire as the *tributarii* of those estates; and when he ceded the lands and revenues of the old villa estate of Withington to a new minster he had at his disposal a taxation system sophisticated enough to tell him that this accounted for 20 *cassati* of the hundred which had centred on the *vicus* at Wycomb.

The idea of limited continuity from the Roman period is important to the Domesday story, as it is with the Viking settlements and the Norman Conquest. How much in each case was society changed by these apparent cataclysms, and how much persisted quietly and unrecorded from the earlier epochs? How much is the society and structure depicted in Domesday the product of Normans, Vikings, Saxons, Romans, Celts, Iron or Bronze Age people? Throughout the 600 years between the end of the Roman world and the Norman Conquest, English kings were the rulers in Britain; it is they who created what we call England today. Throughout that time, but especially in the Viking period and after, the Anglo-Saxon kings relied on their churchmen on the one hand, and their thegns on the other, for the

Above left A reconstruction of the fourth-century villa at Chedworth in Gloucestershire. A magnificent walled country house with inner and outer courts such as are still found in the rural south of Italy, it was probably the administrative centre of a large estate.
Below left A colonial society: the hot room in the owner's bath complex at Chedworth. After the sauna, a sundowner on the terrace?

administration of justice, the collection of taxes and the raising of armies. In a society where subsistence living is the lot of most people, vast resources in terms of land, produce and labour go into maintaining such an élite – in this case of a few thousand people. The churchmen, earls and thegns were maintained by the revenues and personnel of large estates, often lots of them; this must have been how the kings of the Hwicce kept themselves in the seventh-century Cotswolds. Right through the period both the royal kin and the landed aristocracy also spent great portions of their landed wealth on endowing religious foundations. This alienation of royal and noble estates would become massive in the later tenth century, until by the end of the Anglo-Saxon era Domesday Book shows nearly a third of all England's cultivated land in church hands.

This progressive movement, which concentrated huge amounts of land into the hands of a small number of powerful lay and church magnates, would reach a peak in the first two decades of Norman rule. At this time a tremendous shift in landownership took place and a true feudal system was imposed, consolidating the increasingly manorialised land tenure of England into a uniform and universal grid of estates held from the king by tenants or sub-tenants: a grid whose grid reference is Domesday Book itself.

The example of Withington may be seen as a model for how the lives of ordinary people could have gone on, little affected in the short term by the arrival of new masters, whether Roman, Anglo-Saxon, Viking or Norman. It may also show us how complete land units may have survived from the Roman period. Armed with that knowledge we can now return to the problem Frederic Seebohm set himself in Hertfordshire. (See p. 42.)

Hertfordshire had been an important area before the Romans. The native tribe, the Belgae, had a sophisticated society with coins and widespread trade. Their great hillfort sites were all to become important Roman settlements. The capital at Verulamium (St Albans), Welwyn, Wheathampstead, Baldock and Braughing all became centres for the network of villas in the Chilterns, many of which seem to have grown naturally out of Iron Age farm sites. The Roman cantonal capital at St Albans had grand buildings and walls, of which traces are visible today, and, remarkably, there were major municipal improvements there under an active city council as late as about AD 460, some decades after direct Roman rule ceased. In particular there is documentary evidence for continuity of worship at the site of the Christian church and shrine to the third-century martyr St Alban himself.

It is not known what happened in the Chilterns after 500, but there are no major cemeteries of Anglo-Saxon newcomers, and according to the *Anglo-Saxon Chronicle*, it was not until AD 571 that this British enclave fell, with the 'towns' of Limbury (near Luton) and Aylesbury. But if we consider the sequel then some intriguing hints emerge. In the seventh century we find the former Roman settlement at Hitchin on the Icknield Way was now the centre of a people who called themselves *Hicce* after the Celtic name of their local river, and the neighbouring peoples also preserved the old British regional and river names, even if their ruling clans were now Anglo-Saxon. Indeed close by Hitchin was a place called *Weala-tun*, the 'farm of the Welsh men'. If we look at some old field names in the parish of Hitchin we see that in 1460 a track was known as *le Walwey* ('Welsh way'), in 1556 a farm and a croft still bore the names *Walshamsted* and *Welshemancroft*; as late as 1608 we find a *Walcott*. All these names preserved the memory over the best part of a thousand years of the survival of the native British population of Hertfordshire. Similar evidence can be gleaned from the names of parishes south of Hitchin, notably King's and St Paul's Walden ('Valley of the Welshmen'). In this case it is probably doubly significant that St Albans itself bears the name of a saint of the Roman period; likewise the ancient church of one of the parishes adjoining Hitchin is dedicated to the Late Roman Saint Hippolytus, who even gave his name to the village, Ippollitts.

It is likely then that the hundreds, parishes and manors of this part of Hertfordshire which are recorded in Domesday actually preserve vestiges of a pattern going back beyond Anglo-Saxon times to Roman and Iron Age Briton; and moreover, that the descendants of the Late Roman population were distinct well into the early medieval period. Our conclusion brings us full circle – back to Seebohm's discoveries a hundred years ago at Great Wymondley, the parish which adjoins Hitchin on the east.

The evidence enables us to turn back to the system at Great Wymondley and conjecture something of its history. The villa probably controlled the manor, with some sort of village on the present village site; a relatively poor farm existed in the more northerly of the two mounded enclosures behind the church. The fields there had perhaps been cultivated long before the Romans, though it remains possible that the estate in its present form was created by clearance in the Roman period. The villa was on the western edge of the estate; the eastern edge was the Roman road to London, the Great North Road. The distance between the two boundaries was exactly nine squares of 50 *iugera* each. Originally there were probably ten: five complete *centuriae* of 200 *iugera* each, each divided into quarters – a common size throughout the Roman empire. These units were divided up into strips, the smallest of which were 6 *iugera*, or 720 by 240 Roman feet; strips in some areas of the estate were 1200 Roman feet long. Similar field measurements have been deduced from at least a dozen villas in different parts of England. These broad strips evidently existed alongside the Celtic square divisions from the Iron Age found in Berkshire, and are presumably a common type of Romano-British field, which was better suited to larger estates and the heavier, deeper-cutting Roman plough.

The hypothetical villa estate at Great Wymondley probably had about 680 acres (1000 *iugera*) of arable land with extensive woodland. From that an informed guess can be made at the size of its workforce. Various Roman texts on estate management survive. In the first century Columella recommended eight workers for each 200 *iugera* of arable land, which would give a labouring workforce for the Great Wymondley estate of 40 – that is, the minimum workforce for the maximum profit. Whether women and children should be added to this total it is difficult to say, but it would probably include a sizeable percentage of slaves. If the estate was further subdivided into smaller farms of a few acres, such as perhaps the poorly built structure in the field next the church, then a few smallholders would have to be added to this. The total square behind the church was estimated by Seebohm at 25 *iugera*, but the smaller, ditched enclosures immediately over the hedge from the graveyard would only be about 2 each: whether these represent the smallest holdings of *coloni* can only be speculation. Only in the ninth century is there evidence of the lives of such people.

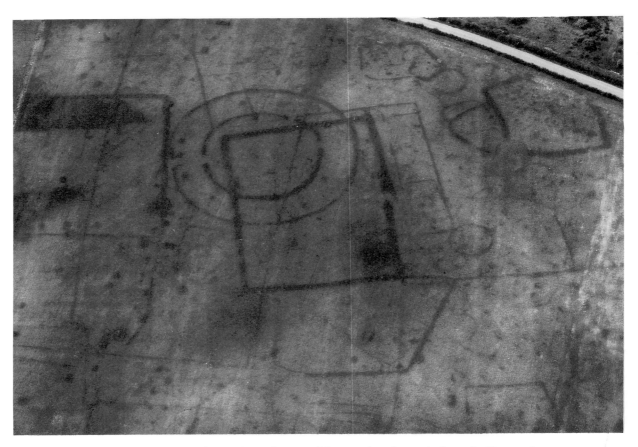

Crop marks near Mucking, Essex, in 1962. The round enclosure is from the Bronze Age; above it are Iron Age circular houses; and the rectangles are part of a Roman villa field system. The small, dark blobs are early Saxon huts – first signs of the impoverished 'Third World' immigrants who would become the English.

Finally, though, something is known of peasant families on similar estates in the Eastern Empire, and this knowledge may have some use in a British context – though marriage patterns in Celtic and Roman Britain need not necessarily have been the same as in other parts of the empire. In one household a man lived with his forty-eight-year-old mother and his eleven-year-old sister, but no wife. A twenty-year-old man lived on his own. The next smallholding had a fifty-six-year-old man living with two sons both under three, plus a forty-eight-year-old woman and another infant boy, apparently orphaned. A forty-year-old man lived with his twenty-year-old son; a thirty-year-old woman in his house was his second wife. A husband and wife, both thirty, had a three-year-old son, but two infant boys were in their care too. A twenty-year-old woman had a two-year-old daughter. One older cultivator, aged sixty-five, and his wife had three sons aged fourteen, eleven and six and a daughter aged twelve. A husband and wife aged sixty and fifty-two had a son and daughter still living with them; presumably, like the other grown-up children in this list, they helped their mother and father run the farm, much as children do today in the Greek islands. Most of these people probably had smallholdings like Theodorus and his wife (see p. 50) – 20 or 30 acres; though some *coloni* in Greece had farms of 60 or 70 acres of arable, with much more land cultivated as olive groves, vineyards and pasture. By analogy the sample from Thera offers an idea of the kind of people who formed the workforce in Roman Britain – at a human level. It also indicates the small size of families: by the fourth century AD there was an acute labour shortage in many parts of the Empire, and presumably in Britain too.

The conclusion of this first stage of our search for the roots of Domesday is inevitably speculative, for there is little hard evidence. But the vital question of continuity from Roman to Saxon times has been addressed. Further evidence will accumulate as we progress into the Anglo-Saxon period with Domesday Book as our guide. But before we turn to the Coming of the English, it is worth remembering that as late Roman society in Britain disappears, in the mid-fifth century, it still functions in urban and rural life in many areas. It may then not be too playful to end with an imagined census return for the Great Wymondley estate, to compare with the return from the Conqueror's surveyors over 600 years later; something like this existed in Britain before the Saxons, and may have been bequeathed to them in some form:

Estate of Melania and Pinianus of the Valerii in the territory of Verulamium of the Catuvellauni, province Maxima Caesariensis, villa name [?]:

Arable 1000 *iugera*; woodland 250; vineyard 100 *iugera*; pasture 250 *iugera*.

Coloni 40 men and women with 17 children, 8 boys under 14, 9 girls under 12. Chattel slaves 20.

Free tenant: Cupitius farms three strips each of 6 *iugera* next to the cemetery: resident in his own house, age 20: total 1. 40 oxen, 100 sheep. Poll tax assessment [?]; land tax [?]; total rating 30 *iugera*.

Though such an entry is inevitably fanciful, for no such record has survived from Roman Britain, indirectly this is what lies behind the following Domesday account:

King William holds Wymondley. It answers for 8 hides. Land for 18 ploughs. In lordship 2½ hides, and there are 3 ploughs. 24 villeins, 1 sokeman, 5 bordars, 5 cottars, have between them 15 ploughs. 6 slaves there. 1 mill at 20 shillings [*solidi*]; meadow for 1 plough and 2 oxen; pasture for the livestock belonging to the villagers; wood for fences.

Adam holds 1 hide and 1 virgate in Wymondley from the Bishop [of Bayeux]. Land for 1 plough, which is there, with 3 bordars. Meadow for half a plough. The value is and was 10*s*; before 1066 20*s*. Alflaed held this land . . . she could not sell without permission.

Gilbert of Beavais holds [another manor at] Wymondley. It answers for 3 hides and 1 virgate. Land for 4 ploughs. In lordship 2 hides and 2½ virgates; 2 ploughs are there – a third is possible. 4 villeins with 3 bordars have 1 plough. 4 cottars are there, and 2 slaves. Meadow for 1 plough; pasture for the livestock; woodland, 10 pigs. Altogether worth 60 shillings [*solidi*], before 1066 60*s*. Swein, Earl Harold's man, held this manor: he could sell.

The constituent parts of the estate then answered in all for 12 hides – probably in this case about 1500 acres, a total very like what would be expected for the Roman villa system. The estate had probably fallen to an Anglo-Saxon chief in the sixth century; in the seventh, as part of the tribe of the Hicce, it fell under the power of the kings of Mercia; in the tenth century it became a royal estate of the West Saxon kings, and as such appears in Domesday. In 1086 the total population on the site was 28 villeins, 11 bordars, 9 cottars and 8 slaves, with two tenants on the land as well as the king's estate agent. The total population within what is now the parish of Great Wymondley in 1086 must have been something in the order of 250 people, excluding the slaves and their families, if they had them. By 1086 the slave system of the ancient world was well on the way to replacement by a new system – manorial feudalism.

5
THE COMING OF THE ENGLISH

In the fifth century AD, the former province of Britain was invaded by Germanic tribes from the continent – Angles, Saxons, Jutes and other, lesser tribes. These peoples settled the lowlands, gradually pushing westwards into what are now the foothills of Wales and the moors of Devon. Eventually these Germanic-speaking settlers formed a culture which they called English, and a geographical entity which they called England. In time, they replaced most of the Celtic place names in southern and eastern England with English ones – though the main rivers, such as Thames, Severn and Avon, retain a form of their ancient names. The further westwards you go, the more are such Celtic names found – in Wiltshire, for example, most of the river names are British: Avon, Biss, Bedwyn, Deverill, Kennet, Nadder, Sem, Wylye. This is not surprising. In historical terms the 900 years or so to the Anglo-Saxon period is not a long time, and Celtic speech survived in Devon till that period. Even in Dorset Welsh seems to have been spoken until after AD 900; in Cornwall, Cornish only died out in the eighteenth century. Even today this lengthy process is still working itself out in the cultural and linguistic border between the Welsh and the English. Domesday Book comes nearly halfway through the period between the very first Germanic settlements in the fourth century AD, and the late twentieth century, and it presents us with a cross-section of British history, with over 13,000 place names in their eleventh-century forms, as testimony to the stage which the transformation of ancient British society had reached.

The old view of the Anglo-Saxons as murderous newcomers who wiped out the native British in the south and east of Britain has been rejected in recent years. Even in eastern England the names of some of the Anglo-Saxon kingdoms retained the earlier Romano-British names – Kent, for instance, is derived from the territory of the Cantii; and Lindsey in Lincolnshire was the Roman Lindis. In contrast with the almost complete lack of documentary evidence from the Roman period, there are many sources from Anglo-Saxon times that help to explain these events – not only Domesday Book itself, but the 2000 or so land grants, leases and land descriptions which date from the seventh to the eleventh centuries. These sources may offer answers to some fundamental questions of British history: how did Roman Britain become Anglo-Saxon England? How

Bede was not only the greatest early medieval historian, but he more than anyone else invented the idea of the unity of the *gens Anglorum* – the 'English people'.

much did the Anglo-Saxons take over – how much did they destroy or introduce their own social structures? What happened to the native Britons? Was it continuity or cataclysm?

The end of Roman rule in Britain is usually taken as AD 410; this was what the English historian Bede thought, writing in 731, and it fits well with scanty evidence from nearer the time. The fifth-century Byzantine historian Zosimus describes the Emperor Honorius in AD 410 refusing a formal request for military aid from the local city authorities in Britain – so by about 410 Roman provincial administration had ceased in Britain, even though local government was still evidently well organised. The British request was linked to the growing external threat of Picts from the north, Scots (from northern Ireland), Angles and Saxons. Zosimus goes on to say that the Britons then organised their own forms of defence, 'freed their cities from the barbarian attacks' and 'went on living on their own without obedience to Roman laws' (that is, without acknowledging external Roman authority). A sixth-century writer, Procopius, underlines Zosimus's account when he says that Rome never recovered Britain, which from then on was ruled by 'tyrants' – self-styled local emperors.

Archaeological evidence suggests that life in some of the cities of Roman Britain carried on with some degree of prosperity until around 450: at St Albans (Verulamium) building projects including an aqueduct point to the survival of urban life until even later, and the *Life of St Germanus of Auxerre*, written *c*. 480, describes a well-to-do élite in a well-governed city at the time of the saint's visit to St Albans in 429. But the country may have fallen back into its constituent tribal areas, with rival local aristocrats and chiefs vying for control. According to later traditions preserved in the *Anglo-Saxon Chronicle* – of which the earliest surviving manuscript dates to *c*. 890 – and Nennius's *History of the Britons, c*. 830, it was this internecine warfare which led to the hiring of Germanic mercenaries to fight for both sides. Bede dated the 'Coming of the English' to 447–9, about the time that two South Gaulish chronicles say that 'Britain fell under the control of the Saxons'. However, such control can only have been confined to certain eastern and southern coastal areas. It is the British Gildas, writing in about 540, who adds to this rather scant picture.

He gives details of a letter written by one faction in Britain to the Roman ruler of Gaul, Aetius, which can be dated between 446 and 453; this was an urgent response to a serious invasion by Angles and Saxons immediately before – in the late 440s. Gildas speaks of the settlement of Germanic federates or mercenaries in eastern England (Kent?) at this time as part of the policy of a British leader whom he calls the 'proud tyrant'. This must be the man remembered in Welsh tradition as Vortigern, who seems to have been an important ruler in western Britain in the period *c*. 430–60. At this point, Gildas says, the Germanic federates became uncontrollable and devastated many of the cities in the south-east, and it may be this news that found its way to Gaul. However, Britain had not fallen 'under the control of the Saxons', as was thought over there. Gildas asserts that the cities in lowland Britain were left depopulated by the fighting in the mid-fifth century, and gives graphic images of unburied corpses in civic piazzas, demolished walls and towers, and overturned altars. He also says that in response to this, though many fled, others 'held out . . . in their own land, trusting their lives with constant foreboding to the high hills, steep, menacing and fortified . . .' So with the collapse of centralised rule, the growth of faction and external threat, and the decline of the towns, the British leadership went back to the hillforts which had been the centres of social organisation before the Romans, and which still formed defensible centres for the rural estates. Archaeologists can point to well over forty Iron Age hillforts which were refortified at this time, the most famous of them the great site at Cadbury Castle in Somerset, which was surrounded by a drystone wall with wooden fighting platforms and a feasting hall with ancillary buildings. Now, says Gildas, the survivors who had weathered the storm around 450 began to fight back, and he continues with this fascinating information which he may have derived from his parents or grandparents:

Their leader was Ambrosius Aurelianus, a gentleman who, perhaps alone of the Romans, had survived the shock of this notable storm: certainly his parents, who had worn the purple, were slain in it. His descendants in our day have become greatly inferior to their grandfather's excellence. Under him our people regained their strength, and challenged the victors to battle. The Lord assented, and the battle went their way. From then on the victory went now to our countrymen, now to their enemies . . . This lasted right up until the year of the siege of Badon Hill, pretty well the last defeat of the villains, and certainly not the least. That was the year of my birth; as I know, one month of the 44th year since then has already passed. But the cities of our land are not populated even now as they once were; right to the present they are deserted, in ruins and unkempt. External wars may have stopped, but not civil ones. . . .
Translated M. Winterbottom.

Cadbury Castle in Somerset. An Iron Age hillfort refortified *c.* 500, Cadbury passed into royal ownership and was used as a mint in *c.* 1012; by Domesday it had been sold.

There are many important clues in this account. Gildas was writing not long before 543, say 540, so the Battle of Badon was in the 490s. If Ambrosius's grandchildren were Gildas's contemporaries, then Ambrosius can hardly have been born earlier than 430. In this case the Ambrosius Aurelianus remembered by Welsh tradition in Nennius as the enemy of Vortigern in the 430s, and the man who fought with one Vitalinus at Guolopp or Guoloph (which must be Wallop in Hampshire) in *c.* 436, is likely to be the father of Gildas's Ambrosius, and presumably the parent who had 'worn the purple' (that is, been emperor in Britain) and who was killed in the fighting of the late 440s or 450s.

It is possible to go even further in reconstructing this late Roman revival, which preserved Romano–British society in central southern England until *c.* 550. It must be significant that Ambrosius is the only fifth-century Roman Briton actually named by Gildas. His name and background imply an origin in the highest levels of the late Roman nobility, and perhaps a link with the circle of St Ambrose (Ambrosius), bishop of Milan from 374 to 397, for Ambrose's father was named Aurelius Ambrosius. The remarkable parallel is unlikely to be coincidence: it may be that Aurelius's family were leaders of the Catholic circle in late Roman Britain, as J.N.L. Myres has suggested, and that their enemy Vortigern was leader of a group sponsoring the Pelagian heresy, which became powerful in the early fifth century. St Germanus's visit to the shrine at St Albans in 429 was part of a pastoral tour to combat this threat to orthodoxy. So Gildas's warm approval of Ambrosius's armed resistance to the Germanic mercenaries brought in by Vortigern may also reflect the triumph of Late Roman Catholic orthodoxy. Indeed, if the later scraps in Nennius have a historical value then the mercenaries may have been brought in by Vortigern not merely to fight off Picts and Scots but because 'he feared Ambrosius', as Nennius claims. In some respects, then, the decline and break-up of Roman Britain may have resembled the 'decolonisations' that occurred in modern times in Africa or South-East Asia. But in one important sense it was different – it was accompanied by the migration of so many new settlers into the former colony that its racial character was permanently altered.

For many reasons it is difficult to reconstruct what happened in the crucial phase of the migration, *c.* 450–600, the period between the wars of the British resistance under Ambrosius and the emergence of the Anglo-Saxon kingdoms. The main literary sources are the Northumbrian monk Bede's *Ecclesiastical History of the English People*, completed in 731, and the *Anglo-Saxon Chronicle*. Bede, however, had no reliable information on the dating of any events between 449 and 538. The *Chronicle*'s account, written down as we have it today only in the 890s, attempts to date traditional events, such as the coming of Cerdic, founder of the dynasty which ruled England till 1066, but its year-by-year dating is dubious: most of its dates had been handed down only by word of mouth, and there is no certainty

Her ceaulin feng to rice on wessexum. ⁊ elle feng to norþanhymbra rice...

Her feng æþelbriht to cantwara rice...

Her ceaulin ⁊ cuþa gefuhton wiþ æþelbriht...

Her cuþ wulf feohtaþ wiþ bryt walas æt bedcan forda...

Her cuþwine ⁊ ceaulin fuhton wiþ bryttas...

Her mauricius feng to romana rice.

Her ceaulin ⁊ cuþa fuhton wiþ bryttas...

Her elle cyning forþferde ⁊ æþelric ricsode æfter him ·v· gear...

Her ceol ricsode ·v· gear ⁊ Gregorius feng to papdome on rome.

Her micel wæl feoll wiþ æt woddes beorge ⁊ ceaulin wearþ ut adrifen...

Her ceaulin ⁊ cwichelm ⁊ crida forwurdon ⁊ æþelfriþ feng to rice on norþhymbrum.

Her Gregorius papa sende to bryttene Augustinum mid wel manegum munecum þe godes word engla þeoda godspelledon.

that any of its dates before the 550s or even the 570s are even approximately right. But there is another way of looking at the English takeover, and that is by examining the most ancient holdings of the Anglo-Saxon dynasties in Domesday Book and the earlier records, grants and wills, and comparing them with their late Roman and Iron Age predecessors. Here, if anywhere, a connection may show itself.

On the eastern edge of Salisbury Plain, in a loop of the Wiltshire Avon, stands Amesbury, in the centre of perhaps the most remarkable historical landscape in Britain. Stonehenge, Woodhenge, the Cursus and the Avenue, along with innumerable ditches, barrows and field systems, testify to the extraordinary Bronze and Iron Age cultures which thrived here millennia before the first Anglo-Saxon speaker stepped on to British shores. Immediately over the river from the town centre is the huge Iron Age hillfort, known locally as Vespasian's Camp, which gave its name to the present town. In the ninth century, when it is first recorded, it appears as Ambresbyrig, 'the burh of Ambrosius'. The fort has never been excavated, though its archaeological potential must be immense: finds made when a road was cut through its southern end suggested that, like many other hillforts, it was refurbished in the fifth century. Was this place one of the forts mentioned by Gildas as springboards for the battles against the Anglo-Saxon invaders? Could it have been the base of Ambrosius?

Amesbury's history as an English centre can be taken back two centuries before the Norman Conquest. It was evidently a royal vill when Aethelbald, king of the West Saxons, stayed there in 858; in his will, drawn up in the 880s, Alfred the Great left it to his son. Amesbury remained a favoured royal residence throughout the tenth century; King Athelstan spent Christmas 932 there with an immense court, and Ethelred was there for Easter 995. The place was still a royal possession in 1086, when it still paid the archaic royal render of one night's supply (*firma*) for the court; it had never paid tax or been assessed in hides. Amesbury was the centre of a hundred which in Domesday amounted to a dozen parishes – an administrative, economic and judicial centre and probably the site of an ancient minster church. Indeed Geoffrey of Monmouth, the twelfth-century chronicler, had tales of a Romano-British monastery at Amesbury, though the most that other sources allow is the probability of a pre-ninth-century minster, and the abbey founded in 979. The present church of St Mary and St Melorus may overlie the tenth-century foundation; presumably the royal palace was nearby. Domesday Book adds a final intriguing pointer to Amesbury's early history: some estates which had contributed to the royal vill before 1066 lay not only outside its hundred, but as far away as the Isle of Wight.

Left The earliest manuscript of the *Anglo-Saxon Chronicle*, now in Corpus Christi College, Cambridge. Written *c.* 890, this folio relates events from the accession of Ceawlin (the top line reads: '*Her ceawlin feng to rice on wes seaxum*').

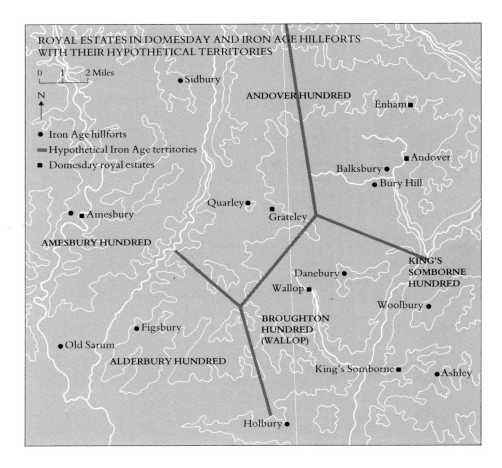

ROYAL ESTATES IN DOMESDAY AND IRON AGE HILLFORTS
WITH THEIR HYPOTHETICAL TERRITORIES

0   1   2 Miles

N

● Iron Age hillforts
━ Hypothetical Iron Age territories
■ Domesday royal estates

● Sidbury

ANDOVER HUNDRED

Enham ■

● Balksbury   ■ Andover

● Bury Hill

Quarley ●   ■ Grateley

● ■ Amesbury

AMESBURY HUNDRED

KING'S
SOMBORNE
HUNDRED

Danebury ●

Wallop ■

Woolbury ●

● Figsbury

BROUGHTON
HUNDRED
(WALLOP)

● Old Sarum

ALDERBURY HUNDRED

King's Somborne ■   ● Ashley

Holbury ●

The history of Amesbury seems to suggest that – like Cadbury Castle in Somerset – it was an important Romano-British strongpoint in the fifth century, centre of its own territory, which fell into West Saxon royal hands in the sixth century and continued to be the centre of an important local unit, even though the hillfort was abandoned. The date at which its ownership passed over can be roughly estimated from the *Anglo-Saxon Chronicle*, which describes successful battles at other Wiltshire Iron Age hillforts – in 552 at Old Sarum, 5 miles south of Amesbury, and in 556 at Barbury Castle, about 20 miles to the north. If these dates are roughly right, the big fortified centres of Wiltshire fell between ten and twenty years after Gildas wrote. Up to that point, however, we must assume that the descendants of the *servi* and *coloni*, the tied farmers and serfs who worked the field systems around these forts, continued to live and work, to reap their harvests and bring their surpluses into barns in these hillforts as tax in kind payable to leaders like the Ambrosii. The towns by now were for the most part desolate and overgrown, inhabited by squatters and the odd local chieftain; civic amenities had gone; the villas had been abandoned, but the estates dependent on the hillforts must have continued to work in some form. When, reinforced by a new influx of immigrants and no doubt aided by the terrible plague which devastated the Roman world in the 540s, the Anglo-Saxon chiefs and their warbands overcame the natives, they would have taken immediate steps to ensure the continuance of the system of collecting and rendering food supplies to the local authorities. For the British-speaking survivors among the peasantry, the *servi* and *coloni*, it simply meant a change from one landlord to another.

If this interpretation is applied to Domesday Book, some interesting patterns emerge. In Wiltshire, for example, the Domesday commissioners found that Amesbury, Calne, Warminster, Chippenham, Bedwyn and Tilshead all paid the archaic render of a night's *firma*; all but the last two were the centres of Domesday hundreds, and Bedwyn was the administrative centre of its hundred. A second group of places, slightly overlapping the first, is Amesbury, Bedwyn, Westbury, Bradford-on-Avon, Warminster and Wilton. All these seem to be early West Saxon royal estate centres with a neighbouring Iron Age hillfort, as at Amesbury, and may well have continued to operate in direct succession to them. Other royal estates in Domesday whose organisation looks ancient may have connections with local Roman towns. Chippenham and Calne, with their dependencies, look as if they were originally estates contributing to the town of Verlucio; Bedwyn and Ramsbury to Cunetio.

This Domesday evidence is striking. Not all the survivals of the royal 'farm' mentioned in Domesday need be so old – those in Dorset were probably more recent, but in Somerset too an ancient substructure may be detected. In Hampshire only vestiges survive, such as the complex renders at Nether Wallop, the centre of a hundred and perhaps the estate successor to the hillfort at Danebury; Wallop seems to have been where the elder Ambrosius fought in the 430s (battles at royal vills are common through the Old English period). Its early importance may well be reflected in its control of no fewer than six hundreds in Domesday Book; recently, fine Anglo-Saxon wall-paintings have been identified in the church there, so it found wealthy patrons as late as *c.* AD 1000, despite its later unimportance. Wallop is also significant in that it preserves its British name, as do a number of very important West Saxon royal residences in Hampshire, some of which were centres of hundreds too – Andover, Candover, Micheldever and Clere. Andover is particularly interesting in that the Anglo-Saxon royal vill succeeded the important Iron Age fort of Balksbury, which is actually within the area of the modern town, and remained a favoured residence of the West Saxon kings, retaining its British name. Within the hundred of Andover were other residences used by the ninth- and tenth-century kings, such as Enham and Grateley; in fact Grateley lies close to another major Iron Age fort, at Quarley, and in the immediate vicinity of the Anglo-Saxon residence where King Athelstan held a great lawmaking synod in 930 are a late Roman farm and an important late Iron

Above Nether Wallop church, Hampshire. Originally a late tenth-century royal church, it is mentioned in Domesday. Recently, Anglo-Saxon wall-paintings of flying angels have been discovered.
Right Anglo-Saxon royal genealogies going back to the period of the migration, including (centre right in larger lettering) the Northumbrians (*nordanhymbrorum*). These probably represent traditions invented by fledgling dynasties in the seventh century.

Age complex with aisled halls. The large hundred of Andover perhaps incorporated the territories of the hillforts at Quarley and Balksbury, just as that of Wallop was the territory of Danebury, and King's Somborne that of the Woolbury fort – see the tentative reconstruction in the map on p. 76. In all these cases there is a strong suggestion of continuity between Iron Age and Anglo-Saxon royal landholdings.

So the West Saxon kings were in a sense the heirs of Ambrosius, and Alfred's royal vill of Amesbury is that rare thing in the English landscape, a site which has left on the modern map clear evidence for the name of its Roman owner. Of course by no means all the royal estates possessed by the crown at Domesday can be assumed to have their origins in the late Roman period, or to have been owned by the crown since as early as the sixth century. But it is plausible to think that the oldest royal possessions of the Anglo-Saxon dynasties go back to the struggles of that time. Interestingly

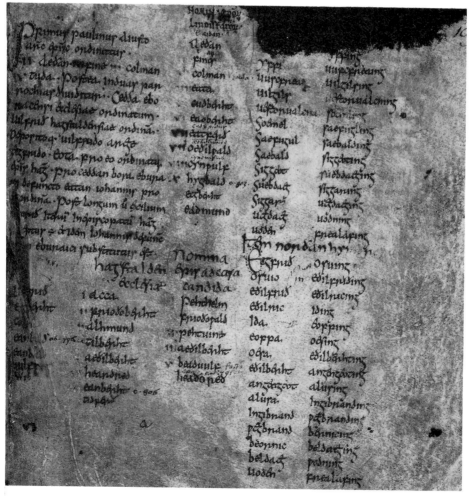

enough, for example, three of the four royal 'towns' which the *Anglo-Saxon Chronicle* says were captured by Cuthwulf from the Britons in 571 – Aylesbury, Benson and Limbury – were still held by King Edward in 1065, according to Domesday Book (so were twenty of the places given by Alfred in his will).

Domesday, then, can be a most remarkable guide not only to the later Saxon period, but to patterns which emerged over six centuries or more before. The possibility exists that the social structures of the late Roman world need not have been destroyed by the English – indeed it is most unlikely that they were. What emerges in *c.* AD 600 in southern Britain is a Germanic culture which has taken over the native culture, adopted its forms of lordship and servitude to suit its own, and lived side by side with its people for long enough to blur its racial identity. Whoever the Anglo-Saxons thought they were in the seventh century, we may be sure that their racial identity was neither Germanic nor Celtic, but a fusion of the two. Their civilisation had become a mixture of Germanic and Celtic law and social organisation, Christian and Roman religion (the religion, after all, of late Roman Britain) and Germanic culture and language. Such were the origins of the English.

Right The king as 'keeper of the kin', from a tenth-century book: kingship was one of the great institutions created by the Anglo-Saxons in Britain. By 1066 there was no aspect of life it did not touch.

PART TWO

THE STATE
BEFORE DOMESDAY

harde adelinga aldon pira v huno pintua þahe

David the warrior, from a Northumbrian book of the
eighth century. Once converted to Roman Christianity,
the kings of the 'Barbarian West' reinterpreted militarist
aspects of their society in biblical terms; they were
impressed above all by David, as both teacher and fighter.

6
THE BEGINNINGS OF ENGLISH GOVERNMENT

When the various Anglo-Saxon kingdoms (see map on p. 87) began to adopt Christianity, starting with the Kentish in 597 and leading to the West Saxons in the 630s and the Mercians in the 650s, they began to keep written records – in Latin, the language of the Church – and from then on the sources offer concrete evidence for what was happening to English kingship. Records of the earlier period generally consist of oral traditions written down long afterwards, but some genuine seventh-century records of land grants have survived, including one original of 679. By then the charter was in wide use as a way of recording the disposal of land, and most of the great bishoprics in England preserved documents like this. It was the kind of material available to Bede for his *Ecclesiastical History* written in 731.

Bede had access to many traditions about the earlier history of the country, with very detailed information on the deeds of the Northumbrian kings of the seventh century; he also used documents from a number of church archives. He interpreted the overlordship of certain early English kings as some sort of hegemony which enabled them to exact tribute not only from their subjects but from other kingdoms in Britain, and even from native British peoples such as the Welsh and Scots. It is in this light that Bede's frequent references to various of the peoples of England should be considered. They seem to be based on some sort of written assessment system, and this could be the first hint of what lies behind the last great record of the Old English geld, Domesday Book itself. Bede gives these estimates in units which he calls the 'land of a family', clearly a translation of the English term 'hide'. He gives 7000 to the South Saxons, 7000 to the North Mercians, 5000 to the South Mercians, 960 to Anglesey (an area within the Welsh kingdom of Gwynedd), 300 and more to Man, 600 to Thanet, 1200 to the Isle of Wight, 600 to the Isle of Ely, 87 to the land of Selsey and just 5 to Iona. Was there already in the seventh century a system of tribute assessment which enabled kings like Oswald to levy from his subject kings a payment based, however loosely, on 'households' – like the Roman poll tax? This question is of great interest in terms of the origins of Domesday, and can be answered with some certainty because of the survival in later copies of two of the most remarkable – and enigmatic – sources for early British history.

Pride of place should go to the *Senchus Fer nAlban*, the 'History of the men of Scotland'. It records the genealogies of the ruling families of Dal Riata, the heartland of the original kingdom of the Scots in western Scotland and the Isles, but also incorporates a census of the military and economic resources of the kingdom founded there some time around AD 500. The following is an extract from it:

The expeditionary strength of the Cenel Loairnd, seven hundred men, but the seventh hundred is from the Airgialla. If it be an expeditionary force, moreover, for sea-voyaging, two seven-benchers from every twenty houses of them. . . . This is the Cenel nGabrain, five hundred and sixty houses, Kintyre and Crich Chomgaill with its islands, two seven-benchers every twenty houses in a sea expedition.

Cenel nOengusa has four hundred and thirty houses, two seven-benchers every twenty houses in a sea expedition.

Cenel Loairnd has four hundred and twenty houses, two seven-benchers every twenty houses in a sea expedition.

It is thus throughout the three thirds of the Dal Riadda.
Translated J. Bannerman.

In its present form the *Senchus* is a late copy of a tenth-century compilation, but its origins almost certainly lie much earlier, probably in the seventh century. It was based on an assessment of households, as Bede's information was, and gives 1410 for the three principal divisions of Dal Riata; in the naval section, at two seven-benchers for every twenty houses it gives 70 ships for a naval force. As far as the army was concerned, we learn that the muster of men for the three districts was 1500. Compared with Bede's estimate for the households on, say, Anglesey, these seem perfectly realistic totals. In other respects the *Senchus* has marked similarities to passages in the early Old English laws from Kent of King Ethelbert (*c.* 600) and the late seventh-century code of the West Saxon Ine. As internal references suggest the *Senchus* in its original form was completed by 660, it has been connected with Bede's account of Northumbrian claims to overlordship of the Scots under Edwin, Oswald and Oswy. Bede says of Oswald that 'all the nations and provinces of Britain, which are divided between four languages, that is British, Pictish, Scottish and English, he brought under his rule' (III 6) and that Oswy 'laid the Pictish and Scottish peoples under tribute' (II 5). Hence another writer of the time, Adomnan, calls Oswald 'overlord of all Britain'. Only with the defeat and death of Ecgfrith of Northumbria deep in Pictland in 685 did the North British, according to Bede, 'regain their liberty' (IV 26). The best current theory, then, would suggest that in its original form, the *Senchus* was drawn up in the middle of the seventh century at the behest of one of the Northumbrian overkings. If so it is one of the most extraordinary documents in the history of government in Britain. It also provides us with a base point from which to pursue our search for the roots of Domesday Book itself.

How were the government and taxation of early England organised in the main kingdoms? Again, Bede and other eighth-century sources give clues. Bede refers several times to what he calls 'regions' or 'provinces' in a

The *Senchus*. Perhaps the earliest taxation list from the British Isles, this is a seventh-century survey of the households of the kingdom of Dal Riata in Scotland.

way which strongly suggests he is describing specific units of organisation: the *regio* of Loidis (around Leeds), the *regio* In Feppingum (around Charlbury in Oxfordshire), the province of the Hwicce in the Severn valley, and the province of the Gyrve in the East Anglian Fens. These primitive units are especially apparent in Northumbria: Bede mentions the *regio* Incuneningum (dependent on Chester-le-Street?), and a contemporary *Life of St Cuthbert* speaks of *regiones* of Kintis and of Ahse (between Hexham and Carlisle). Many of these strange names are very ancient, deriving from the pre-English place name, such as Bede's names for Ripon (In Hrypum) and for Oundle (In Undalum), both of which are Celtic names for places which Domesday Book shows to have been the centre of probable Celtic units of organisation, the so-called 'multiple estates'. In the Anglo-Saxon period many of these units were based on blocks of 100 hides: Oundle, for example, appears as the centre of eight hundreds in Domesday Book – probably including the area of the ancient, primitive *regio*, and pre-English in origin. These blocks of 100 hides can be connected with Bede's remarks about such districts being composed 'according to English custom' of so many units of 'land for one family' – the English translation of which was 'hide': originally the amount of land which could support one peasant family. The hide, of course, was an abstract idea, whose actual area varied greatly from region to region depending on local conditions, quality of soil and so on; it could therefore be employed as a form of tax assessment whose rating could be moved up or down. Seventh-century Latin charters sometimes use the term '*terra unius tributarii*' for the hide, and evidence from western England suggests that the use for tribute purposes of the 100-hide unit may have connections with the Roman *tributum* on land and people. The Gloucester grant from 679 granting the '*tributarii* of three hundreds' to St Peter's church gives a fascinating glimpse of the possibilities of such continuity (see p. 57), but by then the system extended right across England.

One of the most interesting sources for early English history is the *Tribal Hidage*. This is a complete translation from the earliest manuscript, written in a hand of around AD 1000. It is a list of early tribes, largely of the Midlands, from before the time the country was divided into shires.

The land of the Mercians is 30,000 hides [that is] what is called the original Mercia. [Of] Wocen saetna is 7000 hides. Westerna the same. Pecsaetna 1200 hides. Elmed saetna 600 hides. Lindes farona 7000 hides including haeth feld [i.e. Hatfield] land. South gyrwa 600 hides. North gyrwa 600 hides. East wixna 300 hides. West wixna 600 hides. Spalda 600 hides. Wigesta 900 hides. Herefinna 1200 hides. Sweord ora 300 hides. Gifla 300 hides. Hicca 300 hides. Wiht gara 600 hides. Nox gaga 5000 hides. Oht gaga 2000 hides. That is 66,100 hides. Hwinca 7000 hides. Ciltern saetna 4000 hides. Hendrica 3500 hides. Unecun g[a]ga 1200 hides. Aro saetna 600 hides. Faerpinga 300 hides [margin: Faerpinga is among the Middle Angles]. Bilmiga 600 hides. Widerigga the same. East willa 600 hides. West willa 600 hides. East angles 30,000 hides. East saxons 7000 hides. Cantawarena [i.e. the Kentish] 15,000 hides. South saxons 7000 hides. West saxons 100,000 hides. All of which is 242,700 hides.

Strange and archaic though many of these names sound, the reader will recognise some still current regional ones. W[r]ocen saetna were the people dependent on the Wrekin; Westerna the border folk of South Shropshire; 'Peak dwellers', 'Elmet dwellers' and the people of Lindsey and Hatfield Chase still make sense on today's map. The Gyrwa were met in Bede, who says Peterborough was in their territory, while a later source explains that 'the Gyrvi are all the south Angles living in the great fen in which the Isle of Ely lies'. The Spalda gave their name to the Fen town of Spalding. The name of the Herefinna has been traced to Hurstingstone hundred in

ANGLO-SAXON ENGLAND
IN THE EIGHTH CENTURY

Huntingdonshire, while the tiny 'kin' of the Sweord ora have left their trace in the local name of Sword Point, which on old maps projected into the now drained Whittlesey Mere east of the Great North Road in Huntingdon. Moving southwards, the Gifle are the people of the river Ivel and the Hicce the folk of Hitchin in Hertfordshire, whom we met settling around Great Wymondley in Chapter 4.

The *Tribal Hidage*, a tribute list drawn up from a Mercian viewpoint, is very important in reconstructing early English geography. However, as so much of it is still impossible to place accurately on a modern map, it remains difficult to use. As it stands, even its date is uncertain. Any one of several Mercian kings might have initiated it; the great kings of the eighth century, Aethelbald and Offa, have inevitably been suggested, as they are known to have claimed overlordship of the English peoples south of the

Humber. The *Hidage*, however, has a very archaic feel and may date from one of the earlier Mercian rulers, perhaps Wulfhere (657–74). Many of the folk names in the list may have ceased to be used in the later period, though it is known that the five earldoms of Mercia in the ninth century were of the Mercians, the Middle Angles, Lindsey, the Hwicce and the Magonsaeten (Westerna?), while the terms Hwicce and Magonsaeten continued to be used as regional and even administrative divisions into the eleventh century.

Other evidence shows that some of the *Hidage* divisions include earlier folk groups. An early eighth-century charter grants land in the Stour valley in north Worcestershire in the *provincia* of the Husmerae; the name survives in Ismere House near Kidderminster. Another of the same time speaks of Wootton Wawen in Warwickshire as lying 'in the region anciently known as Stoppingas'. Further north, in Staffordshire, charters give a clearer picture of the territory of the South Mercians and penetrate below the simple division of the *Tribal Hidage*. Bede had hidage figures for the North and South Mercians, 7000 and 5000 respectively; the southern part dependent on Tamworth, the northern on 'Northworthy', the pre-Danish name of Derby. Charter evidence shows that the South Mercians were actually divided into two folks, the Tomsaetan and the Pencersaetan. Two charters give the ninth-century extent of the Tomsaetan, from the Trent at Breedon on the Hill in north Leicestershire 30 miles southwards to Cofton Hackett in North Worcestershire; it is clear that they took their name from the river Tame – they are the 'Tame dwellers', and Tamworth was the 'enclosure by the Tame'. The charter dealing with Cofton Hackett (AD 849) mentions that on its northern boundary was the 'boundary of the Tomsetna and the pencer setna', the only reference to what was evidently the other main South Mercian folk. This people must have taken their name from the British river name Penk, with its Roman settlement site of Pennocrucium, near modern Penkridge. Penkridge was still an important residence in the tenth century, and Domesday Book has preserved the pattern of estates which were dependent on it in early times.

From the details of the *Tribal Hidage* it can be seen how, long before Domesday, a system of tribute and taxation was imposed on the whole of England south of the Humber – a system based on the same unit used by the Conqueror's surveyors in 1086. Bede believed that, from the earliest days of the Anglo-Saxon kingdoms in Britain, some sort of overlordship was imposed at times by the most powerful kings. Like all kings, these barbarian newcomers needed to exact dues in the form of military service, food, raw materials, gifts and treasure. The Romans of course had their census, on land or on people, which could be rendered in money. Coins had ceased to be used after the decline of Roman power in the fifth century, but in the seventh century coins began to be used again, and from then on money was closely tied to tax and compensation in law. The *Anglo-Saxon Chronicle* contains a reference to the Kentishmen paying the West Saxons 'thirty thousands' in compensation in 694 – these would be the little silver coins known as sceattas. From then on, tribute systems which demanded both money or precious metal, and renders in kind – stock, food rents and so on –

Left The *Tribal Hidage*, beginning '*Myrcna landes is thrittig thusend hyda.* . . .' A copy written *c.* AD 1000, by then perhaps just 'interesting facts'; the last six lines list national traits including 'the dullness of the English' and the 'libido of the Irish'!

probably existed in tandem; as late as the tenth century King Athelstan exacted tribute from the Welsh in gold and silver, but also in oxen and other goods. Anglo-Saxon and Celtic law provided an elaborate system of tariffs for translating animals and goods into cash reckoning, and this could be applied at the local level in the proportions decreed by a tribute list such as the *Hidage*. If the overlord wanted to exact a particularly punitive render all he needed to do was raise the hidage assessment of the territory involved – the *Hidage*'s assessment of the West Saxons at 100,000 sounds suspiciously like that.

So with documents such as the *Senchus* and the *Tribal Hidage* the Dark Age 'emperors' of the seventh and eighth centuries imposed their will on their subject peoples, kept their thegns and armed troops loyal, and filled their treasuries. In this way they financed their building projects and were able to endow the many monasteries founded at this time. Such ideas lie behind the system revealed in Domesday Book. But between the age of Offa and the time of William the Conqueror dramatic changes took place in the governance of Anglo-Saxon England, and the old system of local organisation was swept away in favour of a system which would survive virtually unaltered until 1974: the system of shires and hundreds. This would be achieved by kings who were able to override the deep regional tendencies of early England and create – for the first time – something like a single unified kingdom.

7
THE VIKINGS AND THE ENGLISH: THE ORIGINS OF THE ENGLISH STATE

By gently instructing, cajoling, urging, commanding and (in the end when his patience was exhausted) by sharply chastising those who were disobedient, he [King Alfred] carefully and cleverly exploited and won over his bishops and earls and nobles and his thegns and reeves to his own will. But in the course of this campaign of education commands were not carried out because of the people's laziness, or else they were not finished on time . . . and enemy forces burst in by land and sea (or, as frequently happens, by both), then those who had opposed his commands were humiliated. . . . But even though they are, alas, pitifully driven to despair, and having lost their parents, spouses, children, servants, slaves, hand-maidens, the fruits of their labours and all their possessions, are reduced to tears, what use is their repentance, when it cannot help their slaughtered kinsfolk, nor redeem those captured from a hateful capitivity, nor even sometimes be of use to themselves who have escaped, since they no longer have anything with which to sustain their lives? They . . . are now sorry they so negligently scorned the king's commands; now they praise his foresight and promise to make every effort to [fulfil the obligations] they had previously refused – that is, with respect to constructing fortresses and to the other things of general advantage to the whole kingdom.
Asser's Life of King Alfred, *AD 893. Translated M. Lapidge and S. Keynes.*

One of the most serious difficulties in Old English history is the nature of the process by which the manorial colouring came over the rural economy of Alfred's time. The Danish invasions of the ninth century are the only known force sufficient to account for the change. . . . No contemporary has described the reaction of the English peasantry to the disasters of the ninth century, but the bare record of events is enough to show that far-reaching social changes are likely to have followed from them.
Sir Frank Stenton.

During the second half of the ninth century English society was shaken by a traumatic series of events. Attacks from Scandinavian seagoing freebooters – 'Vikings' – had already been a cause of concern to King Offa before his death in 796; in 793 Lindisfarne had been sacked. From the 830s the threat had grown, with Sheppey ravaged in 835, Devon attacked in 838, further raiding in the 840s, and then armies wintering on Thanet in 850–1 and Sheppey in 854–5. By then the invaders were bold enough, and numerous enough, to launch frontal attacks on walled towns such as London and Canterbury. The attacks grew in number and size until in 865 what contemporaries described as 'the Great Heathen Army' cut a swathe through England, reducing the kingdoms of East Anglia, Northumbria and Mercia to submission, and ending the royal lines of the first two.

When the Vikings turned on Wessex in 871 the West Saxons only hung on by the skin of their teeth after a series of desperate battles and the payment of tribute to buy time. Under the leadership of King Alfred

Above Offa's Dyke. This 140-mile-long linear defence work was built *c.* 790 by the Mercian overlord Offa, perhaps using labour from his tributary kingdoms.
Above right Chisbury, Little Bedwyn, Wiltshire. A small Iron Age fort reused by Alfred the Great in his burghal system, Chisbury was abandoned in the early tenth century, but at its east gate there is still a tiny chapel dedicated to St Martin.

(871–99) they attempted to consolidate their position, but what military measures they took were clearly inadequate, for in the winter of 877–8 they were overwhelmed and only survived by an astonishing victory in battle at Edington in May 878, a victory which came quite out of the blue but which was crushing enough to discourage the Vikings from persevering with their attempt to conquer Wessex permanently. Long before Alfred's day a system of taxation had existed under which kings granted land on condition that certain military obligations were fulfilled – repair of fortresses, bridges and roads, and the provision of armed and equipped men for the king's mobile fighting force. Bishop Asser's passage is clear evidence that even after the crisis of 871 the king had been unable to exact these traditional obligations from the mass of his landowners. Whether this was because he lacked the support of some areas of Wessex, or whether other kinsmen in the royal house were hostile to him, is unknown; but even in 878, when Alfred won that decisive battle, he could only call upon thegns from Somerset, Wiltshire and western Hampshire to fight at his side.

The victory at Edington, then, was more than just a victory against the Viking outsiders. It gave Alfred the political clout, in modern terms, to push through a comprehensive overhaul of the system in Wessex and greatly to extend royal power. He and his son Edward did all they could to consolidate the resources of the royal family, appropriating church lands if need be, and confiscating the lands of noble families who they felt had supported them inadequately during the campaigns against the Danes. It was during this period, from 878 to 892, that Alfred constructed a series of fortified centres across Wessex, all of which had to be garrisoned and supplied by an elaborate support system. The way in which the royal army was raised was also reformed, so that one force could be permanently in the field while its replacement was working on the land. Society, in short, became geared for war, and the more successful the dynasty became, the more it was able to place precise and heavy burdens on its landowners, and below them on the peasantry. The end result of the long period of external attack was that the social system became much more stratified: and the increasingly manor-oriented economy was the means by which the king of Wessex raised large sums of money and exacted wide-ranging obligations with very heavy penalties for failure to respond.

The fruits of this reorganisation were soon apparent. When the Viking army returned to England in 892, Alfred's system of forts (burhs) and his mobile royal army were put to the test and were able to resist and contain the enemy. In 896 they dispersed, unable to fight their way out of the King's defensive network. The scene was set for Alfred's son and grandson to extend their power over the areas which had fallen to the Vikings in the 860s and 870s, and eventually to bring about the political unification of England.

It would be fascinating to know more about this period, but there are few sources. We have no description of Alfred's defence measures; it is only in an incidental remark that his biographer, Bishop Asser, mentions the construction of burhs:

What shall I say of the cities and towns [which had] to be rebuilt, and of others to be constructed where previously there were none? And what of the royal halls marvellously built of stone and wood at his command? And what of the royal residences of masonry, moved from their old position and splendidly reconstructed at more appropriate places by his royal command? And what [in all this] of the mighty disorder and confusion of his own people . . . who would undertake of their own accord little or no work for the common needs of the kingdom?

However, one crucial document has survived, which in conjunction with remarkable new advances in archaeology enables us to interpret the revolution which seems to have overtaken the southern English in Alfred's day. The *Burghal Hidage* is a list of the fortified sites which formed the defensive network in Alfred's time, together with an assessment of how much land was attached to each fort or town to provide its garrison and support. It also shows how the number of hides for each burh was determined by the length of defended wall, on the principle that each pole (5½ yards) of wall required four men, and that one man would be supplied by each hide: 'for the maintenance and defence of an acre's breadth of wall [i.e. 22 yards] 16 hides are required: if every hide is represented by one man, then every pole can be manned by four men.' The *Hidage* goes on to give examples of how the sum worked up to 12 furlongs of wall, which required 1920 hides: 'If the circuit is greater, the additional amount can easily be worked out from this account, for 160 men are always needed for one furlong, so every pole is manned by four men.' Archaeological excavation on the sites of the West Saxon burhs has shown that the *Hidage* is accurate: Wareham's assessment, at 1600 hides, gives 1600 men defending 2200 yards of wall, and the surviving three-sided banks of Wareham measure 2180 yards.

Whoever drew up this account clearly had before him a list of the lengths of the defensive walls of all the boroughs built by the king; he was also in possession of detailed knowledge of what we would call the logistics of the areas dependent on each borough. The system embodied in the *Hidage* was carefully planned, and expected to work; in short, it is an official document from the highest level of the administration:

324 hides belong to Eorpeburnan; to Hastings belong 500 hides; to Lewes 1300 hides; to Burpham 720 hides; to Chichester 1500 hides. Then 500 hides belong to Southampton; to Winchester belong 2400 hides; to Wilton 1400 hides; to Chisbury belong 700 hides (and to Shaftesbury likewise); to Twynham 500 hides less 30; to Wareham 1600 hides; to Bridport 800 hides less 40; to Exeter 734 hides; to Halwell belong 300 hides; to Lydford belong 150 hides less 10; to Pilton (by Barnstaple) 400 hides less 40; to Watchet 513 hides; to Axbridge 400 hides; to Lyng 100 hides; to Langport 600 hides; to Bath 1000 hides; 1200 hides belong to Malmesbury; to Cricklade belong 1400 hides; 1500 to Oxford; to Wallingford belong 2400 hides; 1600 to Buckingham; to Sashes 1000 hides; 600 hides belong to Eashing; to Southwark belong 1800 hides.

The inclusion of Worcester and Warwick, two places in Mercia, in one version of the list gives a valuable clue to its composition. The main text, and the only one which explains how to work out the assessments, appeared in an early eleventh-century manuscript immediately after a copy of King Alfred's laws – perhaps emphasising its 'official' origin? This manuscript was destroyed in a fire in 1731 and is now known only through a transcript made in 1562. The *Hidage* list alone is also found in six later medieval manuscripts, which give a number of variant readings. There are some indications that these variants go back to a slightly later version of the text, but still a pre-Conquest one: the inclusion of Oxford and Buckingham – both Mercian towns – in a West Saxon document suggests that the surviving text of the *Hidage* was drawn up after 911, when Alfred's son Edward the Elder took over those areas, and indeed after 914, when the *Anglo-Saxon Chronicle* records the building of the burh at Buckingham. The inclusion of Warwick and Worcester in the second version of the text likewise suggests a date after 919, when Edward took control of English Mercia: so this version would be from a tenth-century updating of the *Hidage*. The original text as it exists today could have been drawn up between 914 and 919 and subsequently revised: the reference to the burh at Pilton being at Barnstaple could even imply the closure of the burh within the Iron Age rampart at Pilton, and the foundation of a new burh at nearby Barnstaple, which may have taken place as late as Athelstan's reign (925–39). It is still likely, though, that the date of the compilation of the *Hidage* was in the 880s or 890s, and that it represents the burghal system which Alfred created during those years, as exemplified by the now fragmentary inscription which may once have crowned the gate of Alfred's burh at Shaftesbury, and which was seen by the Anglo-Norman historian William of Malmesbury in the 1130s: 'In the year of the Lord's Incarnation 880, King Alfred made this town [*urbs*], in the eighth year of his reign' (actually the ninth: perhaps William misread an already weathered inscription).

The *Burghal Hidage*, then, is a tremendously valuable testimony to the power of the West Saxon kings of the late ninth and early tenth centuries, and an indicator of their ability to carry out far-ranging administrative reforms. Recent archaeological evidence has entirely backed up this verdict; the *Hidage* was part of a master plan with a long-term strategic eye. The burh sites were carefully chosen to control the main road and river routes into Wessex, and in the main populated areas of southern England there seems to have been an effort to ensure that no one lived more than 20 miles or so from a burh. It is also fascinating to see how the planners of the system – who obviously knew the country very well – often used existing forts; for instance the Iron Age defences at Chisbury, Pilton and Halwell were refurbished as short-term burhs; Roman sites like Portchester, Exeter and Winchester were also reused. Other large-scale burhs seem to have been substantially new creations, laid out with an internal grid pattern, such as

The former Roman Saxon Shore fort at Pevensey in East Sussex – now with a Norman castle inside it – was probably also refurbished in Alfred's time, along with a number of Roman and Iron Age sites.

Wareham, Wallingford and Cricklade, where in each case impressive Anglo-Saxon defences can be seen today. Even in former Roman towns, such as Winchester, new grid patterns of streets were laid out ignoring the Roman pattern, with plots running off the streets to provide for the citizens land for houses and cultivation within the walls. Many of the burhs were clearly intended only as defensive sites, but some of the big centres were planned from the start as centres of urban life, trade and manufacture.

The evidence of the *Hidage* and of archaeology shows that Alfred and his successors were able to put into action massive resettlement programmes. The total *Hidage* figure for the garrisons of the burhs of Wessex exceeds 27,000 men. When this is added to the two shifts of the field army, it makes an extremely high percentage of the population geared to war. Even if a place like Wallingford had some kind of urban nucleus before the 880s, and this is not certain, the size of population implied in the *Hidage* must have been of an altogether greater dimension. A garrison of 2400 men was required to defend its walls; if most of these men had families, then some 10,000 people would have been living either in the burh or its outlying land. In Domesday Book a particularly detailed account of the town of Wallingford is given together with a number of dependent villages and dwellings in Oxfordshire and Berkshire, and at least 400 houses within the town, suggesting a population of 1500–2000 within the walls.

It seems a fair assumption that in the 880s, when, as Asser says, King Alfred 'cajoled' and eventually 'forced' his vassals to fulfil his requirements for defence, large numbers of people were compelled to move into the new burhs or their immediate environments. It is possible that inducements were offered by the government to help people make the move: for instance, the burhs were usually constructed on royal land, or on land specially bought by the king for that purpose. The king would offer favourable terms for people of the thegn or burgess classes, to encourage them to take up residence in the newly laid out towns: low tax assessments, or more likely, land, in exchange for military obligation. In general during this period the West Saxon kings never relinquished their essential tax demands; only for a brief time during the heyday of Athelstan's reign (931–4) did any of them lease land without the customary obligations of 'burh work', bridge repair and military expedition. As Asser relates it, it had taken too long to force the king's rights on the people. Compulsory purchase may have been involved in some cases; Alfred's son Edward frequently extorted one-sided leases, even from the Bishop of Winchester, and a number of his charters show him dealing in land in order to secure in royal hands certain strategic sites, such as Portchester (from the church of Winchester – a burghal site) and Plympton on Plymouth Sound (from the Bishop of Sherborne). So hard were the bargains Edward struck that churchmen begged him not to be so ruthless; these were not times for faint-hearted rulers.

Government in societies such as that of late Saxon England is all about taxation and war. Kings must be able to impose obligations on their peoples and raise money and armed forces. Under the ferocious impact of the Viking attacks of the ninth century and the prolonged struggle to fight back, southern English society was transformed by war. Large-scale construction of deliberately planned towns may have involved large-scale forced movement of population such as happened in the 920s and 30s under King Athelstan. Moreover, the very existence of the *Burghal Hidage* shows how, as the needs of government grew more complex, the requirement to record them in detail became vital. Soon enough (between 917 and 937) the West Saxons would remodel the administration of the Midlands into a shire system like that in Wessex, based on the shire towns, with a regular pattern of assessment so that each shire should if possible contain 1200 hides, or twice that. A mysterious document known as the *County Hidage* is thought possibly to come from this period; it lists the shires of English Mercia and the East Midlands on this basis, giving 2400 hides to Oxfordshire, 1200 to Warwickshire, 1200 to Worcestershire, 2400 to Gloucestershire, 1200 to Bedfordshire, 2400 to Shropshire, 1200 to Cheshire, and other assessments based on proportions of these figures. Though the *County Hidage* is only concerned with English Mercia and the East Midlands (it excludes the Danish areas, which were not hidated), for some reason it also includes Wiltshire in Wessex, for which it gives an assessment of 4800 hides, a figure which agrees very well with the *Burghal Hidage* total for the four burhs of Wiltshire – Malmesbury, Cricklade, Wilton and Chisbury.

The Alfredian burh of Wareham in Dorset, looking south. This photograph shows the town still contained within the ninth-century defences between the Rivers Piddle and Frome.

The thinking behind the *Burghal Hidage*, therefore, was to provide taxation assessments for defence which could be correlated with the shire system, so that renders in money or kind could be broken down into local assessments levied on the hundreds, the shire subdivisions. The military character of the system comes out clearly in the *Chronicle* annal for 914, which tells how a Viking army in the Severn valley was defeated by 'the men from Hereford and Gloucester, and from the nearest boroughs'. The assessments themselves were ultimately based on the hide, as the *Burghal Hidage* shows. But the hide was an abstract rating which could be moved up or down, and on occasion the Old English government gave huge rating reductions to areas which had suffered badly through devastation in war – or, conceivably, to areas where they wanted to win 'hearts and minds'.

An interesting example appears in the *County Hidage*, where Northamptonshire is given a rating of 3200 hides. At the time of Domesday Book the shire had 32 hundreds – so the figures make good sense if the shire really did originally have 3200 hides. Domesday, however, shows that this was not the case by 1086, for although most of the Midland shire hidages correspond very well to the *County Hidage* totals, Northamptonshire has only 1244 hides. But this is not a mistake; the disparity exemplifies one of the characteristic features of late Old English government, for the shire received no fewer than two rating reductions before 1086.

Northamptonshire's case is complicated by the fact that it was conquered by the Danes in Alfred's time, and from about 887 to 917, when it was captured by Edward the Elder, its ancient assessment in hides was replaced by a Danish assessment in carucates. Soon after 917 the English government decided to bring the shire into line with the south for tax purposes, and imposed a new hidation for tax only. In 940 the shire fell into the hands of the Vikings of York after being devastated in the fighting; when the English resumed control in 942 they immediately reduced its tax assessment by about one sixth. We know this because of a document known as the *Northamptonshire Geld Roll*, which dates from before Domesday Book; here the shire's assessment can be very precisely calculated at 2663½ hides, which is stated to be the pre-Conquest figure, too. The reason for this reduction could be that land was lying waste and was therefore exempted from tax because of the devastation suffered in 940; alternatively it may have been preferential treatment for Danish landowners whose loyalty the West Saxons wished to ensure – or reward. But how does one explain the *Geld Roll*'s difference from the Domesday assessment made less than twenty years later, when the shire's hidage was halved? The *Geld Roll* shows that many manors were lying waste soon after 1066 and were returning no tax. Had the devastations in Northamptonshire in 1065, recorded by the *Anglo-Saxon Chronicle*, caused such damage that another massive rate reduction was given by the new Norman government, perhaps at the behest of their English advisers? Whatever the reasons, the shire was rated in Domesday Book at 1244 hides, an assessment which continued until the late twelfth century when the hidage system was phased out.

The history of tax and local government does not make exciting reading, though then as now it was vital to a government's ability to achieve its policies. This chapter has tried to look at Domesday roots in terms of taxation systems, on town and shire, to see how the system inherited by William the Conqueror and revealed in Domesday Book can be traced back to the tremendous changes wrought by the Viking invasions. The survival of documents like the *Burghal Hidage* enables us to make a plausible reconstruction of the development of English government before Domesday. What is certain is that, from Alfred's time onwards, the kings of Wessex had a system of government at their disposal which paved the way for the creation of a kingdom of all England. With Edward and Athelstan, Alfred's gifted successors, this was soon brought about. Because of the social disruption of the Viking age power had become concentrated in the hands of the king and the most important families. These powerful landowners succeeded in curtailing the liberties of the peasantry in southern England, and widening the gulf between them and the few hundred 'lords of the manor'. In this period the society seen in Domesday was created.

We can add force to that conclusion with the help of recent archaeological discoveries. Despite the great amount of evidence which now exists for the transformation of English towns in the late ninth century, historians have not, as yet, faced its obvious implication: that the countryside must also have been reorganised to sustain the burghal system. There is not a hint of this in our scanty sources, but there are important parallels in Germany where Henry I achieved a military revolution between 924 and 933 which may have been modelled on the English successes against the Vikings. In this case the strengthening and founding of towns, reshaping of the army, and reorganisation of the countryside went hand in hand. There was, exactly as in England, a mobile royal army of thegns and nobles, and also rural local forces – poor freemen – who participated in communal labour and crop rotation schemes, as is described in the near-contemporary account by Widukind of Corvey:

Every ninth man was chosen from the troops from the countryside and made to live in the fortresses and build shelters for his fellows and receive and store a third of all the produce there. The other eight were to sow and reap the crops of the ninth. And when the citizens were accustomed to this rule and practice, the king took the offensive.

Something like this procedure is indicated by the *Anglo-Saxon Chronicle* for 893, which describes how Alfred 'divided his army in two, so that always half of its men were at home and half out on service, except for those who were to garrison the towns'. This account may refer not only to the élite royal army, but to the local forces. Either way we must assume that those at home did the sowing or harvesting for those in the field. This was perhaps on a large scale, for as the garrisons required by the *Burghal Hidage* total

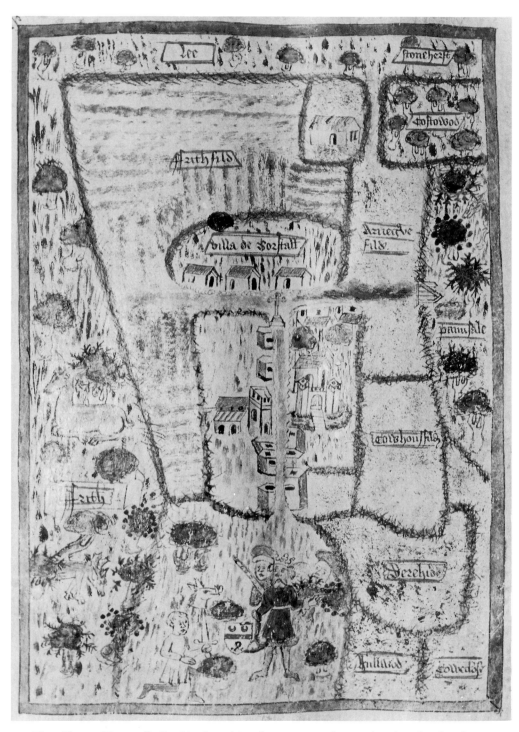

The village of Boarstall, Buckinghamshire, from a map of 1444, showing the church, moated manor, peasant houses and open-field strips: a layout dating from the Viking era.

over 27,000 men, we may be talking of total manpower of five or ten times as many. The reorganisation of the countryside would have made it far easier to gear society to war. In the last resort everything depended on the king's ability to ensure food production; if the harvests were disrupted, so was the military effort.

Remarkable new discoveries could suggest that this hypothesis is right, and that ninth-century southern England went through a 'hidden' agrarian revolution. Surveys of the field systems of some ninety Domesday parishes in Northamptonshire, with excavations on some deserted village sites, have revealed that the classic pattern of open fields dates from before the Norman period, and that they were often laid out over early Saxon sites which apparently had been deliberately deserted to form the present nucleated villages. Most surprising of all, many of the 'long' or 'Great' furlongs – up to 400 yards long – seem to have been laid out as part of a single planned large-scale division of the landscape.

This revolutionary change was well advanced in parts of southern and central England by the later ninth century. Charters in Wessex from the 850s contain very much more detailed descriptions of the estates than before, with a wealth of field details. Tenth-century charters from several parts of Wessex give us our first hard evidence of open-field systems with their intermixed strips; these are particularly detailed in the series of royal charters from Berkshire mentioned on p. 35. There, under Ashdown at Harwell, Drayton, Hendred, Ardington and Curridge, the classic signs of open-field cultivation are described, overriding the boundaries of earlier bigger estates which were now being broken up into smaller 'manors' to reward the thegnly class.

The move to the cultivation of 'common land' and away from small-scale independent farming makes sense in the light of the war effort of the ninth century. The replanning of fields, the change from dispersed settlements to nucleated ones, the shifting of large numbers of people into the boroughs, would be necessary corollaries. We can conjecture a number of other possible explanations for the growth of the open-field system – population increase, royal tax needs, even the wider use of the heavy plough – but war is surely the biggest reason, as Sir Frank Stenton hinted in the quotation at the beginning of this chapter. By 900 a fundamental change had overtaken landowning in England with a massive centralisation of royal power. There is a distant parallel in the Second World War, when British society was rigorously organised with conscription of labour and wide state control and coercion. War as always was the catalyst.

As yet this interpretation is speculative, but if it can be proved, it has profound implications for our understanding of the origins of English society, for it suggests that the manor-based society we see in Domesday Book was created in the ninth century under pressure of war, shaped by the disasters which shook Old English society in the Viking era.

8
THE ANGLO-SAXON EMPIRE:
WAR, LAND AND TAXATION

The late Anglo-Saxon system of government . . . was uniform and sophisticated and reflected not only power, but intelligence. If, ultimately, England avoided the fate of the rest of *ancien régime* Europe it was largely thanks to a framework established by a regime yet more ancient.
James Campbell, Transactions of the Royal Historical Society, *1975.*

Less than thirty years separates the end of Alfred the Great's reign and the proclaiming of his grandson Athelstan as 'Emperor of the world of Britain' in 928. But in the interim war was the theme of English history, as it had been for so long before. Alfred's successor, his son Edward, immediately faced a dynastic crisis and possible civil war with the revolt of his cousin Aethelwald. It ended in a bloodbath at Holme on the edge of the Fens in 902, with terrible casualties to both the Danish and West Saxon aristocracies. The next years were marked by a patient build-up of forces, making treaties, paying gelds to buy time, punctuated by occasional devastating Danish raids into West Saxon territory. The preamble to a royal land grant from those years reflects the fears felt by many in the face of the sacking of cities and ravaging of fields: 'It is by no means evident that what we commit to the written word will survive the terrible dangers which imperil us.' Other documents back this up. A lease issued to the Bishop of Winchester, *c.* 909, with rent payable in kind (ale, loaves, meat, cheese and other produce from the estate), makes allowance for a situation arising when the rent is not paid 'because of the stress caused by a [Viking] raid' – and this on an estate only 6 miles from the 'capital' at Winchester. Most graphic is the statement of the same bishop in a lease for the estate at Beddington in Surrey, *c.* 908, that 'when my lord [the king] first let it to me it was completely without stock, and had been stripped bare by the heathen men'. The bishop had been able to restock his land, but at a cost increased by bad weather, which had further crippled the estate:

Now of the cattle which survived the terrible winter we have nine full-grown oxen with 114 full-grown pigs and 50 wethers . . . and there are 110 full-grown sheep and seven bondsmen [*theowae*] and twenty flitches; and there was no more corn there than could be prepared for the bishop's farm: we have 90 sown acres [the estate was 70 hides – several thousand acres]. Then the bishop and community at Winchester beg in charity for the love of God and for the sake of the holy church that you [the king] desire no more land of them, for it seems to them an unwelcome demand.

This tiny detail brings home how the annual devastations during the Viking wars must have impinged on life. If the principal bishopric in Wessex found it so hard to make ends meet, what was it like for small freeholders? Surely many must have been forced into subordination to powerful, wealthy lords who could protect them.

All the hints from the law codes show that, though the growth in the power of the royal family and the Church can be traced far back, the tendency to a dependent, manorial economy such as is seen in Domesday received a massive boost during the Viking era. In the Dark Ages, as in modern times, a really far-reaching war effort involved great inroads on personal liberty as the government attempted to impose heavier obligations on land and service in order to maximise returns in armed forces, tax or supplies. In peacetime it is unlikely that a Dark Age ruler would have been able to overcome the massive opposition which a deep-rooted peasantry always makes to changes in its way of life. But in time of war, when that peasantry relied on the royal power for its preservation, things were different. In the quotation at the beginning of Chapter 7 Sir Frank Stenton noted that no contemporary source describes the reaction of the English peasantry – and the freeholding class – to the disasters of the ninth century, but the record of events suggests that far-reaching social changes resulted from them. In short, the population of southern England ended the period far more heavily obligated than before; and though society remained mobile in the sense that movement between classes was possible, the gap between the smallholders and peasants on the one hand and the noble, royal and ecclesiastical landowners on the other became very great.

Just how concentrated the war effort was in the first quarter of the tenth century can be judged by the *Anglo-Saxon Chronicle*'s constant record of military campaigns. In the steady, remorseless progress north and east, when between 910 and 920 Edward and his sister Aethelflaed 'liberated' – perhaps we should say conquered – Danish Mercia and East Anglia as far as the Humber, Aethelflaed was in the field every year from 910 to 918. She also built fortresses at Bremesburh (910), Scergeat and Bridgnorth (912), Tamworth and Stafford (913), Eddisbury and Warwick (914), Chirbury, Weardburh and Runcorn (915); in 916 she campaigned in Wales, in 917 she captured the Danish army base at Derby, and in 918 the Leicester army submitted to her. At the same time, and working closely in collaboration with Aethelflaed, Edward of Wessex built a parallel series of fortresses at Hertford (south of the River Lea, 911), Witham and Hertford (north, 912), two at Buckingham (914), Bedford (915), Maldon (916), Towcester and Wigingamere (Castle Camps, Cambridgeshire, 917), Colchester (917), Stamford (918), Thelwall and Manchester (919), Nottingham (south of the Trent), Bakewell (920) and Cledemutha (Rhuddlan, 921?). The military and logistical effort involved in this campaign is unequalled in Dark Age warfare.

In the meantime the field armies of Wessex and Mercia had proved themselves in mobile warfare and in pitched battles, as well as in storming enemy fortresses. Within a few years, under Edward's successor Athelstan, they would confirm the English empire by campaigning as far afield as Bamburgh, Penrith, Hereford and Exeter in one season's campaign (928). With that the overlordship of the West Saxons over Britain was achieved: a powerful and well-organised kingship south of the Humber, client-ruled north of it, and a system of tribute, hostages and personal attendance imposed on the kings of the Celtic lands. This was enforced by a punitive expedition by land and sea deep into Scotland in 934, and a tremendous victory at Brunanburh in 937.

The resources required to wage what amounts to three generations of uninterrupted warfare were immense. It should also be remembered that manpower resources were limited. Old English society was aristocratic, hierarchical and militaristic: the men who did the fighting were not the peasantry but the landowning class, the thegnhood; they were the people who provided the well-armed and well-trained élite, and the investment in their skills and equipment was considerable. A thegn's fighting equipment, which he was required by law to bring to battle, included very expensive items such as helmets, chainmail, swords and horses. As in any mounted aristocracy the horse itself was an important possession, a noble animal in every sense – oxen were the beasts of the field – because of the investment in training, equipment, stud farms and so on. Athelstan's laws prohibited their sale abroad (to Vikings?), and good ones are often named as royal

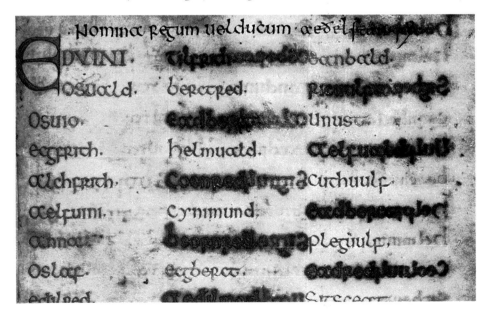

A sign of the times: the eighth-century roll call of the great Northumbrian kings – Edwin, Oswald, Oswy – has Athelstan's name added (top right), *c.* 934, as 'the first king to rule all England'.

gifts. Great expense was also lavished on the best weapons, with fantastic ingenuity and skill going into the creation of the great pattern-welded sword blades. Earl Aelfgar of Essex, for example, who died in the 940s, left in his will a mass of weapons including a single sword 'worth 120 mancuses of gold' with another 4 lb of silver plated on the sheath. In straight cash terms that amounted to 3600 silver pence worth of sword and another 930 pence for the sheath, at a time when you could buy an ox for 30 pence and a slave for 240 pence.

The rewards for such fighting men were often astronomical at this time, and several of the great families became the Dark Age equivalent of millionaires, with vast amounts of movable wealth and estates running into tens of thousands of acres. Most, of course, were tied to the royal house by marriage or blood. But the thegnhood bore the brunt of the fighting in these years – when Aethelflaed, 'Lady of the Mercians', stormed Derby, 'four of her thegns who were very dear to her were killed right there within the gates'. So as the kingdom expanded, and eventually extended its overlordship over most of Britain, the need to increase the thegnly class became paramount. It was no longer possible for the West Saxons and Mercians to provide the backbone of their mobile armies from the ranks of their royal and hereditary landed families alone. The royal land grants of the 930s say something about the expansion of the thegnly class, and show how well they were rewarded by the king. In these grants the ruling class of Anglo-Saxon England is set out in graded ranks, and it is possible to provide a kind of *Who's Who* of them at this crucial moment in English history.

The king himself probably held more land than in 1066, having taken possession of many of the royal estates in Mercia and East Anglia. Below him were a group of prominent families whose roots lay in ninth-century Wessex and which held all the great earldoms in the tenth century – land-rich families whose daughters provided royal wives and which exercised great political power. It is the stratum below them which is of most interest as we try to penetrate to the roots of the manorial structure revealed in Domesday. The backbone of the armies which created the Anglo-Saxon empire in the tenth century was probably something like one or two thousand landowners of the thegnly class in Wessex and Mercia, many of whom could also bring into the field several heavily armed retainers. These people by law held 5 hides and had their own residence. Of the lesser ranks of thegns little is known, but the grants of the empire period say a great deal about the top men, the ones who were most rewarded for the victories of 910–30, who held court office or travelled around with the king on his frequent itineraries.

The exceptionally detailed land grants for 931–4 show that there were about 120 of these top thegns, a figure which can be compared with Domesday's picture of about 180 feudal tenants-in-chief, including earls. These thegns were by no means socially insignificant; most were connected with the royal families of Wessex and Mercia, many held court office or would in time become earls; many held several estates. But if the great earldoms of the tenth century were to pave the way for the vast concentration of power into William's hands after 1066, the growth of this thegnly class in the tenth century helps account for the growing gulf between the free and the unfree classes in Anglo-Saxon England long before the Conquest. Domesday represents the culmination of these tendencies, accentuated by the ease with which the Normans were able to appropriate the system and make it work for them. To show how this power developed let us now look at one of those thegnly families and its tenth-century holdings; its head was Wulfgar of Inkpen, dishthegn or court officer of King Athelstan, who held several thousand acres of fine farmland in the Kennet valley.

On 11 November 931 King Athelstan celebrated the feast of St Martin, 'leader of the saints of the west', with his court at Lifton in Devon. It had been a long year in which the king's itinerary had taken him in the spring to Colchester, at Whitsun to Winchester, and in early June to his residences in Hampshire, such as East Wellow, with a great summer assembly of his tributaries at Worthy; he may have been up in Mercia in the summer, and by October he may have stayed at Kingston-on-Thames before making the long journey down to Devon – a typical year for a Dark Age king, constantly on the move. This was a society with few means of delegating power safely, especially outside the heartland of the dynasty. In his own country a king could rule through his local earls, through the local assemblies. But in the outer reaches of the *imperium* cohesion and unity were always at risk, and constantly showing yourself to friend and foe alike was a reliable means of communicating, controlling, reassuring allies and cowing enemies.

There were also economic reasons for the itineraries. With no centralised system, in a modern sense, it was necessary for kings like Athelstan, Edgar or William the Conqueror to be constantly on the move. They had to staff and keep in good repair a string of royal residences, each one of which was the centre of a local network which drew in the agricultural produce of the neighbourhood to feed the court. Many of the royal residences which provided the king's 'farm' are still recorded as such in Domesday. The king would travel from one to another, stay for a few days at most, use up all the supplies which had been laid in and then move on, constantly preceded by messengers checking stocks of food and standards of accommodation.

Lifton was a tiny royal vill, perhaps no more than a hunting lodge, by the River Lyd – at Domesday its staff numbered a mere fifty workers and a dozen slaves. In the king's company that November day, perhaps mainly lodged in tents, were many of the most important figures in Britain – both archbishops, King Hywel Dda of Dyfed, King Idwal Foel of Gwynedd, 17 bishops, 15 earls (many from the Danelaw), 5 abbots and 59 top thegns – over one hundred magnates in all. If one adds to this enormous assembly the service staff, retainers, hangers-on and the rest upwards of a thousand people would have been 'rejoicing under the wing of royal generosity'. On the day after the feast the king turned to business. One of the jobs of kingship was to reward the thegnly class, particularly in land. Several times a year the king supervised the transfer of estates to his thegns, usually giving a charter – a kind of mortgage – for three lives (the recipient, his son and his grandchildren).

On 12 November Athelstan rewarded a young thegn, Wulfgar, with land for his services. Wulfgar had been with the king throughout the year on his travels, acting as a court officer, a task performed in rotation with other noble companions. The special significance of the Lifton grant is that the original copy of the charter still exists, with all the witnesses laid out in order of precedence; this document found its way into the archive of the bishopric of Winchester after Wulfgar's death, and still attached to it is Wulfgar's will, also in a contemporary hand. Together these two remarkable survivals give a close-up view of how landholding was developing under the Anglo-Saxon empire.

Wulfgar and his wife Aeffe lived at their farm at Inkpen on the borders of Wiltshire, Berkshire and Hampshire. Here would have been the ancillary buildings mentioned in contemporary estate management texts – stables, barns, cowshed, pigsty, threshing floor and stove, ovens, kiln and hen

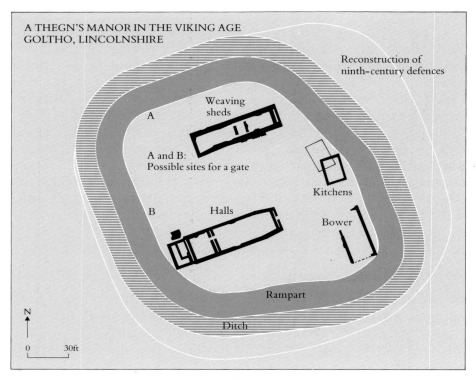

A THEGN'S MANOR IN THE VIKING AGE
GOLTHO, LINCOLNSHIRE

Reconstruction of
ninth-century defences

Weaving
sheds

A

A and B:
Possible sites for a gate

Kitchens

B   Halls

Bower

Rampart

N

Ditch

0   30ft

roost. The family church was not at Inkpen, but down in the valley at Kint-
bury. To this church Aeffe would give a quarter of her crop after her husband's death – here were buried Wulfgar's father Wulfric, and his grandfather Wulfhere. The family were in fact old landed gentry from these parts
and had held estates here for nearly a century. Grandfather Wulfhere had
brought disgrace on the family by somehow failing his duty and 'deserting
his king and his *patria*' during the Viking wars, but the family had not lost
out in the long run. Wulfhere had been 'earl' in Wiltshire in the 860s, and
Wulfgar would be promoted to the same rank in 938. Wulfgar's will shows
that he owned estates at Inkpen, Crofton, Ashmansworth, Denford,
Buttermere, Ham and Collingbourne Ducis, a total of over 60 hides of land;
the original holding of the family had probably been in the Wylye valley in
Wiltshire. Related charters tell how the family came by all these holdings.
Buttermere and Ashmansworth, for instance, had been owned by Wulfgar's grandfather. Collingbourne, on the other hand, had been part of the
lands with which Edward the Elder had endowed his New Minster at
Winchester in 903; but within a few years, as we have seen, the clergy were
getting such a poor yield on some of their properties because of depopu-
lation and war damage that they sold them for ready cash – Collingbourne
came back to the king before being granted to Wulfgar.

The will mentions Wulfgar's kinsmen or tenants, Wynsige and Wulfsige
at Crofton, Athelstan and Cynestan at Denford, and Brihtsige at
Buttermere; whether Wulfgar and Aeffe had children is not known. Of the
dependent population on the estates we have to rely on Domesday for a
rough estimate: in 1086 Inkpen had 10 villeins, 15 bordars and 20 slaves (so a
total population of around 200); Denford perhaps 40 or so; Collingbourne
probably 300 or 400; Crofton 40 or so; Ham 80 or 100; Buttermere a mere
handful; and Ashmansworth perhaps around 100. So Wulfgar had between
700 and 1000 unfree labourers, men and women and their children,
working on his estates. Wulfgar's will makes no mention of the poor people
on his estates, nor does it refer to any manumission of slaves; it is related,
however, that his possession of Collingbourne was conditional on him
supplying 'ten poor people with food and drink at All Saints'. What these
people owed in dues around this time is given in a document from an estate
neighbouring Wulfgar's at Hurstbourne Priors in Hampshire:

Here are written down what obligations shall be fulfilled by the peasants [*ceorlas*] at Hurstbourne. First from every hide they shall pay forty pence at Michaelmas, six large buckets of
ale and three measures of wheat for bread; they must also plough three acres in their own
time and sow them with their own seed, and in their own time bring it to the barn; they must
give three pounds of barley as rent, and mow half an acre as rent, in their own time, and they
must make the hay into a rick; they must bring four cartloads of split wood as rent, stack it in
their own time, and provide 16 poles for fencing as part of their rent, likewise in their own
time. At Easter they shall give two ewes with two lambs – and we count two young sheep to
a full-grown one – and they must wash and shear the sheep in their own time, and work as
they are bid every week except three: one at Christmas, one at Easter and the third at
Ascension.

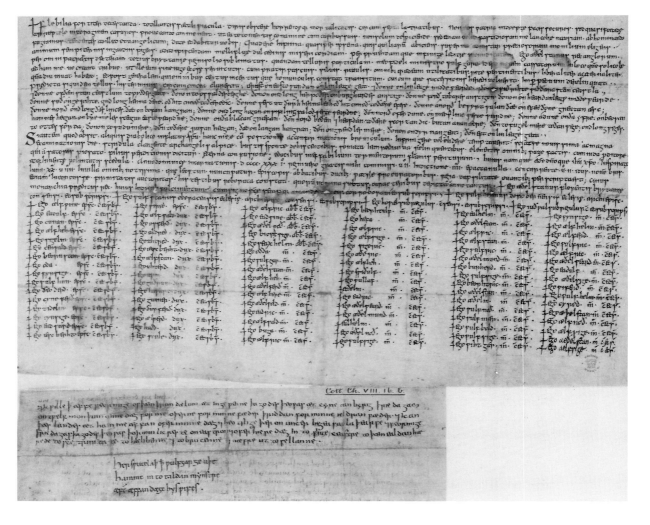

Customs varied in different parts of England. In some places the dues were heavier than these, though if Alfred's laws are anything to go by, people got more holidays elsewhere: 'all freemen' get 37 days a year; here they have to settle for three weeks.

The Hurstbourne dues show how thegns like Wulfgar created their wealth in return for fighting against the Vikings. Wulfgar himself went north with the king into Scotland in the summer of 934, and was doubtless among the king's troops at the Battle of Brunanburh late in 937; his reward was an earldom. He died in 948, probably in his forties, which was about par for the course for men in the Dark Age West. His wife Aeffe outlived him, as women usually did; in that respect, if nowhere else, women had the better of it. Her name survives at Collingbourne, in Wiltshire, in Aughton, whose name in the fifteenth century, Affeton, shows it to have been 'Aeffe's farm' – this was land left her in Wulfgar's will.

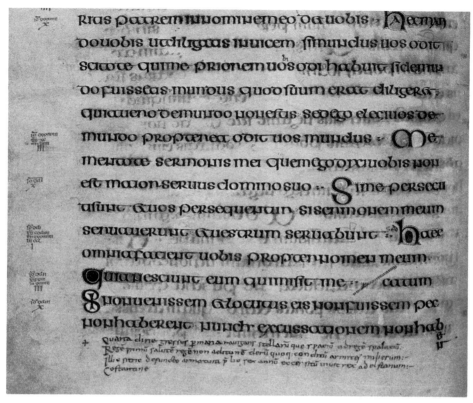

RIUS PATREM INUOMINEMEO OA UOBIS · ŊEC man̄
ŌOUOBIS UTDILIGATIS INUICEM · ſimundus uos ōDIT
SCITOTE QUIME · PRIONEM uos ōDI habuIT · ſideīp
ŌO fuISSETIS · munDUS QUOD ſuum ERAT diligERT ·
quiauero ōemunDO NOUeſTIS · SeOEO eleciuos ōe ·
munDO PROPTEREA ōDIT nos munDus · Ōe ·
menTOTE SERMONIS mei quem eΘO ōIXIuobis non
eſT maion SERuus domino suo · Ѕ ime perſecu
'uſmt aquos perſequentin · si ſennonem meum
ServaverInT aueſTRIM Servabunt · ḧ ac
omniafacient uobis PROPTER nomen meum ·
Ǫuianeſciunt eum quimiſIT me · catum
Ѕ nonvenissem aΘlocutus eis nonfuissem pec
nonhaberent nunch excuſatIonem nonhab·

+ quarta linc grefſur ę mana mangarꝯ ſtellārū que ꝛ paciꝯ a brege ꝛpalacū.
Reſe primū ſalure regē non adtrunē clerū quoꝗ con dꝛū armūreꝯ imperium:
Ille ſnore defuncto armavura ꝗ̄ lio ꝛex annū ecceꝯ ſtai inure rex ad elſtanum:
coſtanrane

Above At the bottom of a page in a magnificent Northumbrian bible of the eighth century is an abbreviated version of a poem written in 927 in praise of King Athelstan, heralding 'this united England' – a crucial moment in British history. From then on the mechanisms were created which made Domesday possible.
Left Athelstan's charter for Ham, made at Lifton, Devon, in 931. Attached is the will of the recipient, Wulfgar of Inkpen, endorsed at the foot: 'Here it is confirmed that Wulfgar has granted Ham to the Old Minster Winchester after the death of Aeffe his wife.'

The defeat of the Vikings and the reconquest of the Danelaw, then, was a crucial factor in the political and social development of later Anglo-Saxon England. Military victory was made possible by sweeping changes in the organisation of towns and urban life, and in the countryside. Society would never be the same again. The West Saxon kings from Alfred to Edgar progressively expanded the power and landed wealth of the monarchy and were successful on the one hand in building up several powerful families in what had been the old kingdoms, with a thegnly class below them, and on the other hand in imposing extremely heavy obligations. By about 930, when King Athelstan issued his law code at Grateley, landowners were required to provide two mounted men for every plough when the king went to war: presumably this tax was commuted into money or kind in time of peace, but clearly the crown possessed the means and the records to assess the whole kingdom in terms of hides and plough teams for each landholder. In the end, as always, such heavy obligations must have transferred themselves on to the workforce. No wonder that the royal chronicler Aethelweard, writing in the 980s about the 930s, said that 'from then on the fields of Britain were consolidated into one, and there was peace and abundance of all things'. That was how it appeared from the viewpoint of a West Saxon aristocrat. Indeed, so successful had Athelstan been in that period that for a while he had been prepared to waive the rights which kings always reserved on land they leased – the right to demand bridge work, fortress work, and especially service in the army, from every 5 hides. Coming after decades of unremitting war it must have seemed like the highest form of tax relief to the lucky few who got it.

The tenth century, then, was a golden era for royal power, when many of the mechanisms were set up which proved so useful to the Normans when they took over the system in 1066. It may have been in the years immediately following the capture of the 'Five Boroughs', the chief Danish towns of the East Midlands, in 917–19, for example, that Edward or Athelstan was able to shire the Danelaw on the West Saxon model, retaining the Danish army boroughs as shire towns and adopting the courts of the wapentakes into the developing West Saxon system of hundred courts. The Danes could administer their own law, with their own lawmen. But no man now could be without a lord – so said Athelstan's Grateley code. It was a symbolic moment, for in theory it embodied two central ideas: everybody could be brought to justice, and everybody could be taxed. Domesday was in sight.

Above right Part of the Domesday Book entries on Middlesex. The actual page size is 380mm × 280mm. Though often compressed, the writing is clear and formal, bearing witness to the extraordinary mind of the scribe-editor who produced the final version, collating and checking the local returns – a mind which 'delighted in synonym and paraphrase'. This double-page spread would have taken a day or two to write.
Right Part of a page from the famous 'shorter illustrated' version of Domesday, the thirteenth-century *Exchequer Breviate*.

KENT

TERRA REGIS

Above The Vale of the White Horse, with Uffington Camp and the Ridgeway.
Above right A prehistoric landscape: the Lambourn Downs. One of the ancient estates of the West Saxon royal family, and still so in Domesday.
Right Remains of the open-field strips at the former West Saxon royal estate of Wantage, pictured on an eighteenth-century estate map. Charlton was the farm of dependent peasants who serviced the estate (ceorl-tun).

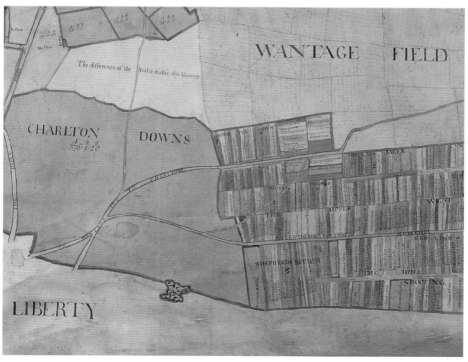

Above Verulamium (St Albans): the second-century-AD Roman theatre.
Below A peasant from Roman times working in the fields, depicted in a mosaic from North Africa.
Right Ceiling decoration from the house of a Roman aristocrat in St Albans.

Above The Saxon church of
St Lawrence at Bradford-on-
Avon, Wiltshire.
Left The interior at Bradford-
on-Avon church, now thought
to be late tenth century.

rgen tpam gnapum phaŋao moette pethej todt beanne ta. j hiin ſp un
ƿuht ƿerhær nâŋeton uŋ oŋhom rloʒe rnoŋon ræʒne oŋon ŋumhʒ

Above The duties of kingship illustrated in a tenth-century Anglo-Saxon manuscript. *Below* Portchester: one of the massive Roman forts of the Saxon Shore, refurbished by Alfred the Great in his system of fortified burhs *c.* 890.

Above Greensted, Essex. Probably mid-ninth-century, it is a remarkable survival of a wooden Anglo-Saxon church.
Below Brixworth, Northamptonshire (eighth-century): in Domesday a royal estate church.

ecclesiae loco

Inprimis

in memorato praefatae
eclypsis et mox sequitur
pestilentiae quo et colman
uincente catholicorum
intentione suplantatur
et suorum paucissimis est·
Cuius dedit sextum
eclesiae donum praesir
episcopus obiit pridie ioui
iulicarum; Sed et tuconbercto
post tantum annorum eodem minre
ecclesiae deputatur· et bercto fili
o reddin nezim noliquit;
Quem ille suscepta·m phinx et no
isin annos tanto;
Tunc et seccato ti pacisco tampone
episcopatu· missus est nomam
abipso simul et cenete nondan
hymbronum osiiu urdinpnaeede din
te libno pecuir diximus urthecend
pus prin· Usin ineclesiae sciar
discipulis doctus simus desinsie

anglorum· Pactirqb: huic eclesiae
anglorum conthi episcopum ondi
nacru· Mysis paruitis apostolico
papae donaturs ereunsis atei on
shtchis uicasis ti pecueris; qui ubi no
mcen psirchito· Cuius sedi apos
tolicae tampone illo uraelia cruru
psirate· post quam scrisiurs sui
ceru scati p faro papae apostolico
papae psirto· Uon multo post
et ipse et omnes psine qui cum eo
eddusihuaccruo soen suirs psirsirsit
ee supirsirsinsirsce deleysunt;
at apostolicuirs papae haebreo
delurs consilio· quae esiuro se
dulurs quam eclesiurs anglorum
conthi episcopum mirresuitt;
Et act hr inmonaesuirio prinidacno
qsi sit non longe aeneapoli caem
pacinaee aebbaes hacdniacnur·
Unnacrione aepen saccrurs liactsiurs
dilirsirchin imbircurs·
Monaesesiu aclibursimul et eccle
siactsiar disciplinir insacrarus·
Tyaece paruthsirs et laeinaee bircurs
psirturs simurs; huic aedreaeci
tum papae iursrto episcopatu
acceshto bnurtaeenaeacin usittuo';
Qui inellsrignum setaecirto quaecdin
responderit·

Left An eighth-century copy of Bede's *Ecclesiastical History of the English People* —
the formative text of early English history.
Above Three illustrations from a calendar of *c.* 1030. Top and middle: images of
Anglo-Saxon agriculture, scything and ploughing. Bottom: the other side of the coin:
the pleasures of the hall — aristocratic culture on the eve of Domesday.

Above The eleventh-century church at Rothwell in Lincolnshire superimposed on the reconstructed village of West Stow gives a vivid impression of an Anglo-Saxon settlement, though the houses of the better-off peasantry would have been grander.
Below Old Sarum: an Iron Age hillfort, Anglo-Saxon royal mint and Norman new town (the abortive cathedral foundations of which are still visible).
Right Norman style: the magnificent small church at Iffley near Oxford is one of the best-preserved twelfth-century village churches in England.

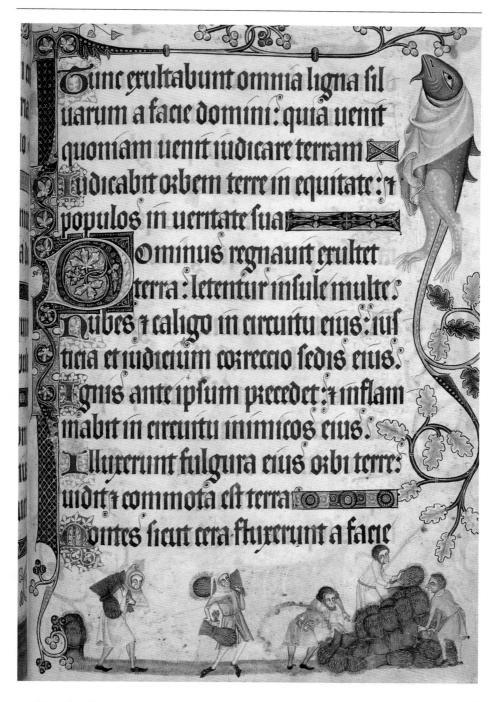

Tunc exultabunt omnia ligna siluarum a facie domini : quia uenit quoniam uenit iudicare terram

Iudicabit orbem terre in equitate : ⁊ populos in ueritate sua

Dominus regnauit exultet terra : letentur insule multe.

Nubes ⁊ caligo in circuitu eius : iusticia et iudicium correccio sedis eius.

Ignis ante ipsum precedet : ⁊ inflammabit in circuitu inimicos eius.

Illuxerunt fulgura eius orbi terre : uidit ⁊ commota est terra

Montes sicut cera fluxerunt a facie

Left Southwell, Nottinghamshire: a Norman church built on the site of the Saxon minster founded in 956.
Above and overleaf Scenes from the *Luttrell Psalter* (1335–40), showing peasant labour before the Black Death.

Below A scene from *Queen Mary's Psalter* shows the lord's reeve overseeing the harvest: such was the life of Michael Gorman or Christina Cok. (See pp. 192–195.)

Above A marriage fête at Bermondsey around 1600 by J. Hoefnagel. From this time a general lowering of the marriage age contributed to a dramatic population increase which would transform British history.

Below Nineteenth-century progress: a cartoon of 1841 marks the passing of an age with the arrival of the railways. Rural society had always been mobile, but now it would be changed for ever.

9
DOMESDAY ROOTS:
THE VIKING IMPACT

It is easy to view the history of England in the ninth, tenth and eleventh centuries from the standpoint of the southern English, to regard the triumph of the West Saxon dynasty as somehow inevitable, and to see the whole historical process with the hindsight of our knowledge of a united England. But in the north and east of the country in the tenth century it did not appear that way. Domesday Book shows that the Viking invasions and subsequent settlements in those parts left a permanent mark on what became known as the Danelaw. An Ordnance Survey map of anywhere north and east of Watling Street will show the distinctive character of the place names, especially the further north and east one goes. The *Anglo-Saxon Chronicle* gives the key moments in this transformation: in 876 they 'shared out the land of the Northumbrians and they proceeded to plough and to support themselves'; in 877 'in the harvest season the army went away into Mercia and shared out some of it'; in 880 'the army went from Cirencester into East Anglia, and settled there and shared out the land'. The annals record free-born Danish soldiers settling as farmers dependent on the army bases established at the main towns – Derby, Nottingham, Northampton, Huntingdon and so on. The large Danish armies were probably several thousand strong, and each army based on the Danelaw towns could muster several hundred men or more.

This military origin was long reflected in the social organisation of the Danelaw towns. In the tenth century they called themselves 'armies', even a century after the settlement. Around 962, when King Edgar issued a law code to include the Northumbrians, he addressed it to Earl Oslac 'and all the army which lives within his ealdormanry' – perpetuating the idea that the by now often well-to-do landowners of the Vale of York still viewed themselves as an army established on the soil. A fascinating local document from 983–5 underlines this impression with a vivid local detail on a matter of securities on the purchase of an estate in Northamptonshire by Earl Aelfric, Cild of Mercia: 'When Abbot Ealdulf bought the toft [homestead] from Godric of Walton, his sureties were Ulf and Eincund and Grim of Castor. When Earl Aelfric bought the estate at *Leobrantestune* from Fraena at a meeting of the whole army [*ealles heres gemote*] at Northampton, the whole army was security on his behalf that the estate was unburdened.' The Scandinavian character of these regions is evident in Domesday Book, and just as pronounced in the personal names in the twelfth century. Indeed as late as Edward I's time (1272–1307) ancient phrases of Scandinavian origin are found in the legal customs prevailing in Leicester. In the Lincolnshire countryside the Scandinavian impact lasted even longer.

A journey across Midland England today enables the traveller to trace this impact on the ground. Coming up the Fosse Way from the heartland of 'English' England, the Forest of Arden, you reach Watling Street at High Cross, the greatest road junction in early England. From here, all the way down to the River Lea in Bedfordshire, Watling Street marked the border of the lands living under English law, and those under Danish law. Indeed even on the Warwickshire side some of the place names indicate Scandinavian settlers, such as Wibbe (at Wibtoft) and Copsi (at Copston). Once into Leicestershire the Scandinavian names come thick and fast: Ullesthorpe, Bittesby, Ashby and Wigston, a name which combines a Danish personal name with the commonest place name element in English: 'Viking's *tun*'.

At Wigston, as at the other Scandinavianised villages in the Danelaw, a considerable class of free peasant landowners is found in Domesday – 31 sokemen at Wigston as against 32 villeins, 12 bordars and 3 slaves: this class of people can be traced right down to the enclosure of the village fields in the nineteenth century. At Domesday there were over two thousand of these people with their families in Leicestershire. Further east, in Lincolnshire alone there were over ten thousand; their subsequent history is dealt with in Chapter 14. All the evidence suggests that these newcomers moved in alongside the native Anglian peoples, rather than drove them out or made them subject. Indeed it is quite likely that many of the sokeman class were English in origin. In this chapter we shall look at one Danelaw settlement and try to see how it developed in the Viking era, while Alfred and his successors were fighting their way into Mercia.

Standing on the dry ground above the valley of the River Wreake in Leicestershire is a little village called Grimston – the *tun* of a Viking called Grim. It is not known precisely when this village got its name – whether, for instance, there had been an English village there before the arrival of Danish settlers (the word *tun* is Old English) – nor whether the Viking Grim whose name is perpetuated in the village name was one of the 'Great Army' of 877 or part of the later influx of immigrants who came in via the Humber and the Trent, often with their womenfolk, to take plots of land and plough. But we will assume that Grim was one of the settlers who carved up this part of the East Midlands between 877 and 886.

Within a short time English local government surfaced in a new form. Grim owed his allegiance to the 'army' council in Leicester, one of the Five Boroughs which formed a confederacy in the East Midlands. Whether they had kings is unclear, though the Northumbrian and East Anglian Danes seemed to have acknowledged a king. Here the boroughs seem to have been run by oligarchies led by important landowners, 'earls' (the word is Viking)

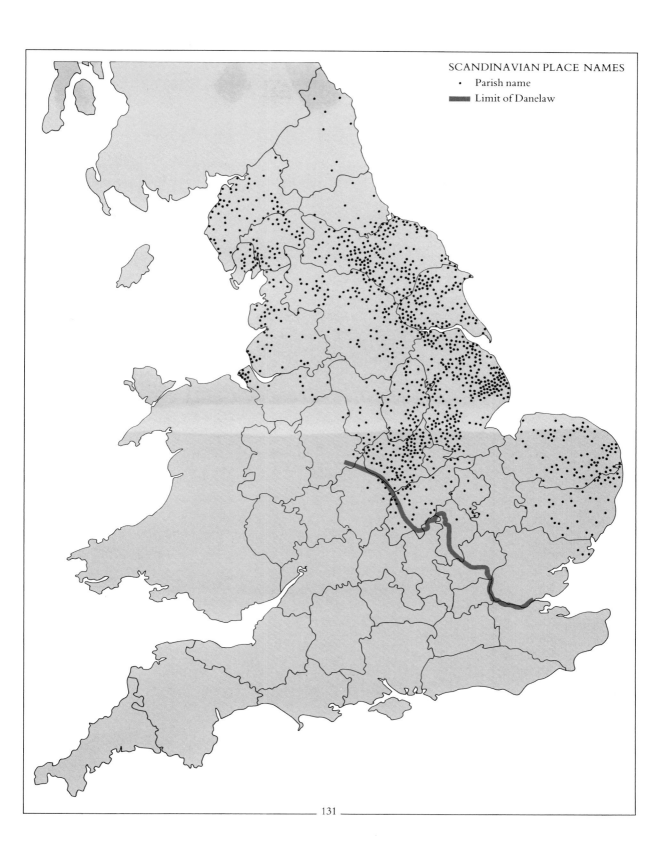

SCANDINAVIAN PLACE NAMES
• Parish name
▬▬▬ Limit of Danelaw

In 1086 about thirty people lived at Grimston in Leicestershire. Now it is shrunken, surrounded by the earthworks of the medieval village and the ridge and furrow patterns of the old fields.

and 'holds', with a council of the 'army' of Leicester in which all the free-holding landowners of that part of the Five Boroughs had a say. The land dependent on each borough was not yet known as a shire, as it would be in Domesday Book, but as the 'army' of Leicester. Its administrative divisions were wapentakes, as compared with hundreds in the south – a word which originally meant the symbolic brandishing of weapons by which decisions at a public meeting were confirmed. The larger territories within the Dane-law were too unwieldy to have a single council and were divided into what the Danes called 'thirdings' or 'third parts', later ridings – not only in Yorkshire but also Lindsey, which had three ridings too. For the next three centuries the Scandinavian influence ran deep into the fabric of life in the Five Boroughs and Yorkshire, and the differences in organisation, language, land tenure and names of people and places were just as marked in 1186 as in 1086. How exactly did this come about?

The Great Heathen Army which had attacked East Anglia in 865 first turned its attentions on the East Midlands in 865–8. But it was in the winter of 874–5 that the crisis came. Then the raiders moved their ships up the Trent into the very heart of the ancient kingdom of Mercia, sacking Not-

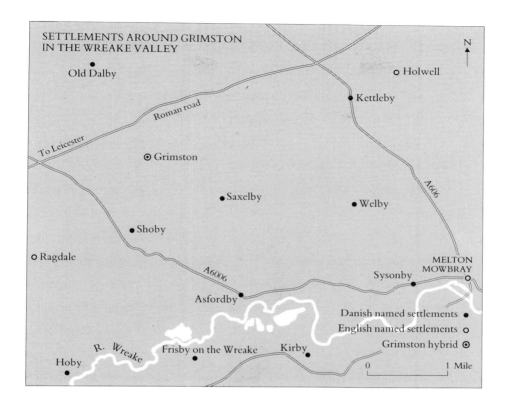

SETTLEMENTS AROUND GRIMSTON IN THE WREAKE VALLEY

Old Dalby
Holwell
Kettleby
Roman road
To Leicester
Grimston
Saxelby
Welby
Shoby
A606
Ragdale
MELTON MOWBRAY
Sysonby
A6006
Danish named settlements •
Asfordby
English named settlements ○
Grimston hybrid ◉
R. Wreake
Frisby on the Wreake
Kirby
Hoby
0   1 Mile

tingham and sailing up the wide valley along the northern edge of what is now Leicestershire. On the way they probably sacked the ancient church of Breedon on the Hill, a great monastery founded in 675 which had been reduced to an impoverished parish church when the Domesday commissioners recorded the neighbourhood in 1086. The army established itself for the winter at Repton, on a bluff above the flood plain of the Trent. Repton had been a royal residence in the days of Offa, a royal mausoleum where Mercian kings like Aethelbald and saints like Wistan were buried in the crypt which still survives.

Recent dramatic archaeological finds have revealed details of this winter's events: traces of the riverside ship docks, the lines of the defensive ditch which enclosed the 3½-acre site, and above all the burial place of about 250 adult men who can only be members of the Great Army. The men seem not to have been killed in battle, so presumably these are the remains of those who died of disease. In all early armies such 'wastage' was treated as one of the concomitants of campaigning, and it is often reckoned that a 10 per cent casualty figure from such causes is realistic. This gives an idea of the size of the Repton army: perhaps 2500 armed men. So a bleak and dangerous midwinter's foraging may have been Grim's first experience of England.

Over that winter the army used its position at Repton to defeat King

Burgred of Mercia, who fled abroad. 'And they conquered all the land' (i.e. of Mercia) says the *Anglo-Saxon Chronicle*. At that time they installed a puppet king, Ceolwulf, who would co-operate with them. In 875 the army divided, part going to Northumbria where, in a crucial annal for the following year, they 'shared out the land of the Northumbrians and proceeded to plough and to support themselves'. The intent now becomes clear, and in the following year's annal comes a statement of great interest to us: 'Then in the harvest season the army went away into Mercia and shared out some of it, and gave some to Ceolwulf.' The *Chronicle* seems to suggest that deliberate division of the land had taken place between the English and the Danes, under some kind of enforced treaty, with holdings apportioned to the members of the army – possibly as many as two thousand men – land earmarked perhaps in between English holdings, or taking over the holdings of Mercian landowners killed or exiled by the war. Let us see what the evidence for this is on the ground.

The evidence for the Viking settlement in the Danelaw centres on the great number of place names of Scandinavian origin which appear in Domesday Book in 1086, and in odd cases in earlier sources. There are over three hundred village names in the Five Boroughs ending with the Danish suffix *-by*, one of the commonest place name suffixes in Denmark today; nearly two hundred of these are compounded with personal names of Scandinavian origin, such as Rotherby (Hreidar's *by*). Over a hundred place names in the East Midlands contain the Scandinavian word *thorp*, meaning farmstead, such as Ringolthorpe (Ringulfr's *thorp*). In addition, a number of place names are completely Scandinavian in origin, such as Eakring in Nottinghamshire (circle of oak trees). A number of earlier English names have been transformed by the substitution of a distinctively Scandinavian word or sound for an Old English one, such as Carlton in Leicestershire, which otherwise would be Charlton today. Finally, and most interestingly for our purposes, there are about sixty examples in the territory of the Five Boroughs which are known as Grimston hybrids, where an English name ending in Old English *tun* (farm, village) has a Scandinavian personal name as its first element.

The picture that emerges from the distribution of these names looks like this. First, of course, it is quite possible that Danes settled in an existing village without changing the name of the place or necessarily dispossessing the native English, but there is no means of telling when this happened. The Danes certainly renamed a few settlements, and presumably in some cases this involved taking over the village itself. More important, examination of the three hundred '-by' names in relation to the geology and soils of the

Right The last open-field village, Laxton in Nottinghamshire, has survived enclosures, World War II and post-1979 privatisation. The pattern of fields probably developed here in the tenth century.

landscape demonstrates that many of the colonists came as settlers developing virgin land and establishing new settlements where there was no existing English village; it is likely that much of this settlement took place in the first wave of colonisation in the late ninth century. Many of these '-by' sites are close to main Roman roads and ancient trackways, suggesting the importance of lines of communication for settlement; they also tend to lie in valleys of tributaries and small streams, whereas the older English villages lie on the main rivers. So for their settlements the Vikings opted for the unused land in secondary areas. In fact a feature of the '-by' village sites is that their founders tended to prefer sandy or gravel lands: this feature is so pronounced that the colonists may have been motivated by a desire to choose land like that back home in Scandinavia. Put together, these facts strongly suggest that this settlement was not achieved by an army of a mere few hundred men, as has been proposed recently. The fact that up to five hundred places in the Five Boroughs alone bear Viking names indicates that the actual number of settlers ought to have been many times that figure. And although all those foundations need not have been the result of the military settlement of 877 and after, it stands to reason that the bulk must have taken place at that time or in the following decades. The most obvious interpretation is that, in the period from 877 to 918, migration took place from Scandinavia into the East Midlands under the protection of the armies of the Five Boroughs, who from 886 held the Watling Street frontier as the boundary between Danish and English England. Whether the English attempted to stop or limit immigration into these parts after they gained control there in 918 is impossible to say.

If this pattern is correct, then the circumstances which led to Grim and his companions taking over 'Grim's *tun*' above the valley of the Wreake can be reconstructed. Leaving the Danish quarter of Leicester we travel northwards along the Fosse Way with the River Soar to our left. At the bridge over the Wreake we turn off in a north-easterly direction up the narrow, twisting valley of the tributary. To right and left are English villages: Ratcliffe, Goscote, Cossington, Rothley, Syston and Queniborough. But within a couple of miles the Scandinavian place names come thick and fast: Rearsby (Reidarr's *by*), Thrussington (Thorstein's *tun*), Brooksby, Rotherby, Hoby and Frisby (Frisian's *by*). Above the valley on both sides are further groups of villages: to the south Dalby, Ashby, Gaddesby (Gadd's *by*) and Barsby (Barn's *by*), and to the north Asfordby and up to Shoby and Grimston itself. Finally, around the large English manor of Melton are another handful of Scandinavian settlement names: Kirby (church *by*) and the farms of Ali (Welby), Saxulf (Saxelby), Ketil (Kettleby) and Sigstein (Sysonby).

The pattern of names in the Wreake valley suggests that the migrants came down the Trent, or used the Fosse Way down to the Middle Anglian territory of Leicester, before leaving the Soar valley for the less-populated banks of its tributary. The earliest core of English settlement had been in the Soar valley, with its broad, fertile terraces above the river flats; this had been heavily settled from the sixth century, so the newcomers turned to the river gravels, sandy shale, sand and limestone patches of the Wreake. Perhaps the ruling earls of the army of Leicester held a moot with local Middle Anglian landowners and negotiated the confiscation of estates in suitable areas with which they could reward their followers, so that the area of the Wreake was deliberately ceded to some Viking chief. Unfortunately there is no charter evidence from Viking Age Leicestershire, so this can only be speculation.

Be this as it may, some of the English *tuns* near the Soar kept their English names, with one or two exceptions where earlier *tuns* took the names of Vikings like Thorstein or Thormod. But 2 miles up the valley a cluster of settlement names by the river, and a spread on to the hills north and south, suggests a definite takeover, filling in between the English areas. Many of these were doubtless new settlements, and may, like Rearsby, Hoby, Gaddesby and Frisby, have had parishes created round them at this time. But the parish system was already established in these parts, and it is quite possible that many of the parishes in the Wreake valley, such as Thurmaston, Syston, Thrussington, Queniborough and Grimston itself, were already in existence. Unfortunately the diocesan organisation has left no record. Despite populations which must have been over a hundred at Thrussington, Queniborough and Syston, the last-named is the only one of all these 'Scandinavian' villages in the Wreake valley with a church recorded in Domesday. In addition, no church in the valley seems to have any pre-Conquest fabric, so there is no means of judging the process by which the newcomers became Christian.

Of the density of settlement, however, there can be no doubt. One particularly eloquent detail is evident even on the most up-to-date Ordnance Survey map. The Wreake is only called by that name from its confluence with the Soar up to Melton; from then on it changes its name to Eye, an English word meaning 'river'. Wreake, on the other hand, is Viking speech for a twisting river course – perhaps the colonists called it something like 'the twister', a name which well fits the stream's tortuous course. So the newcomers were numerous enough to change the name of the river – if only the bottom of it.

There has been much discussion of the way such place names have developed. Scholars were inclined to think that the settlement of the Wreake valley happened in one fell swoop after 877, when a unit of the Danish army from Repton was deliberately settled in that region to protect the borough of Leicester. But more recent studies have been able to distinguish the phases of settlement by suffixes like '-*by*' and '-*thorp*' and the Grimston hybrids. These have suggested that the army based on Leicester settled its own men in the immediate surroundings of the city, and that when the next phase came, with 'second wave immigrants' coming from Scandinavia into the valleys of the Humber and the Trent, and especially into the Lincolnshire Wolds, the ruling oligarchies in the boroughs probably filtered these immigrants into unused land and to new sites that could be cleared and colonised. In the light of this picture some English sites in the lower Wreake valley would have been taken over after 877; the rest would have been the result of progressive settlement over the next two or three generations, a kind of gold rush with land-hungry Scandinavian free farmer-warriors leaving their homeland as the word spread there that their kinsmen and friends had found new homes and fertile land over the North Sea. In many places they must have taken over the existing social structure and become lords of the local peasantry. The main period of migration was probably over by 918, when Alfred the Great's son Edward conquered the Five Boroughs.

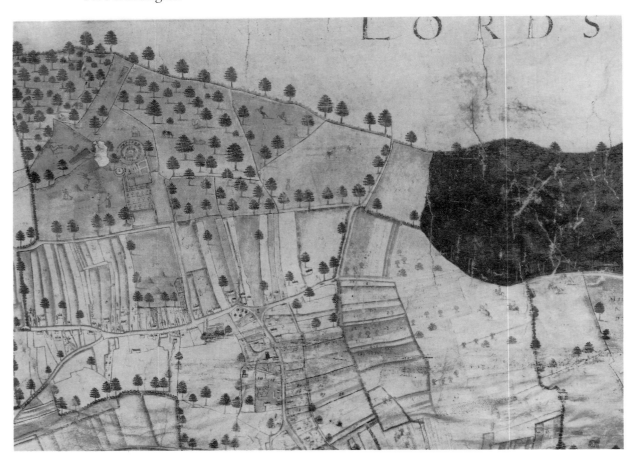

This seventeenth-century map of Laxton shows the burghal plots of the later medieval town and (above) the earthworks of the Norman castle. Though Laxton retained an English name, its population must have been Anglo-Scandinavian.

The Grim who gave his name to Grimston may then have been one of the first wave, who settled after 877; he may have been the equivalent of a retired veteran who settled down after years of campaigning. Maybe he married a local girl, as many Vikings did, for these people would have lived alongside each other. The geographical context of Grimston makes this clear.

The village lay on the edge of what may have been English territory, hence its hybrid name which can only have come from English neighbours describing Grim's farm in their own language, not as a '-by' or a '-thorp' but as a '-tun'. Similar comments can be made about other local villages. In short, everything points to a mixed society right from the start of the settlement period. This would also explain the apparent anomaly, even in places whose name is English, of many of the field names and agricultural terminology showing Danish influence – a classic case is the surviving open-field village at Laxton in Nottinghamshire: the name is Old English (Lexington in Domesday), but there is a prevalence of Danish words in the field names, such as syke, toft, flatt, gate and wong.

So from the place names alone a great deal can be learned about what happened on the ground when the Vikings settled in England, helping us to understand why the society of eastern and northern England in Domesday is so different in character from that of the southern and western parts. What Domesday implies about the differences in the classes of society in the Danelaw will be looked at in Chapter 14. But before we leave Grim at his farmstead we should not forget that the Viking settlements made a major impact on the towns, too. In recent years the exciting excavations at Coppergate in York have brought a new awareness of the Viking character of the city in the tenth and eleventh centuries, but it is easy to forget that the main cities of the Five Boroughs also changed greatly at this time; indeed Derby (formerly Northworthy) owes its name to the Vikings.

Grim owed allegiance to the 'army moot' at Leicester, and no doubt travelled there to buy specialist supplies and luxuries – perhaps selling some of his produce there in the market outside the eastern gate of the old city. Leicester – a former Roman provincial capital with some impressive buildings, such as the bath-house, still standing, along with the partly decayed Roman wall – had probably been a bit of a backwater in the ninth century. In the seventh century it had become the cathedral town for the Middle Angles and the market for the Anglian people who lived round about. Now it was the centre for a Danish army, and for a while may have had something of the feel of a garrison town; the army associations here too lasted for a long while, for Domesday Book says that the great wood which stretched from the north gate of the city into Nottinghamshire – and which is still called Leicester Forest on the M1 signposts – was called Hereswode (The Army's Forest); perhaps its resources in timber, animals and grazing were reserved for the military.

Inside Leicester, the circuit of the old city seems to have remained in the jurisdiction of the Church – though it is not known whether there was a bishop still there after 877. As in York, a number of the main streets are called 'gates', from the Old Norse *gata*, meaning street. But whereas at York these names are found within the Roman walls right up to the Minster, and not just in the Danish quarter, in Leicester they are found outside the Roman circuit, on the northern and eastern side of the town leading to the medieval market at the former east gate. So just like Danish Nottingham and Stamford, Leicester was a twin town, with English and Viking quarters. The Viking area faced the area of thickest Scandinavian settlement, but presumably could use the Roman walls to defend itself in an emergency.

In 1086 Domesday Book recorded a city of perhaps two thousand inhabitants with several parish churches and a hinterland which, even in the incomplete record, was well served with churches. When did Grim and his companions become Christian? Many may have been converted early on, as they lived next to English neighbours who went to church. But the key moment must have been in 918, when Aethelflaed, 'Lady of the Mercians', 'with God's help peacefully obtained control of the borough of Leicester, in the early part of the year, and the greater part of the army which belonged to it was subjected' (*Anglo-Saxon Chronicle*). From that moment, some sort of diocesan control (from Lichfield?) must have been reimposed, with perhaps a suffragan bishop once more seated in the old cathedral. Recent archaeological evidence has suggested that the parish church of the Danish quarter was on the site now occupied by St Margaret's, and that the remains below the present fifteenth-century building are of a tenth-century church built to serve the Viking burgesses of the city. If this is correct, then it is interesting to note that at Domesday the churches within the walls of the Roman city remained attached to Lichfield – from which the Leicester diocese had been created in 679 – while the Danish church of St Margaret's and the 10 hides of land attached to it belonged to the bishop of the chief town of the Five Boroughs, Lincoln.

Within three generations of the settlement of 877 the people of the Five Boroughs seem to have come to regard the kings of Wessex as their natural lords. When King Athelstan died in 939, they were temporarily overrun by pagan Norse kings of York with their Norwegian-Irish following. At that time there was severe fighting at Leicester, with the young West Saxon King Edmund attempting to storm the city, and the York Viking army 'bursting out by night'. The West Saxons evidently came off worst in this clash, for the archbishops of York and Canterbury negotiated a truce which

Left Coppergate, York. Excavation of part of the industrial quarter of the Viking city revealed evidence of wide-ranging contacts and the rise of a Viking 'middle class' in the tenth century.

once more made Watling Street the boundary of separate English and Scandinavian Englands. Leicester and the Five Boroughs again found themselves not only under Danish law, but under Scandinavian rule. But if a contemporary poem can be trusted, when the East Midlands were reconquered by the southern English in 942 the landowners, farmers and 'army members' of those parts were grateful to be 'liberated' by the West Saxons; as Christian Anglo-Danes they had, it would appear, been hostile to the Norse king of York and his pagan army, who were not of Danish origin. The descendants of the Great Heathen Army of 877 had become respectable 'English' freeholders!

Finally, then, Domesday Book recorded these respectable freeholders in 1086. In Leicestershire, as throughout the Danelaw, many of the smallholders still had Viking names: Ingold, Fraena, Swafi, Feggi; their English neighbours were there too – Aethelhelm, Alfwold and Leofric. Some of the best lands on the Wolds – Grimston among them – were now in the hands of a Norman, Robert de Bucy, and in his turn Robert had leased part of Grimston (3 carucates, the Danish equivalent of the hide) to a Norman called Gerard. The population was tiny: two sokemen (on the same farm, or at outliers?) with five villeins and three ploughs. There was another plough on the lord's land, on which the 'free' sokemen may have had to do boon-work. The two sokemen at Grimston were undoubtedly the descendants of Grim and his family in the ninth century – not necessarily by blood, but certainly by class. There are two thousand or so of these people named in Domesday Leicestershire, nearly a third of the shire's recorded Domesday population. Their lands may have fallen to the Normans in 1066, but Domesday and later manorial documents prove that the descendants of this class of free Viking smallholders remained on the soil. The origins and nature of their personal freedom are one of the most fascinating of Danelaw problems, and Chapter 14 will look at some of the post-Domesday documents to try to give an answer to this most thorny of Domesday roots.

In the meantime we can turn from Grim and his compatriots to the kingdom of which they would soon be members – the Anglo-Scandinavian kingdom of all England. During the tenth century royal power extended over most of what is now England. In the south and the Midlands the West Saxon kings reinforced this by a network of mints; in the Danelaw all the Five Boroughs minted coins, some in large quantity. They, and the work of men like Thurston, the moneyer of Leicester, are the next stage of our Domesday search.

10
MONEY AND TAX:
THE OLD ENGLISH COINAGE

Nine hundred years on from Domesday we take money for granted; indeed we are on the threshold of moving away from metal and paper money to electronic systems and computerised shopping and banking. It is likely that by the time the thousandth anniversary of Domesday arrives money will no longer be used in England. But for 1300 years metal coinage has been in continuous use, and until the reforms of the early 1970s the original Anglo-Saxon monetary system of pounds, shillings and pence, with 12 pence to the shilling and 240 pence to the pound, persisted with no basic alterations; it was not long before that the subdivision of the penny into halfpennies and farthings had come to an end. That system was a clever and complex one, and, as will be seen, was important in the context of Domesday.

'Render therefore unto Caesar the things which are Caesar's': a first-century-AD silver denarius of Tiberius. The use of coinage died out in late Roman Britain, to be revived in the seventh century.

The earliest proper penny coinage started in the time of King Offa of Mercia (757–96) was issued from Canterbury. Later London, Rochester, an East Anglian mint and perhaps Winchester were added. No other mints are identifiable until the time of Alfred the Great (871–99), when the names of Gloucester, Exeter and Lincoln appear. Alfred's son, Edward the Elder, seems to have greatly expanded this system, for although the only named mint seems to be Bath, comparison with his son Athelstan's coins suggests that in Edward's day mints existed at London, Winchester, Canterbury, possibly Oxford, Shaftesbury, Southampton, Wallingford, Wareham, Chichester, Langport, Lymne; several Mercian towns, including possibly Nottingham, Derby and Tamworth, certainly Chester (in large numbers), Shrewsbury, Stafford and Hereford; and several other unplaced mints. Clearly this great increase in the number of moneyers can be connected with Edward's reconquest of the Danelaw, and shows that as soon as English control was established in boroughs like Nottingham minting was

Left Offa of Mercia created the first proper penny coinage, with the Mercian duodecimal system of 12 pennies to the shilling and 240 to the pound.
Right Alfred the Great's coinage marking his takeover of the Mercian city of London in 886 had unashamedly political overtones – he now asserted kingship over all the English.

begun in the king's name. In some cases this can be dated quite closely to the last five years of the reign.

So when Athelstan succeeded his father in 925 important moves had already been made to provide the expanded burghal system with coinage. The motives behind this become clear with the numerous law codes which survive from Athelstan's time. None of them can be precisely dated, but as the early years of the reign were taken up with dynastic crisis and then warfare in many parts of Britain, it is reasonable to think that the first main code cannot date from earlier than 928–30. In terms of the history of tax and money in England, this, the Grateley code, is highly significant:

> There is to be one coinage over all the king's dominions, and no one is to mint money except in a town. And if a moneyer is convicted [of forgery], the hand with which he committed the crime is to be struck off and put up over the mint. . . . In Canterbury there are to be seven moneyers; four of the king, two of the bishop, one of the abbot; in Rochester three, two of the king, one of the bishop; in London eight; in Winchester six; in Lewes two; in Hastings one; another at Chichester; at Southampton two; at Wareham two; at Dorchester one; at Exeter two; at Shaftesbury two; otherwise in the other boroughs one.

Other passages in the same code speak of buying and selling being limited to within boroughs: any goods with a value over 20 pence could not be bought outside a town and had to be witnessed by the town reeve – 20 pence was the value of a cow in Athelstan's day. So the minting of coins within boroughs had a double purpose: firstly, it was a means of controlling and taxing commerce, creating a royal monopoly on trade; secondly, the minting itself allowed the king to make a levy on the moneyers in exchange for the dies, which were supplied centrally. Coins were a very good way of making money, and the West Saxon kings from Athelstan onwards made determined efforts to control the weight and silver content of their coinages and to ensure that no place was more than 15 miles from a mint.

The idea of 'one coinage over the king's dominion' is not to be interpreted too literally. It does not mean one uniform type of coin, but that only the king's coins would be acceptable currency, and finds of buried coin hoards have shown how successful Athelstan was in keeping foreign currency out of the kingdom. Within the kingdom there were distinct regional variations, with the coinage apparently being organised on the lines of the traditional divisions of the kingdoms of England: Wessex and Kent together, Mercia, East Anglia and Northumbria. The Danish shires south of the Humber also seem to have had a separate organisation based on Derby and the Five Boroughs, and there are traces of another regional group on the Welsh border. Recently a major eastern group has also been identified, with mints at Lincoln and Stamford. The distinctive styles, and sometimes types, show that the regions maintained their own die-cutting workshops from which they supplied the neighbouring mints, presumably under royal supervision; the remains of the workshop of the York moneyer Ragnald were found in the Coppergate dig, with dies and a trial piece. Other differences may indicate local preference: the king, for example, is never called 'King of All Britain' on his coins minted in the Danelaw or East Anglia; the Midland group called him 'King of the Saxons'; and unlike the southern mints the Midland group does not use a portrait of the king.

The determination to keep a firm grip on the coinage must be reflected in the fact that over most of the country the mint and minter's names were included on the coins, hence ABBON EAXCIVITA (the moneyer Abbon at the city of Exeter), MO SCEFTES (moneyer at Shaftesbury), LAE URB (Lewes town: a rare use of the Latin *urbs*) and MOT ON TOMIEARÐGE (minter at Tamworth). It is therefore a surprise that before the end of Athelstan's reign the practice of recording mint names seems to have been abandoned, and that this state of affairs carried on until late in Edgar's reign (973–5) when a great reform of the coinage was undertaken, one result of which was that the name of mint and moneyer once more became a regular feature on every coin. Fifty mints are certainly known from Edgar's time, and by Ethelred the Unready's reign (979–1016) another twenty are recorded.

King Edgar's reform coinage of 973 coincided with a wave of imperial ceremonies reinforcing the Old English kings' claim to be 'rulers of all Britain'.

It is from Ethelred's time that modern researchers have been able to detect one of the most surprising and remarkable features of the Old English coinage system, indeed of English medieval government as a whole. By the 980s there appear to have been about three hundred licensed moneyers in some sixty mints around the country. Every five or six years all coins in circulation were 'demonetised'; they ceased to be legal tender by royal decree – presumably there was an amnesty during which they could be handed in and exchanged, and this exchange took place only at one of the mints for coins of the new issue. This enabled the government to do several

Obverse and reverse of the Lamb of God issue of Ethelred the Unready. This beautiful coin was probably only a limited production, rather like today's Maundy money.

things. They could, of course, prevent the clipping of coins – this indeed is given as a reason for the great recoinage by the thirteenth-century chronicler, Roger of Wendover, who records it; they could adjust the weight of the coins; and they could alter the silver content, which they often did – rarely to low levels, often to very high levels. These variations in silver content are hard to explain: they could relate to availability of silver bullion, and it has even been claimed that they could have been a response to inflationary or deflationary pressures in the economy.

The late Old English coinage system was one of great sophistication, with a high degree of political, economic and fiscal expertise lying behind royal management; how all this was done, the level of discussion – and who discussed it – may never be known. It was obviously an expensive system to operate, but it paid for itself and brought profits to both crown and moneyer. For a generation after the Conquest the coinage survived on the old personnel and on traditional know-how, but the Normans had no experience of anything like this scale and sophistication of administration, and a system which had functioned efficiently for 150 years or more virtually collapsed once it fell to the Normans to make it work on their own.

The relevance of the Old English coinage system to Domesday is considerable. Coupled with the administrative organisation of shires and hundreds, it enabled the Anglo-Saxon kings to raise very large sums of money. This becomes very clear during the reign of Ethelred the Unready, but there are indications that it had been used for this much earlier, during Eadred's time (946–55). Between 991 and 1017 the *Anglo-Saxon Chronicle* gives precise figures for the tributes paid to the Danes by Ethelred's government, building up from £10,000 to £48,000 in 1012, and the pay-off to Canute's army in 1018 of £72,000 from the country and £10,500 from London. Seen in terms of coinage, these figures run up to twenty million pennies, and on the worst occasions may have comprised as much as two-thirds of the issued coinage. If this is true, then the psychological sense of national defeat must have been as grim as the *Anglo-Saxon Chronicle* says it was: in fact the cumulative effect of payments made after 1002 may have been more damaging than the loss of the silver itself (ranging from 7 tonnes in 1002 to possibly as much as 30 tonnes in 1018). It may not be an exaggeration to say that Danegeld was so heavy a burden that it transmuted the whole nation. Such were the consequences of continued military defeat in an age when the country was nevertheless the richest in western Europe.

But there is another important point about the payment of Danegeld in Ethelred's reign. Certainly it provides evidence of growing disaster, but it also offers evidence that the system itself functioned all the way through Ethelred's reign, that recoinage carried on, and that the government was still able to maintain close control over its local mints, just as it was with the local shires and hundreds through its appointed officers. Indeed as late as 1016 it still proved possible for the government to raise large armies and fight successfully under good leadership. Paradoxically, then, crippling as the imposition of Danegeld was, all the indications are that the country was rich enough, and its organisation efficient enough, to bear it without breaking down. This is a truly remarkable testimony to the resilience of the late Old English state, and indeed adds to the hints from the *Chronicle* and elsewhere that by this time England had some sense of national identity which had been engendered over the previous century by the most success-ful of the West Saxon kings.

The coinage system can now be seen in relation to the local organisation of Anglo-Saxon England. The shires and hundreds and their courts were the way the central government raised its gelds and transmitted them down to local level. At local level every local court knew the hidage assessment of each manor, and the appropriate amount of geld could be imposed on each landowner. This was the way the Danegelds of Ethelred's time were raised in the countryside, with another form of assessment on the towns, perhaps pegged to income. If we keep this picture in mind when we turn to Domes-day, we will see how the Norman conquerors, just like Canute, were able

A coin die from the 920s, discovered in the Coppergate excavation at York.

to employ this method of raising a geld on the hide to gather vast sums of money from the English people. In the sense that Domesday Book is a geld book, it is a record of its assessment. That is why, according to the Chronicle of Florence of Worcester, it caused so much vexation and violence. Although the full circumstances and custom which lay behind the Old English kings' ability to call a geld are unknown – what, for instance, constituted 'just' and 'unjust' or 'fair' and 'unfair' gelds – enough is known for us to see Domesday Book as part of that long tradition, and once again examination of earlier events shows that the Normans relied on the administrative abilities of their predecessors.

These pennies of Edward the Confessor were struck at the Winchester mint by moneyers mentioned by name in Domesday.

11
THE WORKFORCE ON THE EVE OF THE CONQUEST

Throughout the whole kingdom the poor had very few supporters, if any: not surprising since nearly all the ruling class and landowners were more concerned with worldly than spiritual affairs. Indeed everyone was more bothered with his own particular well being rather than the common good.
Asser's Life of King Alfred, *AD 893.*

Domesday Book shows that all but a small proportion of the English people worked the land. Indeed, four-fifths of the recorded heads of household in 1086 are dependent labourers of some sort, ranging from the villein class – over a third of the entire population – through bordars, cottars, burs and slaves or serfs (*servi*), the last class amounting to nearly a tenth of the recorded population. Even the so-called freemen and sokemen, who are largely found in the eastern counties and who number around 15 per cent of the people in Domesday Book, were often very small-scale landholders whose economic level in practice was generally little different from that of the unfree or semi-free peasants. The mass of the English people, then, were unfree and heavily burdened with obligations in labour and produce to the landlord for whom they worked.

Before the Norman period, however, very little evidence exists for ordinary people's lives. Still less can we expect anything which shows a sympathetic insight into their lives. Occasionally a sermon might include a sudden vivid image – say of a poor beggar in rags crouched in a doorway in winter mud and rain, falling asleep to dream of wealth, warm clothes and fine food, only to wake again to his freezing and starving reality; churchmen of the time often used such exemplary tales to remind the rich of their Christian duties towards the poor, but they clearly came from personal observation. A notable exception is a remarkable conversation piece written for the pupils at the monastic school of Cerne Abbas by their master Aelfric (989–1002). Here the enquiring mind of Aelfric has given us a sharp little vignette of the lives of the rural unfree:

Master: 'What have you to say, ploughman? Tell me how you go about your work.'
Ploughman: 'Oh I work very hard indeed, sir. Every day at the crack of dawn I have to drive the oxen out to the field and yoke them to the plough. I would never dare scive at home, no matter how bad the winter weather: I'm too frightened of my landlord for that. No, once I've yoked the oxen and fastened the share and coulter to the plough, I must plough a full acre or more every day.'
Master: 'Do you have a workmate?'

Ploughman: 'Yes, my lad drives the oxen with his goad: he's hoarse today because it's so cold and he's been doing all that shouting.'
Master: 'What else have you got to do in a day?'
Ploughman: 'Oh, there's a lot more than that, you know. I've got to fill all the oxen's bins with hay, give them water, muck them out.'
Master: 'Oh, my: it sounds like hard work.'
Ploughman: 'It's hard work all right, sir, because I am not free.'

Aelfric's is an imaginary dialogue, but it has the ring of authentic observation. For the earlier English period real detail on the lives of such people is lacking: only the occasional glimpse is given in laws and land grants. In 902, for example, when the Bishop of Winchester leased an estate at Ebbesbourne in Wiltshire to one Beornwulf, at a rent of 45 shillings a year, a postscript states that the clergy asked Beornwulf to allow certain people born on the estate – Lufu and her three children, and Luha and his six children – to remain there; the document also states that with the land Beornwulf received three penal slaves of peasant birth (geburs) and three slave-born (theows), with their offspring, who would also be slaves unless their lord chose to give them freedom. This gives a good idea of how the unfree classes were graded in the eyes of the law, and how they could expect to be moved about like chattels. Indeed, precisely this point is made in a document of 880 which records the transfer of estates at Brightwell and Watlington in Oxfordshire to the see of Worcester. Included in the grant are stock and ploughing equipment and six men who had formerly belonged to the royal vill at Benson: 'These are the names of the men who are written down [to go] from Benson to Readanora [Pyrton] on the estate of the bishopric of Worcester, with their children . . . Almund, Tidulf, Tidheh, Lull, Lull and Gadwulf.' This seems to be the earliest record which names people from the lowest level of English society; at Domesday there were still eight slaves on the Pyrton estate, along with forty-two villeins and four 'freemen'.

Shepherds tending sheep, an illustration from an eleventh-century calendar. As in Roman Britain, wool was a major contributor to England's wealth at the time of Domesday.

Domesday inevitably raises the question as to how detailed such records were before 1066. How closely were people like Lufu and Luha accounted? The answer seems to be that from the later tenth century, the period of the great monastic reform in England, extremely accurate records were kept by some of the great abbeys on at least some of their estates, which included records and genealogies of the villeins and serfs, as well as lists of stock. This discovery has great significance for an understanding of Domesday Book itself. Whether this Benedictine system of accounting has a longer history in England is unclear. It is, however, certain that there were close parallels in continental estate management, and it is a fair assumption that the English reformers, who massively endowed great churches like Glastonbury, Ely and Ramsey in the mid- and late tenth century, drew their inspiration from continental practice. From the time of the Carolingian empire in north-eastern France, the Rhineland and northern Italy, a number of descriptions survive which give astonishingly detailed inventories of the estates of great abbeys such as St Germain des Prés, St Rémy of Rheims, and Prüm. These texts list the church holdings very much in the way that Domesday Book lists the estates of, say, the Old Minster, Winchester, but with careful notes on each individual servile family. If anything, Domesday Book looks like an abbreviated collection of such descriptions organised on a hitherto unprecedented scale. Here is an example from the *Polyptych of Irminon*, in the Bibliothèque Nationale, Paris, of how the Carolingian surveyors recorded a peasant and his family at Villaris near Paris, now in the park of St Cloud, in 811–26:

Bodo, a villein [*colonus*], and his wife Ermentrude, a villein, tenants of St Germain, have three children. He holds one small farm freely, containing eight strips [*bunuaria*] and two [*antsinga*] of arable land, two arpents of vines and seven arpents of meadow. He pays two silver shillings [*solidos*] to the army [a tax owed by his landlord to the king] and two hogs-heads of wine for the right to pasture his pigs in the woods. Every third year he pays a hundred planks and three stakes for fences. At the winter sowing he ploughs three [fields?] and at the spring sowing he ploughs two. Every week he owes his landlord two days of labour service [i.e. ploughing and cultivating his lord's land] and one day of 'handwork' [again for the landlord: repairs, tree felling, carrying etc.]. He also pays three chickens and fifteen eggs and has to perform carrying services when it is required of him. He has a half share in a mill, for which he pays two silver shillings.

Such texts inevitably do not account for the full economic life of the village or the family. On the days of the week when they could cultivate their own holdings, such farmers probably engaged in a wide range of small-scale 'cottage' activities, especially if they doubled as artisans for the locality – blacksmiths, carpenters, wheelwrights, shoemakers, toolmakers. Indeed sometimes this kind of work appears in labour services to the lord along with production of odd luxuries such as honey, wax, soap, rope or oil. Women appear in such texts more often as farmers' wives than they do as farmers themselves, but all the way through the period it is common to find women running their own estates, and it is clear that they formed an equal part of this vast subordinate workforce. Servile women were frequently required to spin or provide completed garments for the landlord.

Such labour services were the way of life for the mass of people across Europe for centuries during the so-called Dark Ages and the feudal era. Several management efficiency texts exist from this period, showing how the stewards of royal estates were expected to maintain high standards of economy and 'neatness'. Most famous is the ninth-century Frankish text *De Villis*, but comparable sets of estate memoranda survive from Anglo-Saxon England which show how thoroughly these ideas had been imbibed by the English ruling class. Here is an example from a management text entered into a volume of Anglo-Saxon law:

The gebur's [villein's] duties vary; in some places they are heavy, in others moderate. On some estates it is such that he must perform such work as he is told for two weekdays each week throughout the year, and three weekdays at harvest time, and three from Candlemas to Easter; if he performs cartage he need not work while his horse is out. At Michaelmas he must pay ten pence tax, and at Martinmas twenty-three sesters of barley and two hens: at Easter one young sheep or twopence. And from the time when they first plough until Martinmas he must plough one acre [of his lord's land] each week and prepare the seed in the lord's barn himself. . . . When death befalls him, his lord is to take charge of what he leaves.

From such material it can be seen how detailed estate inventories of stock and personnel may well underlie many of the laconic abbreviations of Domesday Book: they describe the same society in the same terminology. Virtually all trace of them is now lost, but, fascinatingly enough, we can examine one Domesday estate a century before Domesday Book in extraordinary detail, with the names and genealogies of many of its workforce at the lowest level. This account, of *c.* 980, which is given in full, appears in a detached leaf of a lost book from the abbey of Ely and forms a missing link between the management texts, the continental 'descriptions' and Domesday itself.

Above Sowing and planting in the eleventh century. Most of the workforce were semi-free peasants tied by heavy work obligations to their landlords.
Right The fragment of manuscript from Ely describing the serfs of Hatfield, their jobs and marriages, beginning '*dudda waes gebur into haedfelda. . . .*'

Dudda was a gebur on the Hatfield estate and he had three daughters, Deorwyn, Deorswyth and Golde. And Wullaf on the Hatfield estate had Deorwyn as his wife, Aelfstan at Datchworth had Deorswyth, and Aelfstan's brother Ealhstan had Golde. Hwita was beekeeper at Hatfield, and his daughter Tate was the mother of Wulfsige; Wulfsige's sister Lulle was wife of Hehstan at Walden. Wifus, Dunne and Seoloce were born on the estate at Hatfield; Wifus's son was settled on the estate at Walden, and Dunne's son Ceolmund was also settled on Walden. Seoloce's son Aethelnoth too was moved to Walden. Now Cenwald's sister Tate became the wife of Maeg at Walden, and Tate's daughter was taken as wife by Eadhelm son of Herethryth. Waerlaf, father of Waerstan, was a legal bondman at Hatfield, where he was swineherd.

Brada was a gebur on the estate at Hatfield and his wife Hwite was a gebur's daughter from Hatfield. Hwite was mother of Waerstan, Waerthryth and Wynburg. Waerstan went to the Watton estate, and married Winne's sister; Winne married Waerthryth. And Dunne was sent to the Watton estate (she was born at Hatfield). And Deorwyn, Dunne's daughter, was wife of Cynewald at Munden; her brother Deornath lives with Cynewald too. Dudde, Wifus's daughter, is settled at [Great] Wymondley. Cynelm, father of Cenwald, is a gebur at Hatfield. And Cenwald's son, Manna, is at Watton under Eadwold [presumably the estate steward].

Buhe was Dryhtlaf's maternal aunt; she was moved from Hatfield to Essenden; she had three sisters, Aethelwen, Eadugu and Aethelgyth; Buhe's children were called Tilewine and Duda, and Tilewine's son was Ealhstan; Eadugu's son was Wulfsige; Aethelgyth's sons were Ceolhelm, Coelstan and Manwine. This family [cyn] came from 'Felda' [=Felden?]. Deorulf, son of Cyneburh, and his two sisters, and their uncle Cynric at Clavering – these people are kinsmen of Tate the gebur at Hatfield.

This remarkable, apparently unique and, until now, untranslated document, the barest bones of a source, is important because it gives close detail on the condition, movement and kinship of groups of servile people a hundred years before Domesday on an estate which happens to be well recorded not only in Domesday but also in other pre-Conquest documents. These people, geburs, ancestors of the villeins in Domesday, are the agricultural workforce who till the land of the manor and its appendages and pay rent in money, produce and work. They are effectively serfs, 'tied to the land' (*inbyrde*, or in Latin *innati*, not free to up and go 'where they please'). In them and their children the lord had a proprietorial interest – hence this document's notes on these people's descent and kin. It can be seen from this that, much as one would expect, geburs often married into families with which they worked: brothers marrying sisters in common (the lord's permission was required to marry). It is clear that it was normal for such labourers to be moved from one estate to another – a confirmation of considerable mobility within even the most tied part of the workforce.

The administrative history of the Hatfield estate can be reconstructed from a number of pre-Conquest sources. Originally a royal possession, it was bequeathed to King Edgar from a royal kinswoman called Aelfgifu at some time between 966 and 975. Edgar gave the estate to Ely Abbey: for taxation purposes it was assessed at 40 hides. But at the king's death it was successfully claimed in law by another royal kinsman, Earl Aethelwine of East Anglia, and the monks of Ely had to pay him its purchase price to get it back. It is from the next period (*c.* 975–1000) that the genealogical document about the geburs of Hatfield derives, and other contemporary material confirms the penny-pinching mentality of the landlords; Abbot Britnoth of Ely comes over in particular as a hard businessman. In one case a small local farmer, Alfwold of Mardleybury in Hertfordshire, had to appeal to the local court at Hertford to defend himself from the abbot, who was claiming that Alfwold had bought land illegally since he and his wife, and his sons Aelfwine and Aethelmaer, were actually not free people but *innati*, that is, geburs, born on the Hatfield estate – in other words the same class as all the people in the Hatfield document. The local jury confirmed that the family were free people, but by some legal nicety the abbot was able to impose on Alfwold an extra charge in money.

Notes in other manuscripts give some information on stock management under the estate reeve: 'Aelfnoth was entrusted with his office at Hatfield . . . there were 40 oxen there, 250 sheep, 47 goats, 15 calves, 190 pigs, 43 flitches of bacon . . .' and so on. Livestock could also be moved about to make up local shortfalls: 'Thirty full-grown swine were given from Hatfield and Thorney, each worth six pence, from the herd which Aelfwold had charge of in Hatfield, and 13 sows and 83 young swine, and from the other herd Aelfnoth took 14 sows and 60 hogs.' Such fragments amount to little more than random jottings, but they suggest that estate accounting grew more rigorous in the last century of the Old English state. Even wills begin to show the influence of such ideas. One interesting example can even throw a little extra light on the Hatfield serfs. It dates from 980–90, and belongs to an Anglo-Saxon noblewoman and landowner called Aethelgifu who held estates around Hertfordshire and a house in London. Although a will, it has been drawn up with reference to some sort of estate document, as it deals with often minute transfers of stock between holdings, and mentions not only tenants by name, but even serfs – some with local nicknames, like 'Dufa's son at Munden' (quite possibly a kinsman of the people encountered earlier), and Wulstan *aet cocerenho*', which is now Cockernhoe Farm in Offley, Hertfordshire.

From such material it is possible to speculate that for quite some time before the Norman Conquest the manorial system in many parts of England was already subject to some sort of detailed record taking. This was not a centralised impetus; although the Old English kings had the resources to carry through wide-ranging reorganisation in economic life – for instance in the execution of the coinage or the planning of the burghal system – we have no evidence to set beside the Carolingian texts to the effect that the later Old English kings instituted large-scale estate surveys of their demesne. Rather, the chief hints come from the great abbeys like Ely and Bury, which had taken note of continental economic practice after the Benedictine revival which gave them such vast accretions of land in the late tenth century. This kind of material, then, is what lies behind the Domesday entry for the same Hatfield estate:

The abbot of Ely holds Hatfield. It is assessed at 40 hides. There is land for 30 plough teams. In demesne 20 hides, and there are two plough teams, and there could be three more.

There a priest with 18 villeins and 18 bordars have 20 plough teams and there could be 5 more. There 12 cottars and six serfs [slaves] and 4 mills yielding 47s and 4d. Meadow for 10 plough teams. Pasture for the livestock. Wood for 2000 swine, and 10s from dues of wood and pasture. Altogether it is and was worth £25; T.R.E. [i.e. in 1066] £30. The manor belonged and belongs to the demesne of the church of Ely.

Interestingly enough, one of the so-called Domesday 'satellites', the Ely Inquiry, also covers Hatfield. As the original returns, from which the abbreviated account in Domesday was written, no longer survive, it is fascinating to compare part of the more detailed Ely account which dates from around the same time:

20 plough teams with the men, and there could be five more. 18 villeins each holding 1 virgate, and a priest who has half a hide, and four men with 4 hides. And Adam, son of Robert, son of William, has two hides under the abbot [i.e. rented from him]. 12 bordars [each with] half a hide, and six other bordars with half a hide, 12 cottars, 6 serfs: 4 mills yielding 46s 4d. Meadow for 10 plough teams: pasture for the livestock of the vill. Wood for 2000 swine. From wood and pasture 10s; and 26 cattle, 360 sheep, 60 swine.

Whether in a literal sense or not, the dependent peasantry who were inventoried by William's Domesday commissioners in the wet summer of 1086 were the descendants of the geburs recorded on the estate in around 980. In practice, as we saw, these people were frequently uprooted and moved to others of the landlord's many holdings. But the society is the same, and to all intents and purposes the people are the same, in all their legal gradations. At Hatfield in 1086 they amounted to a priest, a lessee, and 58 unfree heads of households – perhaps representing a total of about 250 men and women. Such were the Domesday roots. This close study of one English estate on the eve of the Conquest, supplemented with the account in Domesday itself, gives a vivid picture of what life was like for the ordinary Englishman and Englishwoman at this time. In some senses it is obvious that something like a 'feudal' system of tenure already existed in England before the Normans. Now let us turn to the Norman Conquest itself.

A peasant digging, from the *Junius Psalter* of *c.* 1000. By that time the main classes of English society were fixed in a rigid hierarchy, though it was not impossible for a hard-working peasant to rise in status. The main pre-Conquest class terms, however, are still with us as pejoratives – villain, boor and churl.

PART THREE

DOMESDAY
AND AFTER

Above Battle Abbey in East Sussex, the site of the Conqueror's triumph in 1066.
The buildings lie along the low ridge defended by King Harold's army.
Previous page The Battle of Hastings as depicted on the Bayeux Tapestry. Mounted troops
of the Norman feudal host attack the thegns and mercenaries of Harold's infantry.

12
THE NORMAN CONQUEST

This was a fatal day for England, a melancholy havoc of our dear country brought about by its falling under the domination of new lords. For it had been a long time ago that England had adopted the customs of the Angles. In the first years after their arrival they were barbarians in their look and manners, warlike in their usages, heathens in their rites; but after embracing Christianity, in the process of time and by degrees, owing to the peace which they enjoyed, they came to regard warfare as only of secondary importance. . . . The Normans on the other hand are a race inured to war and can hardly live without it, fierce in attacking their enemies, and when force fails, always ready to use guile or to corrupt by bribery.
William of Malmesbury, AD 1125.

I have persecuted the natives of England beyond all reason. Whether gentle or simple I have cruelly oppressed them; many I unjustly disinherited; innumerable multitudes perished through me by famine or the sword. . . . I fell on the English of the northern shires like a ravening lion. I commanded their houses and corn, with all their implements and chattels, to be burnt without distinction, and great herds of cattle and beasts of burden to be butchered wherever they are found. In this way I took revenge on multitudes of both sexes by subjecting them to the calamity of a cruel famine, and so became the barbarous murderer of many thousands, both young and old, of that fine race of people. Having gained the throne of that kingdom by so many crimes I dare not leave it to anyone but God. . . .
William's death-bed confession according to Ordericus Vitalis, c. AD 1130.

Ordericus' words remind us that the Norman Conquest was a brutal and violent takeover which necessarily involved the deaths of thousands of people from war, thousands more from famine and disease, the devastation of the land and the destruction of villages and towns. All this stemmed from what happened on 14 October 1066 near Hastings, when King Harold and many of the English aristocracy were killed in battle. As a result of that single day's fighting England received a new royal dynasty, a new nobility, a new church, a new art and architecture, and a new language of government. The leaders and the rank and file of the army which had won at Hastings were the first to benefit. After casualties they may have numbered about five thousand men, and many of them must have expected to qualify for a cut of the cake, namely land in England. Domesday Book reveals a massive shift in ownership in England twenty years on: among the 180 or so tenants-in-chief who possessed large estates – those bringing in over £100 a year in income – only two are English; of the 1400 or so lesser tenants-in-chief about 100 or so are English; of the further 6000 sub-tenants there is a much more sizeable English element, many of them leasing land which they had owned freely before 1066.

Other aspects of the Conquest are just as revealing. By 1080 only one of the sixteen English bishoprics was held by a native, and six of the sees had been moved from their historic centres to bigger towns which were centres of Norman administration: some of the former seats of bishoprics, like Dorchester-on-Thames, Elmham, Selsey and Sherborne, never recovered. In 1125, for example, William of Malmesbury remarked that Sherborne was 'an ugly dead-end place where nothing goes on – it is amazing, and almost shameful, that a bishop's see has been here for so many centuries'. The Norman taste is perhaps best exemplified by Goscelin of St Bertin who spent many years in rural Wiltshire: 'I hate small buildings; frankly I would not allow buildings to stay standing – even if everyone liked them – unless they were glorious, magnificently big, very tall and spacious and simply beautiful. He destroys well who builds something better.' By about 1200 almost every Anglo-Saxon cathedral and abbey had been demolished and replaced by Norman-style architecture, a visible sign of the new regime. As a result no great Anglo-Saxon church has survived to modern times, and the popular misconception has taken root that the Old English did not build large churches. Only through archaeology have we been able to form an impression of what the great churches of the Old English state, such as St Augustine's, Canterbury, actually looked like. The Normans may not have wished the great buildings to remain standing which would remind the English of their glorious past, especially churches like Glastonbury and the Old Minster at Winchester, which had been so closely connected with the West Saxon royal family. The Conquest of England made the Norman élite so rich that they were able to do almost anything they wanted; they erected truly vast buildings, whether castles like Colchester or the White Tower at the Tower of London, halls like that at Westminster, or churches such as Winchester or Lincoln.

Indeed, the Normans often claimed that the Anglo-Saxons had lived in wooden palaces and had wooden churches, and that they had had a kind of natural economy in which royal renders had been paid in kind. Hence Domesday itself would be seen as typical of the Norman achievement in government, whereas it was really a product of the Old English system. English culture and manners were dismissed as insular and out-of-date, which was particularly easy to do since the vernacular played such an important role in Old English society. The destruction of so much of the vernacular literature and records of Anglo-Saxon England, and the relegation of the English language to the underworld of the lower classes, completed the subjugation of the English.

How was it that the Normans were able to accomplish so much so quickly? That they were able to consolidate their military and political power so effectively in only twenty years? The most important reason must be that the English had developed the most efficient system of government in western Europe. 'Countries which are well governed,' wrote R.H.C.

Davis, 'should be able to resist invading armies more easily than countries which are not, but if by chance they fail they are easier for a conqueror to control. They do not lend themselves to guerilla resistance, because efficient governments remove the opportunities for such activities.'

Having looked at the origins and development of the English royal administration before the Conquest, we can see now that William took over a country in which trained officials were in charge of central and local government: in the early tenth century the shire and hundred system was organised so that every man should have a lord, and be reachable by justice and by the tax man. With every village belonging to a hundred, whose court met every four weeks, and every hundred to a shire whose court met twice a year, there was no difficulty in getting the king's orders to the regions. When this is coupled with the taxation arrangements, we can see what power had fallen into William's hands. For generations the English kings had had at their disposal the land tax known as a geld (often Danegeld), a tax levied across the whole country at a fixed rate on each hide. Consider the implications of the system for the Normans.

Once accepted as king (and not only was there no other candidate, but William certainly had a claim), William could ask his civil service how he should raise a tax to pay for his army. He would discover from central documents resembling the *Burghal Hidage* or the *County Hidage* exactly how many hides were in each shire. A demand for tax could be sent to the shire courts by messengers, backed up by armed force if necessary, carrying the king's writ in a standardised letter with the royal seal. In the shire court the local officials knew how to divide the geld among the component hundreds; messages were sent out to the hundred courts where the demand was subdivided among the units which made up the hundred; within each hundred local records showed what proportion each landowner had to pay; if records did not exist, or had been destroyed, local juries on each hundred could testify in nearly every case what the geld burden had been; if the demand was disputed, the local jury would be called upon to judge. The full impact of the reforms of Edward and Athelstan can now be appreciated: in this period nothing like their tax system existed anywhere west of the Byzantine Empire, and it needs little imagination to picture the Conqueror's satisfaction on discovering that by declaring a geld of, say, two shillings on each hide, and sending out the king's writ, he could bring in a geld on the scale of, say, 1017, when Canute collected 72,000 lb of silver coin. This was precisely what he did: he levied his first crippling gelds on a still shell-shocked country in 1067 and 1068.

The governmental system of late Saxon England, then, became an instrument of expropriation once in foreign hands, and could be used to effect the massive transfer of English lands into Norman hands. Inroads were made by simply taking over the lands of those who had fought against William at Hastings, and of those who had been killed. Many others soon went into exile abroad, in Scotland or Scandinavia, and added to the supply of land with which the Norman soldiers of fortune could be rewarded. At this stage William was careful to stress his rights as the lawful successor of Edward the Confessor, and he did this by emphasising the continuity of the Old English administration, just as Canute had done in 1016. William continued to use Anglo-Saxon scribes in his chancery, English sheriffs in his shires and boroughs, some English earls, and an English archbishop of Canterbury. Until Normans had been trained to replace them this was an obvious course, and no doubt there were many patriotic English who were prepared to work for the new regime to help things get back to normal. In order to secure their collaboration, William must have made them believe that what he wanted was a genuine Anglo-Norman state in which equal protection would be given to Normans and English alike. This is what happened when Canute had conquered England fifty years before. But in reality this was never a possibility with William. His army had been drawn from many places outside Normandy, and had been joined by many as a profit-making enterprise. Those who took part must have expected to be rewarded with land, and this was impossible without dispossessing large numbers of English men and women.

Exactly how the transfer of land was achieved has never been properly established. It is known that William had already made some grants of land to his followers before February 1067: perhaps English collaborators, such as the faction who had been opposed to the family of King Harold Godwineson, encouraged him in the expropriation of the lands of some families to which they were hostile. Initially, however, the situation must have been chaotic, and no doubt such chaos lies behind the story told by the Anglo-Norman historian Ordericus Vitalis, that where some Normans found themselves endowed with lands that were rich beyond their wildest dreams, others complained that they had been given 'barren farms, and domains depopulated by war'. In reality, the process by which Normans came to possess English lands must often have involved simple naked force. At this early stage of Norman rule it is unlikely that any of the occupying forces did anything without the presence of troops. Since the lands of the English were not expropriated all at once, but gradually over twenty years, there were doubtless many English who hoped to hang on to their own land by informing on their neighbours, and so aided the takeover. But as any opposition constituted rebellion, presumably the Normans were able to effect their plans by force where necessary. There were rebellions, of course – in a number of shires as early as 1067 – but so many of the military class of the English had died in the campaigns of 1066 that a really powerful regional resistance could hardly have been organised even if the leadership had existed to guide it. The rebellions of 1067 and 1069 were suppressed and became another excuse for expropriation. It is unlikely that the normally taciturn *Anglo-Saxon Chronicle* is exaggerating when it speaks of the terrible early phase of the Conquest, when the 'poor people were sore oppressed and things went from bad to worse' (1066) and when vast sums in taxes were extorted from his people 'most unjustly and for little need, so utterly was he completely sunk in greed and given up to avarice' (1086).

The castles were the most important means of enforcing the subjugation. At the main Anglo-Saxon town sites, during the decade after the Conquest, about forty were constructed, all of which involved massive forced labour projects. Much smaller than the English burhs, they were often sited in a corner of the burhs, after the demolition of scores, even hundreds, of houses, and they made it possible for a few hundred heavily armed troops to dominate the subject population. Recent excavations show that the interiors of these motte-and-bailey castles were actually crammed with buildings – stables, smithies, barracks and fighting platforms – to enable the army of occupation to live, eat and sleep under the same roof. Around the castles space was cleared to prevent any opposing forces getting near the walls; in the countryside the landscape round castles was ravaged so that there was no wood or brush to provide cover for enemies. From such grimly functional bases the conquerors emerged to carry out punitive raids and extortions, burning villages and killing inhabitants in areas thought to harbour guerillas or in places which had not paid up on demand.

In such a situation it was inevitable that there should be many disputes over ownership of land, not least between Normans who had rival claims. Domesday Book records numerous disputes of this kind, in addition to the many cases about which the local jury testifies that someone had not come by their land legally – even in Norman terms. In some cases other records survive which show how Norman landowners attempted to misappropriate land and cloak their deeds in legality. Clearly such a situation could not last. The king had to draw a line under this traumatic series of events and establish a new status quo.

Many other considerations pointed the same way. Since 1066 the king had been constantly involved in military operations: not only against rebels, but in campaigns against the Scots and the Welsh, against the renewed threat of Danish invasion, and against his enemies in Europe, especially the French. Against all these he had not only employed his own vassals, but English levies. In 1085 another series of crises began to loom. 'It was reported – and men said it was true,' says the *Anglo-Saxon Chronicle*,

that Cnut, king of Denmark, son of king Swein [who had attacked England in 1070 and 1075] determined to conquer this country. . . . When King William learned this he was in Normandy (because he owned both England and Normandy). He returned to England with a vast host of horse and foot from France and from Brittany which was greater than any that had ever come into this country. It was so vast that men wondered how this land could feed such a host. The king, however, had the host spread over the whole country, quartering them on each of his vassals according to the produce of his estate. People suffered great hardship during this year because the king also gave orders for the coastal districts to be laid waste, so that if his enemies landed they would find nothing. . . .

The *Chronicle*'s account is crucial in understanding the immediate genesis of Domesday. When Cnut of Denmark failed to attack, William released part of his army, but kept part quartered in England over the winter. It was at this moment, says the chronicler, when the king had gone to Gloucester to spend Christmas, that he had his famous 'deep speech' with his wise men 'about this land, how it was peopled, and with what sort of men'. The Domesday inquiry, then, was born directly out of the difficulties engendered by the military events of 1085. This short-term context makes the survey easier to comprehend.

Early in 1086 the Conqueror's commissioners went round the whole of England south of the Tees, dividing it up into seven main circuits, seven groups of shires. In each shire the king's men went to the shire court where local juries were required to testify to the possessions of the king, the Church and all the magnates; to enumerate the numbers of hides, carucates (in Danish districts) or sulungs (in Kent), to state the amount of ploughland, wood and meadow, number of mills, and so on; to give the taxable

Above The mark of the Conquest: the twelfth-century motte-and-bailey castle at Pleshey in Essex. The bridge is fifteenth-century.
Right Castle Rising, Norfolk: the impressive twelfth-century keep stands inside vast Norman earthworks. Crude but effective, such places give an idea of the mentality of the Conqueror.

heads of household, freemen, sokemen, villeins, bordars and serfs; to state the numbers of cattle, pigs and other livestock. This great mass of information they were to estimate in value for each estate at three different dates – when King Edward was still alive (January 1066); when the present owner took over; and as it actually was in 1086. By what means juries were able to give accurate figures for King Edward's day has never been clearly established: obviously many estates were able to provide records of surveys from that time, especially on the great abbeys like Bury or Ely, but for many estates this can hardly have been the case and the judgement must have been arrived at by estimation. How much coercion was used in arriving at the Domesday figures is not known, but it is believed that they are generally accurate, and that a remarkably close relation exists between the produce of the estates and the Domesday valuation.

In this way William used the machinery of Old English government, which had been refined over the previous century and a half, to establish the exact location, extent and value of the lands he had gained, and the lands he

had given to his followers. From his point of view the three-tier dating enabled all claims to be checked, as all informants had to give the ownership of the estate on all three dates required. Domesday records several cases where false claims to land had been shown up. At Wilksby in the South Riding of Lindsey in Lincolnshire the men of the Riding testified, for example, that though the Bishop of Durham claimed the land against one Gilbert de Gant, 'they say they have never seen the bishop's predecessor given possession of the land either by writ or by envoy, and they give their testimony in favour of Gilbert'.

The Domesday survey drew a line under the Conquest by examining every detail of the Normans' ruthless plundering of England, and giving 'official' judgement on their legality: possession was approved only where it had been done by William's authority, directly or indirectly. This was how it got its name in the common speech (see p. 24), and it was indeed a kind of Judgement Day. No doubt many ordinary English men and women who experienced the inquisition of William's commissioners were put in mind of the sculptures or paintings of Christ which they saw in their local church, with Christ as the supreme judge with the Book of Judgement in his hands. If ever there could be an earthly equivalent, the 'book of King William's great description of England' was it, a true Domesday Book. Its conclusiveness lay in the fact that for every approved land claim of a Norman his name was inscribed in the judgement book and could henceforth be upheld forever by the hundred and shire courts. Possessed of over-whelming military force, the Norman settlement was now permanent.

13
FREEBORN ENGLISH:
AN HISTORICAL RIDDLE

The national character of the English is essentially different. . . . The English have no common interests, only *individual* interests . . . only out of individual interests do they act together as a whole. In other words only England has a *social* history. Only in England have individuals as such, without consciously advocating general principles, promoted the advance of the nation.
Engels, England in the 18th Century, *1844*.

The Norman settlement may have been permanent, but as we have seen the society portrayed in Domesday Book had its roots deep in the British past. And after 1086 it would change only slowly. In broad terms there are three distinctive cultural zones implied by the Domesday account: the old Celtic uplands of the west with their archaic pastoral economy and the survival of older social classes, including slavery; then there is the great open-field belt of central England where the population was predominantly dependent peasantry, villeins and bordars; and finally the east, where the richest and most populous counties were – Suffolk, Norfolk and Lincoln – and where Domesday records a society with a much larger class of 'free' peasantry than elsewhere. These three zones maintained their distinctive character till the end of the feudal era, and even into modern times, and it is to them that we turn as we look at what happened to the Domesday world after 1086.

We can now see how Domesday could be used to give us an extra-ordinary insight not only into English society in the later eleventh century, but into aspects of the social structure going deep into the pre-Domesday past. All along in our search we have found that one of the central historical problems centres on the transformation of the ancient world, and its slave-based economic system, into the so-called feudal order. In Anglo-Saxon England it was suspected that an idiosyncratic 'English' pattern developed in lowland Britain, but in general the decline of the ancient system took centuries. Indeed it may not be too much of an exaggeration to say that Domesday Book marks the end of the ancient world economy. If that is accepted, then we come to one of the most fascinating problems concerning the Domesday evidence.

One of the most distinctive features of Domesday geography is the great body of smallholders who individually enjoyed personal independence. In Domesday Book they are largely called 'freemen' or 'sokemen', and the map showing their distribution (p. 27) gives a clear picture of their geographical spread: they are overwhelmingly concentrated in certain eastern areas, Norfolk, Lincolnshire and the Danelaw; Yorkshire too may have had a sizeable proportion of this class, but it is speculated that the Conqueror's devastation of 1069 hit them very badly. But in the lands of the Five Boroughs, especially Lincolnshire, Nottinghamshire and Leicestershire, long before the Norman Conquest a free population was established whose essential character continued right through into the Middle Ages: indeed the remains of that tenurial pattern are still to be found in parts of Lincolnshire.

First, what is meant by 'free' people at this time? In reality their condition seems to differ little from that of villeins. In the Domesday entries they are put in with the peasantry rather than with those native landowners, however small, who still held estates from the king. It was a principle of English law that every man should have a lord; the question was whether you were free to give or sell your land, or 'go with it to another lord'. The legal implications of this are not certain, but protection and support are implied, and perhaps capital loaned for livestock and equipment, in return for military or even labour service. But the relation was dissoluble; you could seek another lord 'with your land'. Other holdings could not be transferred or sold, and had definite services attached including military service. Domesday contains several references to compulsory military service, often with the rough equation of one armed man from every 5 hides of land: if you bought a lease on such an estate with your charter, the obligation for military service came with it. This smacks of a kind of feudal system, but it was by no means uniform. In fact, there may have been large areas of the country where lordship had no real hold. This is particularly the case in the eastern Danelaw, the main subject of this chapter.

In 1086 over 14,000 freemen and over 23,000 sokemen were still holding land, 80 per cent of them in the eastern Danelaw. The distinction between the two is not always evident. Lincolnshire had 11,000 sokemen but no freemen; sometimes one reads of a sokeman who was 'really a freeman'. Sometimes the freeman is called a thegn; whether one is freer or better off than the other cannot be said; most were very small-scale cultivators indeed: though some held whole manors, at Islington in Norfolk eighteen sokemen held only 17½ acres between them.

After the Conquest the numbers of this semi-free class certainly decreased. Many sank to villein status. At Bergholt in Suffolk the sokemen declined from 210 to 119; on the great royal manor of Northallerton in Yorkshire there had been 116 sokemen in 1066, but now, after the Conqueror's devastation of the north, the place was wasted and no freeholders remained. In Essex, perhaps more than in any other county, the survey records a great reduction in the free or semi-free classes; numerous individual cases confirm the impression that only 7 per cent of people retained such status. In Lincolnshire and other parts of the Danelaw, however, the story is quite different: in Domesday a really huge proportion of the population is described as free. These non-manorial features – they are sometimes seen as non-medieval features – of the eastern English economy have never been satisfactorily accounted for. Many historians have thought that the origins of this society lay in the Danish settlement of the ninth century, but certain features seem to crop up elsewhere in isolated cases: could the 'free peasantry' of the Danelaw perhaps be a regional rather than an ethnic phenomenon? Or, if it is ethnic, is it still possible that it could derive from earlier Anglo-Saxon society – in other words that the Danish settlement of the eastern part of the country preserved between the 870s and the 1080s some of the archaic features of earlier English society, whereas under English rule in the south royal power had made tremendous inroads on individual freedom and the countryside had become much more manoria-lised? To find out, let us look at the eastern Danelaw in the two centuries after Domesday.

Lincolnshire has always been a conservative society. The essential pre-Conquest structure of shire, parts, ridings and wapentakes survived intact until the local government reforms of 1974. Here, as in the other shires of the Five Boroughs, the main county town is still the one on which the Danish army of the ninth and tenth centuries was based, and from where it ran local organisation. In 1086, on one level, its social structures resembled the 'English' areas, being organised into manors with the lord's farm, free and unfree peasants and the vill. But what sets Lincolnshire apart is the enormous proportion of sokemen – half the entire recorded population in the county. Later sources show that these people were bound to a lord by homage and by certain payments of services, but that they were actually their own master in the sense that they could sell their land and go else-where. They had their own place in the courts of wapentake and shire; they could dispose of their land or any portion of it by gift, sale or exchange, and they paid their taxes directly to the officers of the king or the sheriff. In addition, it appears that they were usually free from the customary day work on the lord's land (often, as we have seen, two or more days a week). Exceptions to this do appear – at Scotter in Lincolnshire, for instance, in a Peterborough estate book for c. 1125, where the sokemen owed a day a week; so too with some sokemen in Fenland surveys of the thirteenth century. But the main picture is clear – eastern England had a high propor-tion of free smallholders and cultivators. Domesday figures for Lindsey suggest that over 54 per cent of the population were sokemen; but in some wapentakes the figures go up to amazing proportions – 73.4 per cent in Ludborough, 70.3 per cent at Bolingbroke; in the West Riding, Kesteven and Holland, along with Leicestershire and Nottinghamshire, the propor-tion is still over one third. In Framland wapentake in Leicestershire over 50 per cent of the Domesday population at Waltham on the Wolds were sokemen. Let us look at one of the most typical places.

Old Bolingbroke was the centre of a wapentake in 1086, administrative centre of an area 14 miles by 12 and including 23 villages named in Domesday (there were probably more). At Bolingbroke itself, where a Norman castle was erected in the eleventh century, an Anglo-Saxon landowner called Stori had held two carucates of land in 1066. By 1086 there were signs of renewed economic activity: 'Now Ivo has two teams there (in lordship) and 12 villeins and 8 bordars and 12 sokemen with three teams. There is a church there, and a new market, and three mills rendering 10 shillings, and 70 acres of meadow. Then it was worth £30, now £40. . . .' Attached to the manor of Bolingbroke were holdings in 17 vills with land totalling 36 square miles; in these vills Domesday mentions no fewer than 508 sokemen, with 128 villeins and 33 bordars, and 11 churches. The total population of the manor of Bolingbroke then must have been well over 3000 people – 80 or 90 per square mile as against a Domesday average of 6.2.

Old Bolingbroke, Lincolnshire: the remains of the later castle dominate the present village. Bolingbroke was an important market and administrative centre before 1086, and remained into the twentieth century 'capital' of the soke of Bolingbroke, an economic unit which may go back to pre-Roman times.

Domesday allows us to look closer at such people. At the time of the survey, the local courts of the Bolingbroke and Candleshoe wapentakes had to testify in a dispute between a native Lincolnshire family and a Norman newcomer, Eudo. The family owned a dozen or more estates in the Horncastle and Bolingbroke area and lands in Candleshoe including salt-pans at Wainfleet. Before 1066, Domesday reveals, the father of the family was one Godwin, whose kinsmen (brothers?) were called Tochi, Godric and Gunnewate. The local jurors 'testified that before 1066 [Godwin's sons] Siwate, Alnod, Fenchel and Aschil divided their father's land amongst them equally and share and share alike, and held it in such a manner that if there were a call to the King's army, and Siwate could go, the other brothers assisted him. . . .'

Searching through the Lincolnshire folios, it is possible to identify the brothers' main holdings – Alnod (Alfnoth) at Mavis Enderby and Raithby; Aschil at Spilsby and Eresby; Fenchel at Scremby in Candleshoe; Siwate at East Keal. The Domesday appendix on disputes shows what took place when the circuit examiners heard the brothers' case before the courts of the wapentakes at Old Bolingbroke and Candlesby: 'The wapentake bears witness that the bishop of Durham ought to have the land of three brothers with sake and soke [the right to administer justice], and Eudo son of Spirewic the land of the fourth brother with sake and soke likewise. Their names are Siwate, Alnod, Fenchel and Aschil.' So the family lost the rights to their hereditary land. The tale comes out clear in Domesday's description of Scremby in Candleshoe, where Fenchel had farmed one carucate of land: 'The same man now holds it from the bishop [of Durham] with one plough team there on the lord's land and four villeins ploughing with five oxen.'

Domesday's evidence for Bolingbroke gives us a picture of a society which before 1066 had a large and growing population, remarkably densely settled; a society whose ordinary landholders, the sokemen, enjoyed particular freedom; a society which practised an equitable form of partible inheritance; a society marked by economic growth, rising land values and new building, as instanced in the churches. This picture is consistent with Domesday statistics through much of East Anglia and Lincolnshire.

Over a wide area of eastern England sokemen amounted to over one third of the population, in many places to half, especially in the wapentakes of Ludborough, Bolingbroke and Louth Eske, from where in the two centuries after Domesday Book there is better evidence for the existence of a large free peasant population than from anywhere in the Danelaw, if not in all England – indeed perhaps much wider afield than that. For these areas, there survive literally hundreds of twelfth- and thirteenth-century grants of small parcels of land being conveyed by so-called 'peasants' using the charter and a personal seal, and thirteenth- and fourteenth-century surveys reveal large numbers of free smallholders with no relative decline in numbers since Domesday. The grants are particularly interesting evidence;

a century after Domesday the sokemen and women of that survey are clearly engaged in a flourishing land market which they themselves control. A charter from Kirkstead Abbey in Lincolnshire, now in the British Library, records:

Let it be noted by all who hear or read this charter, that I, Henry, son of Tovi of Askeby [West Ashby, Lincolnshire], concede and give, and with this charter confirm to God and St Mary Kirkstead [the donor's local abbey] at the above mentioned place in pure and perpetual alms one acre, and a quarter acre of arable. And they lie in these places, to whit, first, on the west side of the village the plot I have above Theny next to Edric's land; secondly, on the other side of the village the strip two perches wide between the two ways, next to Eudo son of Norman's land; with pasture appurtenant to so much land. This honour I and my heirs warrant to the aforesaid monks against all men in perpetuity, so that they will have and hold it freely and released from all earthly service, custom and exaction. Witnessed by William, chaplain of Ashby, Roger, son of Norman of Ashby, Walo of Ashby, Henry son of Eudo; Simon of Kirkstead.

Such grants explain many important things about their society. Here are small-scale 'peasants' making grants freely, in perpetuity, and unencumbered by earthly services or custom. They are able to warrant the land in the local court of the wapentake or shire: they have other charters to back them up. They have no seigneurial authority over them, and the grant of pasture rights shows that Henry, son of Tovi, is a member of a village community who is able to deal with his neighbours in connection with the admission of a new person into the benefits of the commons and wastes of the vill. Such documents also call into question the degree of literacy at the disposal of such 'peasants' in the late twelfth century. In short, a man or woman who could do all these things was as free as anyone could be in the conditions of the early medieval world.

Women must not be forgotten in this discussion. It is likely that Domesday figures – whether for 'freemen', sokemen, or villeins and bordars – often conceal women cultivators and smallholders by their constant use of masculine forms in the wording. The Lincolnshire and Danelaw charters are a case in point. Of the hundreds, even thousands, which may survive, Sir Frank Stenton printed twenty-nine examples in 1922 of which none involved women; but of his printed list of 300, in 10 per cent women are conveying land, leaving aside the large number where husband and wife convey jointly. It is certain, then, that women played a fundamental role in the economy of this 'free' Danelaw society, and that they were an important part of the landowning community. The history of this society is also the product of such as Emma and Mabel of Yarborough; Avina, daughter of Athelstan of Saltfleetby; Christiana of Cockerington; Emma and Maud of Skidbrooke; the sisters Sybil and Juliana of Manby; Gunnhild of Saltfleetby, who has left us her seal, 'SIGILL GVNNILD F AC'; the 'lady' Beatrice of Mumby; Hawisa, daughter of Ragenhild of Saltfleetby; and the many other women whose transactions appear in these documents.

Who were these people? The Henry whose grant was considered above bears a Norman name. But his father Tovi had an old-fashioned Viking name which, like many others in the post-Conquest charters, remained in use in Lincolnshire and the Danelaw long after it ceased to be current in Scandinavia. It must be assumed that such names were a survival from long before the Conquest. Henry's ancestors were peasant cultivators of old local stock. His ancestors must be among the sokemen at West Ashby in Domesday Book, where, in the king's soke of Horncastle, 45 sokemen were recorded along with 10 villeins and 18 bordars. In some cases the charters allow such a connection to be made. In the case of Christiana of Cockerington, who was mentioned above, the names are known of her father Ivo, who probably died in the 1170s; of her grandfather Swan, son of Magnus, whose name is certainly Scandinavian; and of her great-grandfather Magnus himself; as Christiana was of marriageable age (twenty-five?) by 1179, it is not unreasonable to think that Magnus could

Boothby Pagnell, Lincolnshire: a surviving Norman manor house of the twelfth century.

have been one of the sokemen of the Cockerington named in Domesday Book less than a century before as an estate of the Bishop of Bayeux:

In Cockerington Aschil and Ulgrin had three carucates of land and one bovate assessed to the geld. There is land for six teams. Ilbert, the bishop's man, has two teams, there is demesne and 7 villeins and 4 bordars and 27 sokemen, having three teams. There are 80 acres of meadow there, and 60 acres of underwood, and 2 parts of a mill rendering two shillings. Then it was worth 60 shillings; now the same.

These were not wealthy people. The holdings of the Lincolnshire sokemen were very small: 20 acres of arable was normal for members of this class – an amount comparable with the holdings of villeins, unfree cultivators, in other parts of England (as, for example, at Great Barton in Suffolk, where the villeins' holdings ranged between half an acre and 80 acres).

The sokemen have a curious position in English medieval society, then, with marked personal and tenurial independence, but with an economic position often inferior to villeins in the south. It is curious, too, that they successfully maintained their position throughout the century after the Conquest; the characteristics of their society were just as marked in 1186. Here and there, of course, individual families can be found increasing their holdings until they passed from peasant to 'thegnly' or 'knightly' class. In fact this is precisely what happened to Ivo, the father of Christiana of Cockerington, who is named in the great return of knights' fees made in 1166 by order of King Henry II. Christiana would end up marrying Roger de Neville, sponsored by her feudal lord, Hugh de Bayeux. There are few better examples of how a family from the Anglo-Danish 'sokeman' class at Domesday could find itself in the organised feudalism of the later Middle Ages, with marriage by feudal charter. Other families, like the Galle clan of Saltfleetby in the Louth Eske wapentake, did well by managing their hereditary lands: brothers Andrew and Odo, and Odo's sons John, Andrew, Philip and Walter, rose to knightly status during the thirteenth century.

But these examples are exceptional. In general the sokemen kept their middling, smallholding position. They were a conservative race, resisting encroachments on their ancient liberties, and many features of the agrarian economy in this region in the sixteenth century seem to connect directly with this 'individualist' pre-Conquest past, handed down from the Agmunds, Tovis, Grims and Halfdans who settled these parts in the ninth century. Such conclusions can also be drawn from other regions in the Danelaw: W. G. Hoskins' study of the Leicestershire village of Wigston Magna, *The Midland Peasant*, showed how continuity could be traced from the thirty-two sokemen of Wigston in 1086 to the freeholders of twelfth- and thirteenth-century surveys. Indeed Hoskins argued that the pedigrees of many well-known Leicestershire gentry families in Elizabethan times very likely went back to this class in Domesday.

14
ENGLISH INDIVIDUALISM?

Fascinating as the Domesday and twelfth-century evidence from Lincolnshire is, however, it does not answer some of our original questions. Are the peculiarities of Domesday tenure in the Danelaw the result of Scandinavian settlement in the ninth century? To what extent were these features of the local economy and society rooted in the ethnic and social heritage of its original conquerors in the fifth and sixth centuries? To what extent in the circumstances of the Danish conquest in the ninth century? And how much are they due to the peculiar relationship between, say, the Lincolnshire people and the environment? To the relatively unlimited pasture in the Fens, with its exceptional fertility? To the possibility of reclamation, the creation of 'new lands' on a larger scale than was possible anywhere else in Britain? Were not the possibilities for expansion, the potential for economic growth – coupled with the impermanence of manorial and tenurial traditions – ready-made for forms of social and economic independence? How far do inheritance customs play their part?

The strong evidence for the continuance of the social system of the Danelaw long after 1086 enables us to link it with the voluminous material from thirteenth-century manorial surveys, and has suggested that one reason why landholding and social structure in these parts differed from that of the typical medieval manor lies in the prevailing customs of partible inheritance which the Danish settlers may have brought with them. But similar customs were found in other parts of England on free or soke land, and where they are found many of the social characteristics of Danelaw society also appear, though in a less extreme form. The difference, then, may be merely one of degree. It may even be possible that when the Danes began to settle, in the 870s, they found a freer and less manorialised kind of society in Lincolnshire and the East Midlands than in other parts, and that the concessions made to them after their conquest by the West Saxons ensured that this more archaic kind of 'free peasant society' – in reality a relic from early English times – may have been preserved long after the south was manorialised.

Interestingly enough, it is in Lindsey – including Lincoln itself – that the clearest evidence survives of Anglo-Saxon invaders indirectly succeeding to an existing Romano-British environment. At the great Anglo-Saxon church of Barton-upon-Humber, archaeology has recently provided evi-

dence for the close association of late Roman occupation with Anglo-Saxon material. At the site of a Domesday manor at Goltho, east of Lincoln, recent excavations have shown that the Norman castle and manor house overlay Anglo-Saxon manorial halls of the ninth and tenth centuries, a Middle Saxon settlement and a Romano-British farm. Both archaeological finds and the testimony of Bede indicate that Lincoln itself could have been taken over more or less intact, along with what remained of its sub-Roman population. The pattern resembles those described in Chapter 5, but here the Roman name of the chief city survived, along with its buildings, towers and gates, one of which still stands; the earliest Anglo-Saxon church also stood squarely in a Roman building. It may also be relevant that in Lindsey, as in Wessex, the genealogy of the sixth-century kings included a name of British origin, Caedbaed. Had the English royal house actually linked itself with a prominent native dynasty? Certainly, the unusual degree of Romano-British survival around the *colonia* indicates a more or less peace-

Above and below Goltho's brick church of *c.* 1640 now stands alone.
Above left Barton-upon-Humber, Lincolnshire: an intact church of the tenth century, built on much more ancient foundations.

ful absorption of the native population, with far less disturbance than at urban sites elsewhere.

The peaceful conversion of the Roman province of Lindum into the English kingdom of Lindsey, the survival of that kingdom until the Viking era, and its subsequent Danish settlement (into a region already very heavily settled – one of the most heavily populated regions of England) could help account for the social character of the province revealed by Domesday. This picture is supported by some remarkable material from thirteenth-century surveys for south Lindsey and Holland Fen country, which reveals how this expansive Fen society 'took off' economically after the Conquest as pressure for new land in this populous and acquisitive society grew.

Even before the Conquest, population pressure had brought people off the Wolds into the fens of the Wash, seeking new land. There had been salt working on these coasts from prehistoric times, but the first major period of actual land reclamation came in Roman times, in the first century AD, with a major period of land settlement in the 120s. Remains of numerous Roman salt workings have been discovered along the northern Wash coast, chiefly at the tidal limit of the creeks; they used the Fen peat as fuel to evaporate the salt. At Wrangle, masses of second-century Roman pottery were found with industrial debris. At the end of the Roman era this area seems to have been abandoned, but major land reclamation projects seem to go back into the pre-Conquest period; some of the great seabanks, like the Leverton Highgate at Wrangle, which is Anglo-Saxon in origin, are still visible. Domesday again records numerous salterns along this coast, with forty-one at Leake alone, and the remains of some of these can still be seen at Wrangle and Wainfleet. Grants of land around 1200 at Wrangle mention salt-pans and land newly reclaimed from the sea.

A veritable gold rush developed in the two centuries after Domesday, as new people came off the Wolds, pushing outwards the Fen edge; and by the time of the tax assessment of 1334, astonishingly, this part of Lincolnshire – Holland – was the wealthiest area in the whole of England. Huge reclamations were accomplished in the twelfth and thirteenth centuries, which have left their mark today on the layout of the land. The parishes in Elloe wapentake are often up to 16 or 17 miles long, and Holbeach, at nearly 23,000 acres, is one of the biggest parishes in England; Elloe indeed is as big as, and was more heavily populated than, a small shire. Much of this work was achieved by co-operation between villages, for which there is much evidence in the manorial records of Spalding, Moulton and Weston, for example (here again with pre-Conquest antecedents: some of the sea dykes in their region are from the Old English period). Hints of this communal organisation came in vivid accounts of Fen reeves adjudicating over matters of common interest, for instance in the case of the Fen reeves of the sokemen of the three sokes of Bolingbroke, Horncastle and Scrivelsby

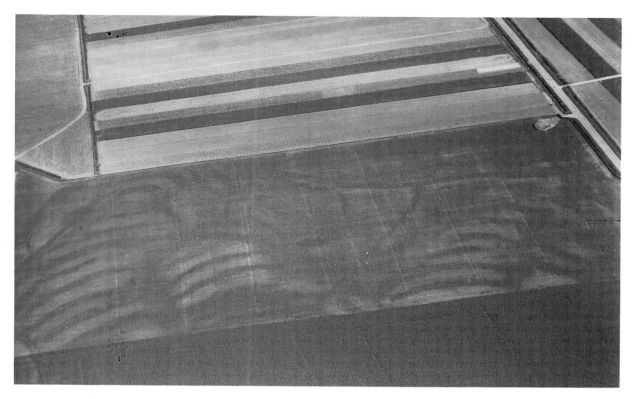

Roman industry: crop marks reveal the site of salterns near Wainfleet, Lincolnshire. In 1086, according to Domesday, there were thirty-one salterns at Wainfleet.

dividing Wildmore from West Fen in about 1150 by common agreement of the soke assemblies: 'eight of the most wisest, discreetest and gravest men of the said Sookes should walk and view the same marsh and make division thereof.' Such land hunger found its rewards in soil so rich that it gave two harvests. Even in the 1980s it was not difficult to find small-scale farmers with less than 100 acres who could make a good living; some had only 25. In 1986, 900 years on from Domesday, these small 'sokemen's holdings' still sold for over £10,000 an acre in prime areas.

The remarkable surveys from Spalding, Weston and Moulton tell much about the continuing prosperity of this part of Danelaw society. The population boomed in consequence. In 1086 Fleet had 8 landholders; in 1315 490. Moulton and Weston had 77 heads of household at Domesday; 378 in 1260. Spalding manor had 73 in 1086, but 426 in 1260, while the town population had risen from 91 to 587. Pinchbeck, manor and town, had increased from 107 to 1067 in the two centuries after the Conqueror's survey. So a tenfold increase is not uncommon. Only where there was no reclamation, as at Gosberton and Thurlby, is any decline detectable.

Various factors aided the triumph of the free Fenland peasantry. First, there was a pronounced weakness in lordship in this region. The same

Domesday figures already discovered apply in the area of the new lands; in Elloe wapentake, for example, over 50 per cent were sokemen – though, curiously, Domesday classes some as villeins here. But what is most telling is that 50 per cent of people lived on unmanorialised land, in other words with no demesne farm of the lord on which they had to pay tribute and do the heavy week work customary on estates in other parts of the country. The areas of greatest reclamation, then, were the greatest areas of freedom in the thirteenth century: for example Bolingbroke, Candleshoe and Skir-beck. Since lordship was much weaker in the Fens the peasantry were more independent and more likely to take the initiative. The difference between Domesday and the great surveys of the 1260s is simply a vast increase in the number of sokemen. Geography and society went hand in hand.

Other factors played their part in this remarkable flowering of the Domesday society of Lincolnshire, the East Midlands and the Fens. Surveys of five of these Lincolnshire villages from 1250 to the 1470s show that by the fourteenth century at the latest the western European pattern of late and prudential marriage was well established; men, for example, married in their late twenties, and in general married not for love or to have children but for practical reasons of economy and 'suitability'. Households were usually nuclear, with an average size of 4.68 including the parents. Husbands on average were eight years older than their wives before the Black Death of 1348, and five years older afterwards. The average length of

Ludborough, north of Louth, Lincolnshire. Thirty-eight sokemen and their families lived here in 1086, but the village shrank after the fourteenth century. House platforms, sunken lanes, gardens and (foreground) fish ponds are all still visible from the air amidst the surviving houses by the thirteenth-century church.

marriage before 1348 was thirteen years; the average age of death in women was thirty-four. Marriages were unlikely to produce more than three children. Since there were more males than females among children, many men remained unmarried, but since the death rate of women was very high (presumably because of the number of failed pregnancies), men lived longer.

This remarkable evidence from the later medieval period shows how marriage patterns contributed to the economic character of the age, with its land hunger and booming population. In the richest areas, it was natural that prudential marriage should be practised. Among the 'free peasantry' of the Danelaw there may be some clues to the origins of modern English ideas about love, marriage, the work ethic and the 'prudential' society. Whether this too goes back before the Norman Conquest we are unlikely ever to know, but there are some pointers. In the late Roman Empire, for instance, the usual age of marriage for pagan girls was around twelve to fifteen, for Christians nearly nineteen; pagan men married around the age of twenty-six, and Christian men at about twenty-seven.

It is hard to pin down marriage age in the Dark Age West, but so thorough were the authors of the Carolingian abbey surveys mentioned in Chapter 11 that we have a good idea of the size of families – and they are remarkably close to those of modern western Europe. At St Germain des Prés, where Bodo and his wife worked with their three children (p. 151), 4316 married or formerly married adults counted in the survey had between them 4060 children – that is, about two children per household. Among married people families were nuclear and small; in addition there were about 850 single adults, mainly men – so about 16 per cent of the adult population were unmarried, which is close to the present western European marriage pattern. Here again the proportion of men to women was high, averaging 120 to 100, so women were in relatively short supply, and therefore men would marry late and women early. Another ninth-century survey from France supports this. Adults who were or had been married amounted to 48 per cent of the population, children to 46.6 per cent. Households usually comprised just parents and children. There were few one-parent families, and few unmarried adult children lived with their parents; only a small number of widowers, widows, bachelors and spinsters are recorded living on their own. Of the adult population 11.5 per cent had never married. Again the picture is very like western Europe in modern times.

The pity is that, although such good English evidence survives from the twelfth century onwards, no detailed surveys of this kind exist with which to compare the tremendous detail of the Carolingian surveys of the ninth century. There is no reason to doubt that the basic pattern would be repeated if such sources existed, say, for tenth-century Ely or Bury; but would the trend be even more pronounced? Is English society, as most foreign observers since the fifteenth century have thought, different even from other western European countries in these important aspects of social life? And if so, where does this 'individualism' – this late-marrying, independent-minded, tenurially 'free', smallholding, land-dealing, 'free-born English' society – come from? Do these roots actually lie long before the Conquest?

As yet there is no simple answer. The main facts can be summarised as follows. The East Midlands and especially parts of south Lincolnshire are singled out in Domesday Book for their species of 'free' tenure, which may well have very deep roots in that part of the world, and which proved very long-lasting, as long as agriculture was the wealth of England. The success of that region, even before 1086, led to population movement into the fen edge. The large-scale reclamations of the boom period which ended early in the 1300s were the outcome of this great population pressure which even in 1086 made some of the villages there the biggest in England. The really enormous increase was between 1086 and 1260. What causes population increase is a question which has long exercised historians. Modern studies of these 'new lands' have shown that free institutions may help such growth to gather strength and take effect, especially free and equitable inheritance customs; as H. E. Hallam wrote, 'A society which gives opportunity for the young to flourish while they are still young is likely to possess a bounding population, full of energy, but if one asks why a society behaves in this way the answer will not appear.' The question then falls back on rather debatable historical arguments about 'national' or 'regional' character. But certainly it is not difficult to go today to the fen villages of the twelfth-century Danelaw charters or the thirteenth-century surveys and find a sentiment of rugged independence and free opportunity for all in the actions and saying of the fenlanders. Does the sentiment produce the society or the society the sentiment? Or the landscape produce both? Difficult questions. In 1086 the Wolds sustained a free peasant society with its roots in the land – a strong, conservative brand of independence; the fen-dwellers, on the other hand, lived from 1086 to 1300 in a colonial society with many of the characteristics of such: they were progressive, grasping, and frequently used violence to get their ends in local feuds. This was a society where youth was at a premium and the way to prosperity open to whoever wanted it. Like many colonial societies, it was also a co-operative society. They were accustomed to act together to drain marshes and fens and to maintain and repair the dykes by which they had gained the new land. The Danelaw peasantry, and especially the fenland communities, formed the most successful culture in medieval rural England. Together they reclaimed the fen and the marsh for posterity, and in so doing left many monuments – the finest parish churches in England, and the great banks of the sea dykes which criss-cross that fertile landscape still today. But it may be that they left another historical legacy which Domesday records – the earliest picture of what has come to be known as English 'individualism'.

15
THE HIGHLAND ZONE

The highlands are as a rule a world apart from civilizations which are an urban and lowland achievement. Their history is to have none, to remain almost always on the fringe of the great waves of civilization, even the longest and most persistent, which may spread over great distances in the horizontal plane but are powerless to move vertically when faced with an obstacle of a few hundred metres. To these hilltop worlds, out of touch with the towns, even Rome itself, in all its years of power, can have meant very little.
F. Braudel, The Mediterranean, *1966.*

We have looked at the Domesday evidence for the 'free' areas of the east of England, and we shall come back later to the main topic, the great central lowland area with its largely dependent villein population. But a third element, the highlands, must not be forgotten. In the highland areas of Britain we touch on the most ancient surviving contact with prehistoric pastoral life in these islands. Here there is not merely a change from the village society, with its arable economy, which has dominated the Domesday story in lowland England, to the hamlet and the isolated farmstead, but a change from one way of thinking to another.

The division, deeply rooted in British history, has been described as the most constant frontier in the history of Britain. The lowlands corresponded to the region of cities, villas and villages when the Romans conquered Britain, while the old British population, in Roman terms the 'uncivilised', gravitated to the highlands. The lowlands have always occupied a more important position in history – they were richer, more populous, better recorded, the focus of political action. The frontier is still recognisable today, even if its lineaments no longer have the same forceful identity that they possessed even as late as the sixteenth century, when to travel into the hill country of Devon was to enter a different world, distinct from the towns and villages and managed landscape of the lowlands: a different kind of social organisation and a different way of life. There, what is called transhumance – moving up to the higher reaches for summer pasture – remained a way of life for centuries; and the traveller on the fringes of Dartmoor will still find the intricate patterns of prehistoric and early medieval field enclosures now abandoned but marking the higher limits of earlier cultivation. Custom and language enshrined the old upland way of doing things; for example, when King Eadwig granted land in Burlescombe in Devon in 958, the scribe noted that outside the bounds of the estate 'there are many hills there which man may till'. The verb used for

'tilling', *erian*, long remained in living use in Devon dialect; in 1566 the
tenants of Clayhidon were told 'they may breake upp or eare any parte of
the lord's waste to sowe any grayne in'.

At the time of Domesday about one fifth of the population of England
lived in the highlands – 200,000 families. The land contained few villages
but many tiny hamlets, and above all thousands of isolated farmsteads:
these settlements were often not equipped with ploughs, but kept livestock
on pasture and hand-tilled small enclosed fields as they must have done
since the Bronze Age, moving on to upland common or waste land in the
summer. This was the way of life in the western third of England, and most
of Wales and Scotland, for millennia. The movement away from this way
of life is still visible in the late twentieth century even though the arrival of
the telephone, the car, the motorway and radio and television have seemed
to blur the distance – both in miles and in way of thinking – between the
upland dwellers and the rest of us.

In Domesday Book, and in its 'satellite', the so-called Exon Domesday,
which gives a more detailed account of the south-western counties, a
minutely detailed record exists of the upland landscape. Something like
9–10,000 farms are implied by the Domesday account in Devon alone, of
which perhaps 8500 were tiny outliers occupied and worked by people of
the villein class, who must have lived at the lowest level of subsistence; in
addition to these, the Devon Domesday gives about 1200 separate manors

Some of the well-preserved hut circles on Dartmoor may date from the Bronze Age.
Later changes in climate brought the cultivation line much lower.

with a lord's farm (these figures are from W. G. Hoskins' *Provincial England*, in which he assumes – surely rightly – that the 4667 bordars or smallholders did not hold anything more than plots). Of the farms we can be sure that the majority were isolated farmsteads; and in many cases a single farm still lies on the spot today, and documents exist showing that this has always been the case since Domesday. Many of the 'demesne' farms became the residences of franklins or lesser gentry in the Middle Ages, and a modern traveller through the byways of Devon will frequently come across the ruins of 'bartons' (farm houses) on Domesday sites, often abandoned only recently. In some cases, such as Collacombe or the wonderful Tudor house at Hareston, the Domesday site remains inhabited and still stands in splendid isolation. Let us look at one of these farms.

Modbert holds Eggbeer from Baldwin. Leofgar held it in King Edward's time. It paid tax for 2 and one half virgates of land. There is land there for 6 ploughs. On the lord's farm 2 ploughs; 2 slaves; 1 virgate. 4 villeins and 4 bordars with 2½ ploughs and 1½ virgates. 10 acres of meadow; 30 acres of pasture; 6 acres of woodland. 3 cattle, 4 pigs, 36 sheep, 4 goats. Formerly worth 15s, now 20s.

Eggbeer stands 10 miles west of Exeter, in deeply folded hills where the wooded valley of the River Teign cuts down from Dartmoor. The land is dotted with single farmsteads. In 1086 the place was called *Eigebere*, and was one of five separate manors within the large parish of Cheriton Bishop. It probably totalled around 700 acres, and the Domesday entry suggests that it contained the lord's farm – on which the two slaves worked – and four farms where the villeins cultivated their own rented holdings of 40–90 acres each. The main farm in 1086 – where Modbert lived – was at what is now Lower Eggbeer Farm, down a minor road from Cheriton Bishop, south of the A30. At 220 acres this is the biggest farm in the 1842 tithe map, and the old farmstead incorporated part of a fifteenth-century great hall; this was clearly the principal house of the locality, home of one of the medieval lesser gentry farmers. As W. G. Hoskins has shown, these houses were usually the descendants of the Domesday demesne farms. The villeins' farms were probably on the sites of the smaller farms that appear on later tithe maps, at Woodbrook, Orchardlake, Haylake and Jervis. At Lower Eggbeer itself Modbert farmed with his wife and family and two slaves who are likely to have been of Celtic descent; in the south-west the Celtic element in the slave population lasted right through to Domesday and after, and in some parts of Devon they probably still spoke Celtic in the eleventh century.

So Lower Eggbeer has been a single farmstead on the same spot for nearly a thousand years, and can be traced in detail throughout that time. It forms a mirror for that upland society, with its villein farms which across the south-west often averaged around 50 acres: nineteenth-century tithe maps of many villages in these parts reveal that the common Domesday division of a virgate of demesne to a virgate or so of 'villein farm' was still fairly closely reflected in the agrarian pattern of the mid-nineteenth century. But in fact Eggbeer goes back far beyond Domesday, as do many of the isolated Domesday farms of Devon. Astonishingly enough, earlier documents allow us to reconstruct the story of Eggbeer Farm – and even the names of its owners – long before 1086.

Upland Devon presents a landscape of dispersed hamlets and small farmsteads. In the centre is the Domesday manor of Germansweek. Around it lie former villein farms including (one mile south-west of Germansweek) Seccombe, which has been farmed by the same family since at least 1310 and perhaps since before Domesday.

In 976 King Edward, the future martyr, granted an estate in Devon to a member of his court, his 'faithful vassal' Aelfsige. He was presumably a figure of some importance in Devon, and it is plausible to identify him with the son of Earl Ordgar of Devon (died 971) who died between 976 and 981 and was buried at the family's foundation at Tavistock. A little later ealdorman Ordgar's other son, Ordulf, freed a slave at the high altar at Bodmin. The event was entered in the church's most valued gospel book, now in the British Library. This act, says the inscription, was done by Ordulf 'for the soul of Aelfsige'. The charter granting Aelfsige his estate describes the land as 'Hyple's old land', which offers another clue. *Eald-land* can mean 'land which has been left untilled for some time', and the name Hyple is almost certainly an English attempt to render the Celtic name Ebell, in Latin Epillus. So the land given in 976 had perhaps been allowed to go out of cultivation since the time of the British owner by whose name it was still called. Where was 'Hyple's old land'? The charter describes its boundary:

This is the boundary of Hyple's old land. First from the three posts to [gate?] spring, thence eastwards along rough [scrubby] down, as far as Stanford [=stone ford]; from Stanford east to Lamford, from Lamford east to the way [or lane]; along the way to the old ditch; south along the ditch to Rooks Fen; thence due south to the big ridge over Middle Hill; from there south to the old ditch; and along the ditch as far as Ecca's farmstead [*ieccan stoc*], then south to the middle of the old earthwork, then due south as far as Cuca's Brook; up along Cuca's Brook to where the little stream discharges; up along the little stream as far as its source; thence west to Frithestan's ditch; west on the ditch as far as Rushbrook, and up by Rushbrook as far as the three posts.

Enough of these landmarks have survived to enable us to pin down this estate on the map today: it comprises the modern parish of Cheriton Bishop and part of Drewsteignton, and as Lower Eggbeer Farm is situated on its southern boundary it must appear in the charter bounds as Ecca's Farm. By 1066 the property of 'Hyple's old land' had been split into two, the northern part around Cheriton farmed by the thegn Aelfstan, and the smaller, southerly part of the old estate, Eggbeer itself, by the thegn Leofgar. Later medieval court records enable us to fill in a few final details in trying to reconstitute the history of 'Hyple's old land'. They show that the Cheriton part of the estate was divided into a number of constituent manors and farms, all of which have names which may go back before the Conquest: Cheriton itself (Old English 'church farm') with Wilson (this name appears only in 1242, as Wolgareston; Old English 'Wulfgar's farm'); Easton Barton (in 1157 Alvrikestone; Old English 'Aelfric's farm'); and thirdly – and most interesting of all – Tryfebel, held in 1242 by Eleanor de Hause. This last name is represented today by Treable Farm, and is Celtic rather than Old English: its first element is Cornish *trev*, 'homestead'; the second part is suggested in the Celtic name Ebell, the name the English scribe in 976 tried to render as best he could by 'Hyple'. This is the Celtic landowner who gave his name to the land, and whose name is still commemorated on the modern Ordnance Survey map by Treable Farm.

How long before 976 he lived in these wooded hills in the Teign valley is unknown: perhaps a generation or two before Aelfsige took over the estate, perhaps longer. The English had conquered Devon by 700, but its Celtic character took much longer to change, though many Saxon settlers took their chance to 'go west' and open up new farms in the wooded uplands. By Alfred's day the West Saxon ruling family owned royal estates in Cornwall itself, though there seems to have been trouble between the colonial settlers and the native aristocracy in the early tenth century. The process of colonisation was emphasised by Athelstan around 930, when he deported British speakers across the Tamar, which was fixed as the border of the Cornish: they were left under their own dynasty to regulate themselves with west Welsh tribal law and customs, rather like Indian princes under the Raj. By then the English element had thoroughly penetrated Devon, and many of the British who had survived had sunk to the servile class, as is proved by the proliferation of British names in the Bodmin manumissions. But there were still British landowners in Athelstan's 'Raj' – men like Maenchi 'the count, son of Pretignor', who spent the festival of All Saints 'in the island of Athelney in the land of the Saxons' at some time in the 930s. The fact that Ebell – or Epillus – survived as a landowner in Saxon Devon so close to Exeter at that time adds another precious detail to the English story; it is also a detail which takes us deep into the British past, for Ebell and his land are a link with the old upland way of life conducted by Celtic-speaking people which survived in the south-west until the eighteenth century. The fact that the Celtic name only re-emerges in documents in the thirteenth century suggests that many similar stories may underlie later English names. We simply do not know how many south-western Welsh were absorbed into the Anglo-Saxon settlement, even adopting English names as second- and third-generation Vikings sometimes did; nor do we know how many Celts were left in quiet possession of their ancestral acres as late as the tenth century. It may be guessed that by survival or intermarriage they formed a significant element in the later Devonian's make-up. Such are the real-life complexities which underlie Domesday's laconic record.

A last piece of the story: 'Hyple's old land', 10,000 acres in 976, is still farmed a thousand years on, though divided among many farms. Ebell's homestead site is still a farm, and nearby a bronze coin of the Roman emperor Hadrian turned up not so long ago, a tantalising hint that a farm has been on that spot since the second century, and probably beyond that, in the Iron Age. Lower Eggbeer Farm, the site of Ecca's home, still preserved its fifteenth-century timber hall until 1970, when it was burned down in an accidental fire. It was not rebuilt, and today's traveller would not guess that one of the most enduring examples of our Domesday roots was once to be found there. But the landscape is still there; the tenth-century bounds can still be followed, and the tale understood on the ground.

16
THE MIDLAND PEASANT:
THE DOMESDAY LEGACY

And I have dreamt a marvellous dream. I saw a fair field full of folk, poor and rich, working and wandering as the world demands . . . in particular the ploughmen who labour and till the ground for the good of the whole community.
Langland, Piers Plowman, *1372–89.*

From the eighth or ninth century until the fifteenth the great central area of lowland Britain was farmed by a dependent peasantry on the open-field system. In this long and formative period of English social history Domesday Book therefore constitutes something like a mid-point. After Domesday written records become much more numerous, and from the thirteenth century the great wealth of manorial records – rolls, rent books, leases, charters, wills, extents, surveys, censuses and customaries – mean that for many Domesday villages life can be reconstructed in remarkable detail. From this material it can be seen that the population of the country increased greatly up to 1250 or 1300, after which it experienced a decline which was accentuated by devastating famine and disease in the early fourteenth century – especially in the Great Famine of 1316–17 – and finally, after 1349, by the shattering blow of the Black Death, in which most village records suggest a death toll of one third to one half. Further plagues in 1361, 1369, 1371 and 1375 ensured an end to the spectacular population growth between Domesday and 1300. There is no certainty over what level the country's population had reached by 1349, but many experts believe that it may have been over five million; some have even thought it was six or seven million. Whatever the truth of that, two broad conclusions can be drawn from this trend in English society. Firstly, a gradual increase of population took place from the later Anglo-Saxon period to about 1300; it attained a level not reached again until the seventeenth century. Secondly, the population boom of the twelfth and thirteenth centuries brought numbers to a level which could not be sustained by the prevailing manorial system; by then as much land was under cultivation as in the early twentieth century. When in the 1600s the population recovered to its 1300 level, the prospect was either another demographic crisis or a new economic system.

One of those open-field villages of central England was Codicote in Hertfordshire. The village was already the centre of a manor in 1002 when King Ethelred the Unready, desperate to raise hard cash for his Danegelds, sold it for 152 mancuses of gold to a thegn called Aelfhelm. The place was called

Cutheringcoton, 'Cuthhere's cottages'. In Domesday Book the population was 16 villeins, 1 Frenchman, 3 cottagers and 4 slaves – allowing four or five to a family, probably a total of 100 or so; the estate was rated at 8 hides, with 3 and a virgate in lordship: there were two mills along with meadow, common pasture and woodland for 200 pigs. The detailed surveys and customaries drawn up between 1284 and 1331 disclose a taxable population of 120 or so – say 500 people, probably its peak until the eighteenth century (the 1801 census reveals 99 houses with 309 taxable males). The lord of the manor during these years was St Albans Abbey; the common fields were farmed by peasant smallholders, who owed boon-work to the lord which is laid out in detail in the manorial accounts.

The general picture provided by the thirteenth- and fourteenth-century records for Codicote agrees with those from the many detailed surveys which survive of individual English medieval manors. Although many aspects relate to the idea of 'communal' life, the most striking feature is that the village was not a closed corporate community – that traditional 'good old days' vision – with an all-embracing, supportive, extended kin network. What is remarkable is that the village is subject to constant change of population – more pronounced from 1350 to 1450 than in the century before, admittedly, but nevertheless an important feature, so that only 10 per cent of the families of 1350 are still recognisable a century later. The family generally appears to be nuclear and small, with few in-laws or parents living in. There was an intense land market at all times, with women frequently appearing as absolute owners, so that marrying widows became one of the ways in which single men acquired land. There was a great deal of violence in village life, with frequent resort to such behaviour to right wrongs and solve feuds. Moreover – and so much for those modern

Above Codicote, Hertfordshire, before the First World War.
Right Codicote around 1800. This tithe map gives an idea of the size that the village would have been in 1350.

commentators who think crime figures do not relate to social conditions –
there is an absolutely clear correlation between crime figures and prices:
murder, violence and serious crime – the only crime recorded in the fourteenth century – rises astronomically when the price of wheat and other
foodstuffs shoots up, as during the Great Famine of 1316–17.

Although a village, Codicote had a number of features which made it
more like a small market town: it had a market and a fair, for example, and
though the villein's lot is generally seen in terms of agricultural labour, it is
clear that during the late thirteenth century the people of Codicote engaged
in all sorts of other economic activity. One villein who ploughed strips in
the manor was Hugh Cok, who was active between 1277 and 1306.
Though a smallholder, and never able to increase his wealth by any large-
scale purchase or large-scale owning of pasture, Hugh is typical of the mass
of post-Domesday English people in the way he wheeler-deals, shuffling
his holdings and making little deals here and there.

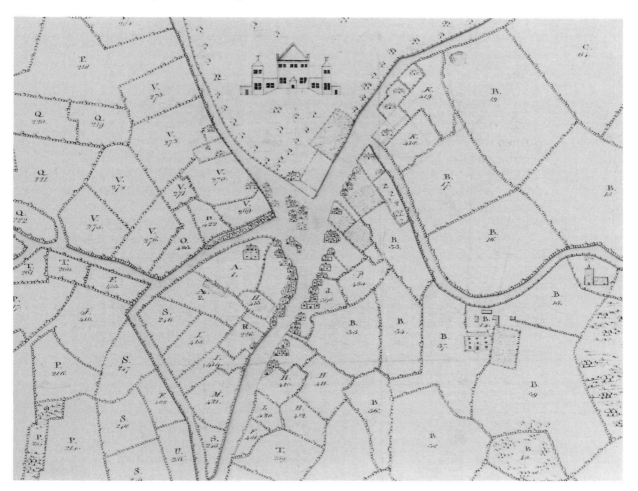

In 1277 Hugh was taxed at 6*d* a year, the lowest in Codicote. Shortly afterwards he took a place in the market where fish was sold, paying 8*d* a year rental to St Albans Abbey; he then took up a 1¼-acre plot for 1*s* 'entry fee', and another for 2*s* and a yearly rent of 4*d*; a plot 'near Ledwell' for 2*s*; 2 half-acres and another plot for 2*s*; two more strips of 2 acres and 1½ acres respectively; another 1½-acre strip on a ten-year lease for a 6*d* down payment; and 1½ acres 'for a term of four crops'. Not long afterwards Hugh was at it again, consolidating his little maze of smallholdings by adding 2½ acres; a house with 3 acres; 1 acre and a hedge; ½ acre in three separate parcels leased for nine years; 1 acre 'for 12 years or eight crops'; and 'a piece of land for 3 years or two crops'. He also got leave to make a ditch 5 feet wide which cost him 10*s* to his landlord – and to cap all this, he and his wife were fined for bad brewing! Finally in 1306, presumably in old age, he surrendered all his holdings to his daughter Christina, who is described in the 1332 customary of the village living in the house 'which was Hugh Cok's, for which she paid 1*d*'. This incredible list of the dealings of one individual tenant of no particular significance shows us how closely the accounting mentality of post-Domesday government and landlord had come to rest on even the semi-free peasantry. Not only that but, as Ada Levett wrote, 'The amount of semi-intellectual energy which must have been absorbed in remembering or forgetting such complex obligations is amazing.'

Such people did not gather many possessions. At another St Albans manor, Norton, the villein John Geiard, who held 4 cotlands, a ferling and a cottage with 2 acres, died in 1385 with a death duty of two cows, a horse and a mare, while his nine-year-old son inherited one plough with a coulter and ploughshare worth 2*s*, a brass pot and a dish, a cart worth 1*s* 6*d*, a bushel measure bound with iron, a lock, a seedcod, a harrow, a fork and a mattock. Another tenant had a horse and plough, a brass pot and dish, a chest, a large barrel (for making beer?), a bushel measure, a cart, a saddle, a pair of traces, a seedcod and a barrel. With such bare lists the everyday existences of the ordinary working men and women of the Middle Ages come to life for the first time; such evidently was the farming tackle on small but accumulating tenements like Hugh Cok's – similar to that of many Third World smallholders portrayed in the media today.

From all these tenants the landlord exacted dues and services. Many were a constant source of friction between tenants and lord long before the Peasants' Revolt of 1381. Already before the Conquest customary law on many estates was worked out in very great detail, with the days to be worked for the landlord itemised along with the tasks to be accomplished. And although the number of real slaves was declining – they had disappeared as a class by *c.* 1200 – serfdom in its various forms would last until the fifteenth century. Manorial villeins were often treated as serfs and in the thirteenth century comes the first evidence of them organising collectively

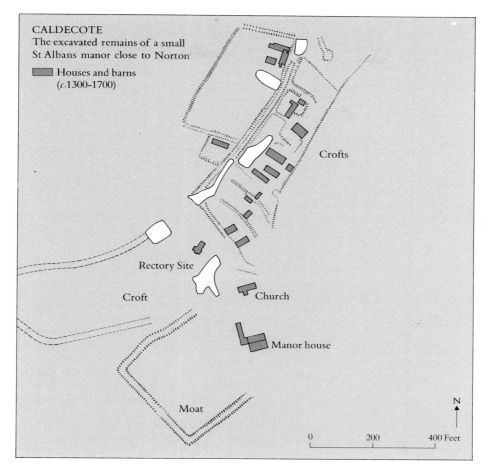

CALDECOTE
The excavated remains of a small
St Albans manor close to Norton

▬ Houses and barns
(c.1300–1700)

Crofts

Rectory Site

Croft

Church

Manor house

Moat

N

0   200   400 Feet

to fight 'uncustomary' or excessive impositions – at Mears Ashby, Northampton, in 1261; at Stoughton in Leicestershire in 1276, when the tenants took their landlord to court after refusing to do services; at Harmondsworth, Middlesex, in 1278; and at Newington in Oxfordshire in 1300, where the entire body of villeins refused to do mowing services and raised a collection of 4d a head for a 'strike fund' to fight the case in court – possibly the first such instance in British labour history.

Customary services at Codicote are known about in great detail as the document known as the extent of the manor has survived from 1332, and is now in the British Library. A villein called John Salecok, for instance, who held a house and a croft of land, with about 15 acres of arable, had to pay each year rents and fees totalling 5s 5½d out of an annual income of, at a guess, £1. He also had to plough 2½ acres of the lord's demesne each winter, Lent and fallow, or pay 6d an acre each. He had to do a day's harrowing, 'providing his horse if he has one'; and to bring his own plough to do additional ploughing at sowing time, providing his own meals. At

Christmas he had to render one cock, one hen and a loaf worth ½d, and at Easter 30 eggs. He had to provide 42 work days between Michaelmas and August (½d each if commuted); one day of hay-carrying at haymaking – the lord provided food; mowing – 'to help till the lord's meadow be finished'; harvesting – 'two men at each boon-work with meals but no drink, or 1d per day' (in other words the lord provided free ale); 'reaping and binding: three acres at the lord's will, or 4d an acre; carrying corn: one day, with all meals, if he has a horse and cart; cleaning the mill-course: half a day, with one extra man when necessary'. Such was the fine print of medieval estate management 150 years on from Domesday: the aspirations of most ordinary people were confined by an extraordinarily oppressive and uneconomic system, though whether things would have developed differently if there had been no Norman Conquest is debatable.

In the first part of the fourteenth century rural society went into crisis. The birth rate seems to have declined and there were serious outbreaks of cattle and livestock pest, together with the plagues and famines already mentioned. At Codicote the village court book, now in the British Library, gives first-hand evidence of the troubles. In particular the surrender of holdings is very revealing, as smallholders and speculators like Hugh Cok were squeezed. In an average year about six or eight smallholdings were surrendered, but in 1316 they went up to 31, with another 28 in 1317. Sometimes these might be simply family deals – aged parents like Hugh Cok relinquishing his hold in favour of his daughter – but most have no family connection and stem from mere economic necessity. Most indeed are tiny plots of 2 acres or under: in a society with a rampant land market and a competitive acquisitive drive, this was what happened when things got tough.

Not all cases were of small men or women selling out to big, but such a story is that of Michael Gorman and his wife from Codicote. Between 1315 and 1317 the Gormans sold out: five parcels of land totalling a house, two pieces of land and 1½ acres – it can hardly have been enough to make ends meet at the best of times. By November 1321, the third year of famine, Gorman was dead. Presumably he died, as he had lived, in abject poverty, and like farmers in the African famines of the mid-1980s was forced to sell off even his tackle, his ploughshare and coulter – if he had one – his horse, his utensils and tools: the court book of Codicote records that there was no death duty (heriot) to pay 'because he had nothing'. The land he had been left with, the land on which his dwelling stood, went to his lord. But another tenant in the same book gained from the Gormans' misfortune. Roger le Heldere made twenty-two separate purchases between 1315 and 1325 totalling 16½ acres and a few small plots. In the 1332 survey of Codicote Roger appears with all this land plus two houses and three shops in the 'forum' – the market.

Evidence from such material suggests that by 1300 the pattern of landholding seen in Domesday was breaking up. People like Hugh and Christina Cok and Roger le Heldere were peasants perhaps, but they were living in a proto-capitalist world with great economic diversity at grass-roots level and considerable economic vitality in the lives of the ordinary workforce as they tried to break free from the suffocating constrictions of the feudal order. This was a commercially minded, class-ridden society with great mobility – many people left Codicote, for example, including villeins, and many newcomers came in. It is the society that can be seen all over western Europe from at least the twelfth century onwards: a society whose members marry relatively late and raise small, nuclear families, where individuals use this 'prudential' marriage and mobility for self-aggrandisement; it is a competitive, acquisitive society, which until 1300 kept some sort of a balance – despite the rising population – between resources and population. These trends in marriage, mobility, decline of serfdom and land-dealing expressed themselves in a work ethic which has traditionally been called Protestant, but which in fact owes its origin to the Latin Christian work ethic whose own roots lie in the management and law of the great Dark Age estates; it is perhaps ultimately derived from the pervasive accounting mentality, legalism and rigid division of time that characterised Benedictine-inspired estate management. This work ethic bred a view of society where the father was a heroic, self-denying labourer who strove hard to keep himself and his family, and leave his children better off than he.

But whatever forces were at work in English society in the 1330s an even more violent dislocation of the feudal work pattern was about to come: the Black Death. No event in British history has had a more cataclysmic effect on the life of the people, and the court books of the possessions of St Albans again give examples in remarkable detail. The court rolls naturally only record the holders of tenements, so the figures which follow are not complete, and normally these are men and women over sixteen years old. But even so the picture is terrifying. At Codicote the court book records the deaths of 59 tenants between 1 November 1348 and 19 May 1349, with 3 before and 6 later. These are holders of plots – the register was not interested in wives, children and next of kin who lived in the same household unless they became heirs. But for those 68 people the book gives dates, names, death duties, fines and the name of the heir with his or her relationship to the deceased. Some of the names are already familiar to us: 'May 22 1348 Christina Cok/holding: 1 house with yard/death duty 1 pig worth 4s/fine 3s 4d/heir: John/relation: son/age: full [over sixteen].' So Christina had had a child, even if there is no sign of a husband. The same list reveals that Roger le Heldere's son Richard and daughter Eva also died of the plague, on 19 May 1349, and that their lands went to Richard's three-year-old son William, whose mother Alicia acted as guardian; the family were still among the wealthier villeins at Codicote, with 3 cotlands and 19 acres.

The blow must have been catastrophic, here in Codicote as everywhere else in England: 68 householders dead in a place whose population had included 121 tenants in 1332. The same picture is found on the other St Albans manors whose court books survive: at Norton 27 deaths in a place which even in 1801 only had 55 houses; at Cashio 73 deaths out of 200 tenants; at Abbots Langley 82 deaths; and at Park 85 out of 150. In these figures few wives appear – five at Cashio, one at Codicote, seven at Norton and one again at Park. But in fact the lists show that the loss among women was almost as severe: 15 women at each of Langley, Norton and Cashio, 17 at Codicote and 22 at Park. Nevertheless life still went on. In all these places virtually every tenement was taken up by a new tenant during 1349–50. At Abbots Langley every one of the 71 vacant tenements was taken up, in 44 cases by a man or woman of full age, in 21 cases by a minor. Codicote offers a similar picture. Moreover, at all these St Albans manors marriages were licensed between May and October 1349 (the height of the plague was the summer of 1349): 17 marriages at Cashio, 3 at Codicote, 21 at Langley, 14 at Norton and 19 at Park.

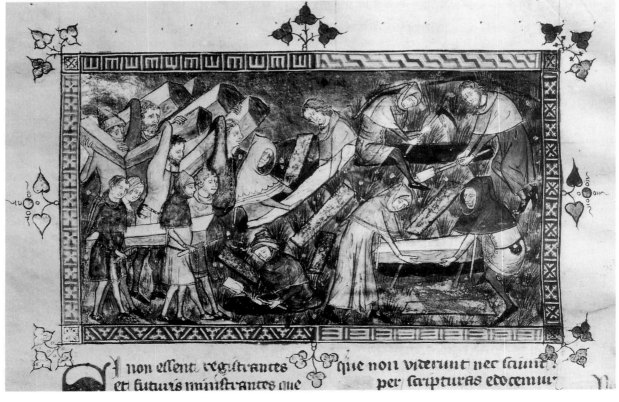

The Black Death: a rare early illustration depicting scenes of the plague at Tournai in 1349. 'No one was safe, whether rich, middling or poor.'

These records show that the landlords carried on running their accounts as carefully as before. In April 1350 the books of all the St Albans manors record that the villeins 'gave of their own free will' 60s from each manor as a newly created tax for the abbot. Obviously the devastating effect of the plague on his villages had not increased the abbot's sympathetic consideration for his tenants. Nor had the system in any way collapsed. By the end of 1350 life on the estates had resumed its normal course and the court books revert to their normal record of purchases, surrenders, fines and so on. No violent revolution followed hard on the Black Death: the only hint of trouble lies in the increased numbers of fugitive villeins – in some villages rising from six in 1351 to ten or a dozen in 1355.

Other social changes only became apparent in the longer term. Most obvious is the long-term stagnation of society, in terms of both economy and population: by 1522 the population of England was still only 2,300,000. Local details give further clues. In village records throughout England evidence for migration grows in the later fourteenth and early fifteenth centuries, with more people moving away, and moving further afield: such is the picture in the East Anglian estates of Ramsey Abbey, and the West Midlands estates of the bishopric of Worcester.

The early fifteenth century may also have seen a growth in social tensions and the frequency of personal violence between the tenants of large holdings and the poorer wage-earners which has been observed in many sets of manorial records. In many places scholars have been tempted to see the progressive break-up of the old 'village community' in the late fourteenth and fifteenth centuries. At Warboys in the Fens, for example, the social atmosphere of the village changed perceptibly after the Black Death; the village had been relatively peaceful before the plague, but afterwards clear signs can be seen of a decline in respect for neighbours' property and the disappearance of the reliance on personal pledge in solving local disputes; there was a marked increase in violence among villagers. Most notably – and this is repeated at many other places – not only do many village names disappear during the plague years, but the rate of disappearance carries on; families were often large enough for part of them to survive the plague, but by the 1370s and 1380s the survivors had been wiped out by new epidemics or the normal process of mortality in a weakened family.

The end of the personal pledge may be a further sign of the breakdown of communal feeling: since pledging another person was a free option, did villagers no longer wish to support each other in this way? It would seem that the disasters and social unrest of the fourteenth century dealt an irreparable blow to the community spirit by which the workforce had ordered their lives since before Domesday. A remarkably detailed study of one village in the Fens, Holywell-cum-Needingworth, found that profound changes in the overall cohesion and co-operativeness of village life are detectable from 1350 onwards; here there was a pronounced turning away from the personal ties of co-operation and dependence of peasant life on the feudal order, towards an increased exercise of independent action. Even if they did not exactly follow a policy of 'every man for himself', nevertheless the peasants of Holywell began to display less concern for the rights and privileges of neighbours, and a greater laxity towards the more formal public and legal institutions through which they had formerly resolved conflicts. Private interests began to supplant communal relations. In the court books here, too, the personal pledge faded away; there was a startling increase in acts of trespass and violence against neighbours; manorial commitments and obligations were disregarded much more frequently than before, with a great upsurge of derelictions in the 1350s. As E. de Windt wrote, 'The pursuit of private interests was assuming a paramount place, and the preservation of a tightly cohesive village community was becoming more and more a matter of secondary importance.'

Above The exterior of the great tithe barn at Lenham and, *right*, the interior of one at Frindsbury, both in Kent. Erected all over England, such buildings are the symbol of an age which specialised in increasingly detailed accounting of its agricultural production.

If conclusions can be drawn from such apparent changes, they seem to be that Domesday England was nearing the end of its lifespan. Promoted by the shocks of famine and then plague, by the steadily decreasing concentration of population in the community, the increased incidence of outsiders, the *adventitii* who wandered in and out of villages like Codicote for various economic purposes; by the changing nature of the exploitative and pastoral economy among the major families, the old cohesiveness faded and private interests grew. The English village did not collapse, of course; but something was missing from a community which, whatever its tensions, had been bound by far-reaching ties of personal responsibility. It can hardly be a coincidence that such social developments have been detected at a time when the decay of the old demesne-oriented manorial economy is apparent – the economy which had been the key to England's wealth since long before Domesday. When that system lost its vitality and withered away, so did the village organisation which had sustained it. Something similar would happen in the late twentieth century to the urban 'communities' of the great industrial cities in Britain, when hit by long-term economic change.

The stagnation and eventual collapse of the manorial economy would eventually bring about a different economic life for the peasant – a life dominated by impermanent, cash-based tenurial commitments and the ready exploitation of properties for quick profit; just so the decline of the 'feudal' village organisation brought forth a society in which behaviour was increasingly independent, individualist and even impersonal. The crux of the matter was that the English peasant was once more displaying his pragmatism in the art of survival, abandoning institutions and patterns of behaviour no longer practical in the light of what would be a new age, a different day. The village community continued to function as a unit of government and a social focus right up to modern times – many only lost their autonomy in the nineteenth century – but in the troubles of the fourteenth century the seeds of destruction of the village were sown. In Christopher Dyer's words, 'The undermining of the common fields, the declining effectiveness of village government and the development of a distinct group of wealthy tenants, would lead to the triumph of individualism over the interests of the community.' Not a new individualism, as we have seen, but an accentuation of what was there before. The late-marrying, land-dealing, property-owning English were, one suspects, already there at Domesday; the cataclysms of the fourteenth century only helped to usher out the feudal age so much earlier than in any other country and to usher in the beginnings of a different economic system in which England would set the stage for the whole world: capitalism.

EPILOGUE:
SHAPED BY THE PAST

Time present and time past
Are both perhaps contained in the same future
And time future contained in time past.
T.S. Eliot, Burnt Norton, *1936.*

It is not the literal past that rules us, save, possibly, in a biological sense. It is images of the past. These are often as highly structured and selective as myths. Images and symbolic constructs of the past are imprinted, almost in the manner of genetic information, on our sensibility. Each new historical era mirrors itself in the picture and active mythology of its past.
George Steiner, In Bluebeard's Castle, *1971*

The fifteenth century witnessed the end of Domesday England and the rise of powerful new forces in English society. Many scholars have seen the rise of the yeoman class – whose interests were strongly identified with making money from the exploitation of property – as the beginning of a different form of class system and economy in England; this was R.H. Tawney's opinion in his famous book *Religion and the Rise of Capitalism*, which was based on a study of the agrarian collapse in the sixteenth century and the rise of the capitalist spirit. Certainly dramatic changes took place in the coutryside in the period from 1450 to 1550, with thousands of villages being deserted – often deliberately depopulated – by new landowners who were buying up the old monastic and ecclesiastical estates which had been built up since the tenth century. One notable case is the Spencer family, ancestors of the late Princess of Wales, who were small yeomen in Warwickshire up to the later fifteenth century when they began to buy up former church and noble property and enclose it for sheep farming. They, like many other Tudor 'sheep ranchers', benefited from the massive depopulations across Warwickshire and Northamptonshire, and still own many of the estates enclosed at that time. One of them, Wormleighton, had been royal sheep land as far back as the mid-tenth century; from the grassy mounds which mark the site of the 'old town' there, the sites of a number of other villages can be seen which were thriving communities at the time of Domesday and which died in the late fifteenth century, their people driven off the land to work or beg in the booming textile town of Coventry.

As always, history meant change. It is in the period of the Reformation, when the Catholic Church was dispossessed of holdings built up since the

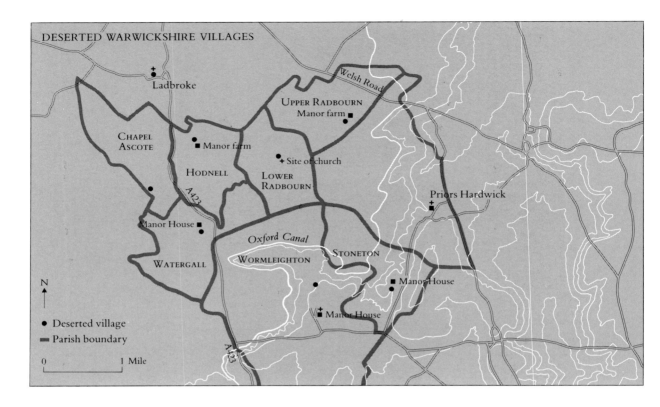

DESERTED WARWICKSHIRE VILLAGES

Welsh Road

Ladbroke

UPPER RADBOURN
Manor farm

CHAPEL
ASCOTE

Manor farm

HODNELL

Site of church

LOWER
RADBOURN

Priors Hardwick

Manor House

Oxford Canal

WORMLEIGHTON

STONETON

Manor House

WATERGALL

Manor House

N

● Deserted village
━ Parish boundary

0   1 Mile

seventh century, that many modern scholars have been prepared to see the origins of a 'bourgeoisie' and of the capitalist spirit in England, the transition from a feudal peasant society to an absolutist state based on market relations. As we have seen, such ideas may go much further back, but the secular spirit of the Tudor age and what we now call the 'Protestant' work ethic are fitting heralds of the modern age.

In the seventeenth century the new middle class with its landed and moneyed interests overthrew the now outdated monarchy in a civil war, which many saw, not altogether unjustly, as overthrowing the 'Norman yoke' imposed by the Conqueror in 1086. But more far-reaching redistribution of wealth did not take place, and by 1688 a restored constitutional monarchy was installed in alliance with a ruling class whose dominant political philosophy was a 'possessive individualism' with a strong emphasis on personal freedom and property ownership in which human relations were seen as market relations. The triumph of this ideology in the seventeenth century laid the basis of nineteenth-century liberal democracy in Britain, the United States and elsewhere. But the period 1540–1688 also saw the beginning of a dramatic change in population which eventually made it possible for England and her individualism to dominate the world.

The population of England was still only two and a half million in 1540: it represented a small, underdeveloped, third-rank kingdom on the fringe of

Above Wormleighton, Warwickshire, the site of the village destroyed *c.*1500. From the air the streets and back ways can be seen, leading up to the row of fish ponds. To the right, in the crook of the canal, is the site of the medieval moated manor. The Spencer family's Tudor manor house, *below*, lies on the hill, at the top left, by the church. There was a church here at the time of Domesday; in the 950s the manor had been royal sheep farming land.

Europe. By 1688 the population had recovered to something like its pre-1348 level: the contemporary survery by Gregory King estimated it at five and a half million people, of which three million were the poor labouring proletariat, successors of the bond peasantry of the Middle Ages. By 1750 it had probably reached six and a half million and it is from that point that really dramatic changes take place which would transform British history and bring the country into the forefront of the world. In the 1801 census the population of England and Wales totalled 8,873,000, and by 1901 it had quadrupled to thirty-two million. A comparison with France is interesting: the 1801 population of England and Wales was only a third of that of France; the 1688 level under a quarter. Not surprisingly, the comparative prosperity of the English peasantry was the frequent theme of French and English travellers in the seventeenth and eighteenth centuries: the English were universally agreed to be far better off, better clothed and richer – though not necessarily happier – and better educated and informed. Indeed one could say that such observations are consistent from the seventeenth century to the nineteenth when writers from La Rochefoucauld to de Tocqueville and Hippolyte Taine commented on the level of education among the English working class and the 'individualism' of the man in the street.

Why this extraordinary population rise happened now seems clear. It was not due to better health or lower mortality, but to a fall in the marriage age. What triggers off such a change – as after the Black Death – still needs explanation, but the late eighteenth century marks the end of a pattern which probably stretches back before Domesday. One contemporary observer was Robert Malthus whose *Essay on the Principle of Population* (1798) remains the classic statement on the connection between food supply, birth rate and 'prudential marriage': a form of marriage now extending to the whole of the world. Malthus thought there would be a social collapse – a 'Malthusian crisis' – as the population rose till it outstripped food supply, but in fact agricultural change was so dramatic that the population was able to rise and feed itself with no check till modern contraception. But by the 1830s there was no longer a living on the land for the bulk of the population.

By then, of course, the real shift from rural to urban life was well under way in England, with the growth of the mass populations in industrial cities, especially in the north of England. What might be termed the second great phase of English history had begun: workshop of the world, prototype of all the industrial civilisations which would follow. It is easy to forget that most countries in the world have only industrialised since the Second World War.

Now, in 1999, the wheel has come full circle in English history: the urban

Left Willicote, Warwickshire: the surviving ridge and furrow patterns of a deserted medieval village; the still visible 'bone structure' of the pre-Domesday world.

Above Ploughmen in Berkshire, *c.* 1880. They have horses instead of oxen, and a heavier iron plough, but the image is still that of the *Luttrell Psalter* of 1335-40 *(below)*.

phase is again undergoing a drastic change. The 1873 'New Domesday', a government land survey, showed the end of the English smallholder whom we have followed through from the Dark Ages – at that date only 900,000 farming people were left who owned less than 100 acres, as against five and a half million in France, for example; by 1973 less than a fifth of England's population worked on the land, while over half still did so in France. In two or three generations England had diverged and become an urban proletariat. This massive shift provoked – and is still provoking – a huge amount of scholarly work in a tradition going back to a host of prophetic works from the early nineteenth century onwards, such as Engels' *The Condition of the Working Class in England*.

Engels was well aware of the relation between agricultural revolution, population rise and industrialisation. Because of industrialisation the population explosion did not lead to stagnation or contraction, as it had in the fourteenth century, but to a period when, for the first time in history, poverty for the mass of humankind became not a necessary part of men and women's lot, but a preventable social evil. Engels saw industrialisation as the final triumph of English individualism: 'England's activity was the work of unconnected individuals which seldom and only out of individual interests act together...' The French historian Alexis de Tocqueville saw the same: 'The spirit of individualism is the basis of the English character' – an individualism he saw as rooted deep in the Anglo-Saxon past, where in customs such as the legal system 'one can find all the elements of present-day procedure'.

Now, 150 years or so on from de Tocqueville and Engels, over 900 years on from Domesday, we have a new problem. As we have seen throughout this story, economic systems run down and are supplanted by others, places themselves – sometimes whole cities – decline and are abandoned or de-populated when they cease to have a function. Now that Britain is undergoing post-industrial contraction – the first nation in the world to experience this, as it was the first to undergo an industrial revolution – changes are perceptible over a much shorter space of time than previously in our history. It is incredible to think, for example, that over two million people were still employed in the coal industry in 1945. What happens when a nation goes through such changes? The answer is that nobody knows. The 'New Domesday' of 1986, an electronic survey of the United Kingdom recorded on video-disc, sponsored by the BBC, was published after this book first went to press, but advance trends indicated further far-reaching changes. The old concentration of work and population in the great nineteenth-century industrial cities of the north and Midlands was clearly seen to be losing its economic vitality to the new microchip belt stretching from Bristol to the Wash, the new or newly expanded towns like Swindon and Milton Keynes with their booming computer-age industries. So, as the medieval textile towns were replaced by the nineteenth-century manufacturing bases, they too are being superseded.

In the role of women too, the 'New Domesday' sees a dramatic shift, this time back to a more medieval pattern of employment: the return of women to being a major – and perhaps eventually equal – part of the workforce after the best part of a century, from 1850 to 1940, when the 'housewife' – a job description which first appears between 1850 and 1870 – defined a woman's role in the world.

Another prominent trend in the 'New Domesday' is the growth of a kind of structural inequality which looks like separating about a fifth of the fifty-five million population of the United Kingdom from the rest, in terms of wealth, income, standard of living and job opportunities – from Domesday to 1999 class continues to exist as a divisive factor in the development of society. External factors obviously play their part far more today than they did in the fourteenth or eleventh centuries. If William the Conqueror was alive today, and contemplating a new Domesday Book, he would have to take into account international banking, the International Monetary Fund, foreign debt, balance of trade, foreign investment and the host of other bogies which haunt newspaper and television accounts of our own society. Here too, though, the 'New Domesday' shows the incontrovertible evidence of historical and economic change: a third of the entire manufacturing base of Britain was lost in the years since 1970, over half of it between 1979 and 1986. What effect do such changes have in the long term on the fabric of a country whose population for the last 150 years has owed its living and its social organisation to industry?

Here again the 'New Domesday' can perhaps offer us the kind of psycho-logical pointers which detailed studies of the medieval workforce have detected: the 1986 survey, drawing on massive computer archives going back to the Mass Observation project of the thirties, and all the modern opinion poll data, concludes that the British are taking one further step in the move away from the communal life and into a 'privatised' and more self-centred existence. The work ethic, the survey seems to show, will no longer be a driving force in society: people now work in order to provide for what goes on inside the home, to pay for leisure activities which are increasingly private and individual. More and more people have come to believe that the state should be responsible for things that the family and the community once did – for instance in the care of the aged or the mentally ill. This tendency, detected in the declining manorial world of the fourteenth century, is now apparent in the declining urban world of the twentieth. Whatever community feelings were built up in the slums of the mass cities of the nineteenth and early twentieth centuries – and the nostalgic 'chumminess' of *Coronation Street* may not be all myth – have perceptibly broken down under the impact of world wars, massive slum clearance, dehumanising tower blocks and the commercial pressures of the commodity age, the era of 'You've never had it so good'. Undeniably, we are better off than our medieval ancestors; we live longer, in better health, and with far

Women gathering and binding cut wheat in Norfolk, *c.* 1900: a vision of the medieval past from within living memory.

more things to fill our minds and time. Technology has brought us the prospect of real freedoms – of leisure, of expanding knowledge and so on. But the benefits of the modern world have also brought the erosion of that religious world view which gave meaning to the likes of Bede, Alfred the Great and even, for all we know, Christina Cok. Materialism has triumphed.

As it is with the village community of 'Merrie England', so it is with the embracing communities of *Coronation Street* and *EastEnders*. Our view of our history is inevitably tinged with a desire for a golden age, for an unchanging traditional society in which neighbours are kind and elders respected, where children obey their teachers and everyone knows their place. Every age constructs such golden ages retrospectively – they were at it in the 990s, as we can read in their sermons, just as we are today; the threats are the same, and always the belief is expressed that society was better in those days, and that the present is a falling off. As we have seen, the medieval village in

which our ancestors lived for most of the forty generations which take us back to the English emigration was never a fixed, closed community of unchanging values. The past is only safe in the sense that it has happened – that is the attraction of history, and at the same time the catch. In fact, the past is always changing – changing in relation to the present, in relation to the point of view of the living. In Britain in 1999, as at every other moment in our history, we have both a real past and a symbolic past. The real past is difficult to recover, for trying to reconstruct it demands a great effort of will, imagination and involvement. Far from being writ handed down by the experts as a single dimension presented for our contemplation, it is – or should be – a three-dimensional image which we ourselves create, setting ourselves in relation to our ancestors; indeed it is an image into which we also put something of ourselves. On the other hand the symbolic past is the past we see all around us: images of greatness, royal ceremonial, son et lumière on the 'Heart of the Nation' advertised with images of Henry VIII, Good Queen Bess, Nelson and Churchill; Beefeaters at the Tower, State Openings of Parliament, wigs on judges and hunting scenes on Christmas cards. This version of the past requires no effort of imagination to enter into: it is symbolic, invented tradition; it simplifies history to advertising slogans, like the Hovis advertisement showing an Edwardian child wheeling down the steep hill at Shaftesbury to the sound of a brass band.

But if history is reinterpreted, then everything else is, too: a new past means a new future. Domesday Book, on its 900th anniversary, was chosen as a symbol of the English past, an image of continuity, tradition and inevitable progress of our history: '900 years of government administration and centralisation'. The nine centuries are not long in historical terms: twenty-seven generations of the real families who can genuinely trace themselves back. The connections are still there, as I have tried to show in this book. Nine hundred years on we still call ourselves 'Anglo-Saxon' in race, we still swear in 'Anglo-Saxon': indeed most of our bread-and-butter words are derived from Old English. Conversely, in this 'them-and-us' equation, our images of greatness are still Norman – The Tower of London, Windsor Castle, Westminster Abbey, the great cathedrals: we still use Norman French in legal terminology; our words for government and power are French. Yet it would appear that whatever the diverse ethnic origins of the people who call themselves English – and there has never been an 'Anglo-Saxon' racial identity, only a linguistic and cultural one – certain crucial aspects of our culture, such as our attitudes to love, marriage and the family, to work, to drink, to common rights and personal freedom, to property ownership, may go deep into our past, before 1086 and Domesday,

Left An alley in Glasgow, *c.*1880. Pictures like this created the popular image of the city as a place of disaffection where people were cut off from their true selves and their rural roots.

to the Anglo-Saxon, Viking and Celtic in the British make-up. So until we understand more about the whole story we will remain ignorant about so many important things which we take for granted; and the whole story includes the anonymous Iron Age farmers of the Berkshire Downs, the villa serfs of Melania, Waerlaf the swineherd at Hatfield, Lufu and her children at Ebbesbourne, Michael Gorman and Christina Cok at Codicote in the 1320s. Their tale is important because the history of this small island off the shore of Europe became world history, its speech became world speech, and, perhaps more importantly, its social and economic experience also became that of the rest of the world.

GLOSSARY

Acre A day's ploughing for one plough team. Now 220 × 22 yards. 120 were reckoned to be the average which would support one family, but the acre varied in real size according to local conditions and soil.

Boon-work Work done on the lord's land by dependent peasants for a fixed number of days per week.

Bordars Smallholding cottagers of lesser standing than villeins but better off than cottars (see below).

Bovate An eighth of a carucate (see below). Sometimes reckoned at 15 acres; land ploughed by two oxen.

Burh, Borough Originally a defended farm or residence but usually used in the meaning current from the ninth to the eleventh centuries, namely an urban settlement, normally fortified.

Carucate Danish equivalent of a hide. The land ploughed by eight oxen; actual area varied locally and like the hide could be reassessed.

Coloni Peasant farmers, free and semi-free, in the later Roman Empire.

Cottars Lowest of the main levels of peasant cultivators at Domesday: 'cottagers' with 4 acres or less.

Danelaw Area acknowledged by the West Saxon kings as under Danish law in the tenth century, owing to the heavy Danish settlement there; hence East Anglia, the East Midlands, Lincolnshire and Yorkshire.

Demesne Land devoted to the lord's profit, whether a manor, or a portion of land within a manor, worked by peasants as part of their obligations.

Feorm (Latin *firma*) 'Farm': renders in land to provide one night's food and upkeep for the court. By 1086 often commuted to cash.

Freeman Not to be understood in the modern sense but a man who was personally free but could owe rents or obligations to his lord; many freemen in Domesday are 'lesser thegns'.

Furlong 220 yards length (×22 yards (1 chain) = 1 acre, 4840 square yards). Then the average furrow in a ploughed field.

Geld The Anglo-Saxon land tax used for military purposes, especially the payment of the royal fleet (geld = payment or tribute in Old English). Hence Danegeld was the tax raised to pay tribute to the Danes in the tenth and early eleventh centuries.

Hidage	Document containing assessment of land, shires or towns, drawn up in hides.
Hide	Originally the land necessary to sustain a peasant household. Sometimes reckoned at 120 acres but in fact the hide varied according to locality, date, and government needs.
Hundred	Subdivision of the shire based on groups of estates adding up to 100 hides: probably artificially imposed in the Midlands 900–939, but in the south based on older units.
Linchet	Artificial terrace allowing ploughing on the slopes of the chalk Downs in Wessex.
Manor	An estate with land and jurisdiction over tenants. Not necessarily a whole village, which might have several manors, just as one manor might own land in more than one village.
Ploughland	Amount of potential arable land on an estate (that is, the number of ploughs there was scope for) expressed as a tax assessment which varied according to regional conditions and class of soil.
Plough team	Often assessed at eight oxen per team; in the richest agricultural areas, like the Severn valley, there were between three and five per square mile. On harsher land like the fringes of Dartmoor, a smallholder might own only one or two oxen.
Reeve	The lord's official on the manor who supervised labour dues and renders owed by peasants.
Serf	Slave; property of the lord.
Sheriff	Royal official in charge of a shire.
Soke (land)	Land attached to a central manor for payment of dues and for judicial purposes. Often large units – perhaps of very ancient origin.
Sokeman	Freeman of peasant status who was free to leave (and often to sell) his land; often owing services or rent, and obliged to attend his lord's court.
Thegns	Pre-Conquest nobles below the level of earls; local estate owners with at least 5 hides of land and a residence. Richer ones had grand halls behind large defences. Backbone of the royal army.
Villeins	The highest class of dependent peasantry, often holding between 30 and 100 acres; above them were 'freemen' and 'sokemen'.
Virgate	A quarter of a hide: often 20 or 30 acres.
Wapentake	Equivalent of a hundred in the Danelaw.

BIBLIOGRAPHY

This bibliography is intended to highlight the main sources used in this book. For the traveller to Domesday England there are certain essentials: Domesday Book itself, now available county by county in paperback editions published by Phillimore, edited by J. Morris (the translation is usually reliable, but sometimes should be checked – as, for instance, where it translates sokeman as 'freeman'); the Ordnance Survey 1″ maps; N. Pevsner's *Buildings of England* series (Penguin Books 1951–); H. and J. Taylor's *Anglo-Saxon Architecture*, 3 vols (Cambridge paperback 1981–4). There is no satisfactory edition of the Anglo-Saxon charters, but the handlist by P. Sawyer, *Anglo-Saxon Charters* (British Academy 1979), gives references to modern translations where they exist.

On Domesday itself, the great book by F. W. Maitland, *Domesday Book and Beyond* (Cambridge 1897, Fontana paperback 1961), is still worth dipping into; the classic modern statement is V. H. Galbraith's *The Making of Domesday Book* (Oxford 1961). See too the important essays in *Domesday Book: A Reassessment*, edited by P. Sawyer (E. Arnold 1985); E. Hallam's *Domesday Book* (Thames and Hudson 1986); S. Harvey's *Domesday Book* (Croom Helm forthcoming) and – a very significant reassessment – *Domesday Economy* by J. McDonald and G. D. Snooks (Oxford 1986). Fundamental to any study of Domesday is *The Domesday Geography of England* by H. C. Darby, 7 vols (Cambridge 1952–77), especially the survey volume *Domesday England* (1977). For wider views of the period, D. C. Douglas's *William the Conqueror* (Eyre Methuen 1969) and *Time and the Hour* (Eyre Methuen 1977). Main sources are contained in *English Historical Documents*, vol. 1, edited by D. Whitelock (Eyre Methuen, 2nd ed. 1979), and vol. 2, edited by D. C. Douglas and G. W. Greenaway (Eyre Methuen, 2nd ed. 1982). For a comprehensive, critical bibliography of all the literature on Domesday Book, D. Bates' *A Bibliography of Domesday Book* (Boydell and Brewer, for the Royal Historical Society, 1986).

On Ashdown, the Anglo-Saxon charters are discussed by M. Gelling in *The Early Charters of the Thames Valley* (Leicester University Press 1979), in *The Place Names of Berkshire*, 3 vols (English Place-Name Society, Cambridge, 1973–6) and in *Signposts to the Past* (Dent 1978). For landscape studies in general the relevant volumes of the English Place-Name Society should be consulted; a model of landscape history is *Village and Farmstead* by C. Taylor (George Philip 1983); see too *A History of the Countryside* by O. Rackham (Dent 1986).

On the later Romans: S. Johnson's *Later Roman Britain* (Routledge 1980) and J. Percival's *The Roman Villa* (Batsford 1976). On Wymondley, *The Agrarian History of England and Wales*, vol. 1, part 2, edited by H. P. R. Finberg (Cambridge 1972); Finberg was also the author of a famous study of Withington in *Lucerna* (Leicester University Press 1964); see too *The Place Names of Gloucestershire*, edited by A. H. Smith (Cambridge 1964). On the Roman census, A. H. M. Jones's *The Roman Economy* (Oxford 1974).

The arrival of the Anglo-Saxons is the subject of a vast literature, most recently J. Myres' *English Settlements* (Oxford 1986). For a different view, C. Hills' *The Blood of the British* (George Philip 1986). Bede and the *Anglo-Saxon Chronicle* are available in Everyman paperbacks; on the Alfredian period *Alfred the Great*, edited by M. Lapidge and S. Keynes (Penguin Books 1983), is indispensable.

On the open fields, *The Origins of Open-Field Agriculture*, edited by R. T. Rowley (Croom Helm 1981). Material in Chapters 7 and 8 is based on my forthcoming study of King Athelstan (British Museum Publications).

On the coins, D. Metcalfe and M. Dolley in *Ethelred the Unready*, edited by D. Hill (British

Archaeological Reports, Oxford, 1978). R. Lennard's *Rural England: 1086–1135* (Oxford 1959) looks at the rulers and the workforce; some of the sources in Chapter 11 are translated in A. J. Robertson's *Anglo-Saxon Charters* (Cambridge 1956). On the Conquest, in addition to the books cited on Domesday there is R. H. C. Davis's *The Normans and their Myth* (Thames and Hudson 1976) and an important article in *History*, vol. 51 (1966): 'The Norman Conquest', which I have used in Chapter 12.

On the sokemen of Lincolnshire, the classic study is F. M. Stenton's *The Free Peasantry of the Northern Danelaw* (Lund 1926, reprinted Oxford 1969); opposed views of the Stenton thesis can be found in *The East Midlands in the Early Middle Ages* by P. Stafford (Leicester University Press 1985) and in *Land and People in Medieval Lincolnshire* by Graham Platts (Lincoln 1985). Post-conquest developments in the Fenland (see Chapter 14) are treated in *Settlement and Society* by H. Hallam (Cambridge 1965), on which I have relied. On the highland zone, W. G. Hoskins' *Provincial England* (Macmillan 1963) and H. Finberg's *West-Country Historical Studies* (David and Charles 1969) and *Early Charters of Devon and Cornwall* (Leicester University Press 1969) are the source of much of the groundwork on 'Hyple's old land'. In Chapter 16 much valuable material is printed in A. Levett's *Studies in Manorial History* (Oxford 1938, reprinted Merlin Press 1962). There are many good recent studies in this area: J. Titow's *English Rural Society 1200–1350* (Allen and Unwin 1969), R. Hilton's *A Medieval Society* (Cambridge 1966, reprinted 1983) and *The English Peasantry in the Later Middle Ages* (Oxford 1975); C. Dyer's *Lords and Peasants in a Changing Society* (Cambridge 1980); *Peasants, Knights and Heretics*, edited by R. Hilton (Cambridge paperback 1981). On women's history at this time: *Medieval Women*, edited by D. Baker (Blackwell paperback 1978); *Women in English Society 1500–1800*, edited by M. Prior (Methuen paperback 1985).

Epilogue: on population, the definitive work is *The Population History of England 1541–1871* by E. A. Wrigley and R. S. Schofield (Arnold 1981); my figures for before the sixteenth century are based on a number of scholars, including H. Hallam's *Rural England 1066–1348* (Fontana 1981). The debate on the family has provoked a fascinating controversy: L. Stone's *The Family, Sex and Marriage in England 1500–1800* (Pelican Books 1979); A. Macfarlane's *Marriage and Love in England 1300–1840* (Blackwell 1986); see too *An Open Elite? England 1540–1880* by L. Stone and J. C. Fawtier Stone (Oxford 1984). The debate aroused by A. Macfarlane's *The Origins of English Individualism* (Blackwell 1978) continues, but his basic argument would not have surprised foreign observers such as Engels (*Articles on Britain*, Moscow 1975) or de Tocqueville, who coined the word 'individualism' to describe what he saw as a distinctive trait in English social history: 'I have always been astonished that a fact, which distinguished England from all modern nations, and which can alone explain the peculiarities of its laws, its spirit, and its history, has not attracted still more than it has done the attention of philosophers and statesmen, and that habit has finally made it as it were invisible to the English themselves' (*L'Ancien Régime*, Oxford 1904).

PICTURE CREDITS

Aerofilms: pages 118 (bottom), 122 (bottom), 158, 164; Institute of Agricultural History and Museum of English Rural Life, University of Reading: pages 12, 206 (top); Alecto Historical Editions: endpapers; Bardo Museum, Tunis: page 52; Mayor of Bayeux and Director of Galerie Reine Matilda: pages 15, 20, 157; Berkshire County Record Office/photo, Denis Jones: page 115 (bottom); Bodleian Library, Oxford: pages 19 (MS Laud Misc 636 f62v), 81 (MS Junius 11), 138, 156 (MS Junius 11); Bridgeman Art Library: page 125; British Library: pages 11 (MS Julius A VI), 70 (Add MS 39943 f2), 79 (MS Cott Vesp B f109r), 88 (MS Harl 3271 f6v), 105 (MS Cott Dom A VII f15), 110 (MS Cott Chart VIII f164B), 118 (top) (MS Cott Claud B IV f59), 120 (MS Cott Tib C II f94), 121 (top, centre and bottom) (MS Cott Tib BV pt 1 folios 6v, 3 and 4v), 125 (Add MS 42130 f173), 126 (top, centre and bottom) (Add MS 42130 folios 163v, 193 and 158), 127 (top) (Add MS 42130 f173v), 127 (bottom) (MS Roy 2 B VII f78v), 150 (MS Cott Tib BV pt 1 f5), 152 (MS Cott Tib BV pt 1 f4), 153 (MS Cott Tib BV pt 1 f76v), 206 (bottom) (Add MS 42130 f170); Courtesy of the Trustees of the British Museum: pages 49 (top), 143 (left and right), 144 (left and right), 146 (left and right); Buckinghamshire County Record Office: page 101; Cambridge University Collection of Air Photographs: pages 29, 31 (bottom), 32, 33, 37, 39, 66, 72, 92, 93, 96, 98, 132, 135, 170, 177 (top), 179, 180, 186, 204; Corpus Christi College, Cambridge: page 74 (MS 173 f6b); Crown copyright/Cambridge University Collection of Air Photographs: page 203 (top); Crown copyright/Public Record Office: pages 16, 23, 113 (top and bottom); Mike S. Duffy/York Archaeological Trust: pages 140, 147; Courtesy of the Dean and Chapter of Durham: pages 82 (MS BII 30 f172v), 111 (MS AII 17 f31v); Elton Collection/Ironbridge Gorge Museum Trust: page 128 (bottom); Exeter Cathedral Library: page 21; Fotobank/Ray Duffurn: page 78; Fay Godwin's Photo Files: pages 31 (top), 36; Sonia Halliday Photographs/Bardo Museum, Tunis: page 116 (bottom left); Hertfordshire County Council, Local Studies Collection: page 190; Hertfordshire County Record Office: pages 43, 191; Michael Holford: pages 116 (top and bottom right), 117 (top and bottom), 119 (top and bottom), 123, 124, 165; *Illustrated London News*: page 62 (top); Mansell Collection: pages 47 (top), 53, 55, 56, 196, 210; Steven Morris: page 122 (top); Norwich Public Library: page 209; Rheinisches Landesmuseum, Trier: page 47 (bottom); Canon M. H. Ridgway/Conway Library, Courtauld Institute of Art: page 203 (bottom); The Royal Commission on the Historical Monuments of England: pages 42, 45 (top and bottom), 58, 59, 60, 62 (bottom), 173, 176, 177 (bottom); Courtesy of the Marquis of Salisbury/Bridgeman Art Library: page 128 (top); John Sims/Daily Telegraph Colour Library: page 115 (top); Spectrum Colour Library: pages 114, 184; Pamla Toler/Impact Photos: pages 198, 199; The Board of Trinity College, Dublin: page 85; Warburg Institute, University of London: page 49 (bottom).

Maps
Pages 24 and 27: reproduced with permission from *The Domesday Geography of England*, 7 vols, by H. C. Darby (Cambridge 1952–77); page 108: reproduced with permission from *Goltho* by Guy Beresford (Historic Buildings and Monuments Commission for England, forthcoming); page 133: Author; page 193: reproduced with permission from *Caldecote* by Guy Beresford (forthcoming). The remaining maps are based on maps found in the following books: page 34: *The Open Fields* by C. S. and C. S. Orwin (Oxford 1967); page

61: *Later Roman Britain* by S. Johnson (Routledge 1980); page 76: (Iron Age information) *Danebury: the Iron Age Fort*, 2 vols, by B. Cunliffe (Council for British Archaeology 1984); page 87: *An Atlas of Anglo-Saxon England, 700–1066* by D. Hill (Blackwell 1981); page 131: *English Place-Name Elements*, part 1, by A. H. Smith (Cambridge 1956); page 202: *The West Midlands* by R. Millward and A. Robinson (Macmillan 1971).

Maps drawn by Line and Line.

INDEX

Page numbers in *italic* refer to illustrations

Teign, River, 185, 188
Thames, River, 56, 69
Thanet, 83, 91
thegns, 105, 106–10, 168
Theodorus, 67
Thera, 50, 67
Thetford, 26
Thurlby, 179
Thurston (Leicester moneyer), 142
Tilnoth, River, 57
Tilshead, 77
Tocqueville, Alexis de, 205, 207
Tomsaetan, 89
Trent, River, 89, 130, 132–3, 136, 138
Tribal Hidage, 86–9, *88*, 90
Tunisia, *52*

Uffington, 30, *36*, 38, 41, 44
Uffington Camp, *29, 114*
Uffington Castle, 35
Uffington Down, 35

Vale of the White Horse, 35, *114*
Valerii family, 50
Verlucio, 77
Verulamium, *see* St Albans
Vespasian's Camp, 75
Vikings, 17, 40, 63, 91–4, 98–102, 103–4, 110–11, 129–42
villages, 34–5, 102
Villaris, 151
villas, Roman, 34, 48, *52*, 61, *62*
Vinogradoff, P., 10
Vitalinus, 73
Vortigern, 71, 73

Wainfleet, 178, *179*
Wales, 18, 69, 90, 104, 163, 184
Wallingford, 30, 38, 97, 143
Wallop, *see* Nether Wallop
Waltham on the Wolds, 169
Wantage, 30, 35, *115*
wapentakes, 132
Warboys, 197

Wareham, 95, 97, *98,* 143
warfare, Anglo-Saxon, 103–6
Warminster, 77
Warwick, 26, 95
Warwickshire, 89, 98, 130, 201
Wash, the, 178
Watling Street, 129, 130, 136, 142
Watlington, 150
Welwyn, 64
Wessex, 61, 91–100, 102, 103–12, 144–5
West Ashby, 173
West Ginge, 30
West Hendred, 30
West Lockinge, 30
West Meon, 63
West Midlands, 197
West Saxons: army, 104–5; Battle of Holme, 103; burhs, 94–100; Christianity, 83; conquest of Midlands, 141–2, 175; in the Cotswolds, 56; defences, 94–9, 104; law codes, 84; royal estates, 68, 75–6, 77–80, 107–8; taxation, 89–90, 111–12; thegns, 105–7, 108–11; under Alfred the Great, 93–7; Viking attacks, 91–3, 94, 98–9, 103
West Stow, *122*
Westbury, 77
Westminster, 9, 160
Weston, 178, 179
Wheathampstead, 64
White Horse, Uffington, *29*, 30, 35; *see also* Vale of the White Horse
Whittington, 59, 60
Whittlesey Mere, 87
Widukind of Corvey, 100
Wight, Isle of, 75, 83
Wigston, 130
Wigston Magna, 174
Wilksby, 166
William the Conqueror, King, 9, 17–25, *20,* 107, 159, 161–6, 202

William of Malmesbury, 96, 159, 160
William of Poitiers, 17
Willicote, *204*
Wilton, 77, 98
Wiltshire, 69, 76, 93, 98, 108–10, 150, 160
Winchester, 9, 25, 26, 41, 55, 96, 97, 103, 107, 108, 109, 143, 150, 160
Windt, E. de, 198
Wistan, St, 133
Withington, 55, 57–61, *58–60*, 63, 64
women: employment, 208; landownership, 172
Woodhenge, 75
Woolbury, 79
wool trade, 41, 55, 201
Woolstone, 34, 36
Wootton Wawen, 89
Worcester, 57, 58–9, 95, 150, 197
Worcestershire, 89, 98
work ethic, 195, 202, 208
workforce, 149–56, 207–8
Wormleighton, 201, *203*
Worthy, 107
Wrangle, 178
Wreake, River, 130, 136–8
Wrekin, the, 86
Wrington, 61
Wudiadun, 58, 60
Wulfgar of Inkpen, 107, 108–10, *110*
Wulfhere, King of Mercia, 88
Wulfhere (Wulfgar of Inkpen's grandfather), 109
Wulfric (Wulfgar of Inkpen's father), 109
Wychwood, 56
Wycomb, 60, 63
Wylye valley, 109

yeomen, 201
York, 26, 99, 139, *140,* 141–2, 145
York, Vale of, 129
Yorkshire, 18, 25, 132, 168

Zosimus, 71